THE CAMBRIDGE COMPANION TO
WALTER PATER

This is the first and only comprehensive introductory study of Walter Pater, novelist, short story writer, literary critic, and philosopher. One of the late nineteenth century's most important and least understood writers, Pater evinced a new mode of hedonism that presented a fundamental challenge to the prevailing moral and social norms of his contemporaries, responding to post-Darwinian sensibility, waning faith, and new philosophies in ethics and epistemology. In his diverse and daring writings, Pater spoke for a generation that encompassed aestheticism, decadence and the emergence of a queer literary canon, including writers such as Oscar Wilde, Vernon Lee, and Michael Field. His defining influence continued to be felt long after his rise to fame and notoriety by such major writers such as T. S. Eliot, James Joyce, and Virginia Woolf. Featuring exceptional detail and thematic breadth of coverage, this *Companion* accessibly introduces Pater's main works and demonstrates his ongoing significance.

Kate Hext is Associate Professor of Decadent Literature and the Arts at the University of Exeter and Visiting Professor of English at Ewha Womans University. Her books include *Walter Pater: Individualism and Aesthetic Philosophy* (2013) and *Wilde in the Dream Factory: Decadence and the American Movies* (2024).

A complete list of books in the series is at the back of the book.

THE CAMBRIDGE
COMPANION TO
WALTER PATER

EDITED BY
KATE HEXT
University of Exeter

CAMBRIDGE
UNIVERSITY PRESS

Shaftesbury Road, Cambridge CB2 8EA, United Kingdom

One Liberty Plaza, 20th Floor, New York, NY 10006, USA

477 Williamstown Road, Port Melbourne, VIC 3207, Australia

314–321, 3rd Floor, Plot 3, Splendor Forum, Jasola District Centre,
New Delhi – 110025, India

Cambridge University Press is part of Cambridge University Press & Assessment,
a department of the University of Cambridge.

We share the University's mission to contribute to society through the pursuit of
education, learning and research at the highest international levels of excellence.

www.cambridge.org
Information on this title: www.cambridge.org/9781316516690

DOI: 10.1017/9781009030892

First published 2026

Cover image: Walter Pater (litho). Photo: © Look and Learn / Bridgeman Images

A catalogue record for this publication is available from the British Library

Library of Congress Cataloging-in-Publication Data
NAMES: Hext, Kate editor
TITLE: The Cambridge companion to Walter Pater / edited by Kate Hext.
DESCRIPTION: Cambridge ; New York, NY : Cambridge University Press, 2026. | Series:
Cambridge companions to literature | Includes bibliographical references and index.
IDENTIFIERS: LCCN 2025033342 | ISBN 9781316516690 hardback | ISBN 9781009015967
paperback | ISBN 9781009030892 ebook
SUBJECTS: LCSH: Pater, Walter, 1839–1894 – Criticism and interpretation | English
literature – 19th century – History and criticism | Great Britain – Intellectual life –
19th century
CLASSIFICATION: LCC PR5137 .C36 2026
LC record available at https://lccn.loc.gov/2025033342

ISBN 978-1-316-51669-0 Hardback
ISBN 978-1-009-01596-7 Paperback

For EU product safety concerns, contact us at Calle de José Abascal, 56, 1°, 28003 Madrid,
Spain, or email eugpsr@cambridge.org

For Francis O'Gorman

For still, in a shadowy world, his deeper wisdom had ever been, with a sense of economy, with a jealous estimate of gain and loss, to use life, not as the means to some problematic end, but, as far as might be, from dying hour to dying hour, an end in itself: a kind of music, all-sufficing to the duly trained ear, even as it died out on the air.

~ Walter Pater, Marius the Epicurean

CONTENTS

CONTENTS

This chronology does not cover all publications

1839	Walter Horatio Pater is born in Stepney, 4 August
1842	Death of Richard Glode Pater, father, on 28 January
1853	Pater begins at the King's School, in Canterbury
1854	Death of Maria Pater, mother
1858	Pater matriculates at the Queen's College, University of Oxford
1859	Spends long vacation in Heidelberg
1861	Pater is coached by Benjamin Jowett
1862	Pater graduates with a BA in Literae Humaniores
1863	Elected as a member of the Old Mortality Society in Oxford
1864	Probationary fellow at Brasenose College, University of Oxford. Pater reads his paper 'Diaphaneitè' to the Old Mortality Society
1865	First trip to Italy; Ravenna, Pisa, Florence, in the long vacation
1866	'Coleridge's Writings' is published in the *Westminster Review*
1867	Becomes a lecturer at Brasenose College
1868	Pater anonymously publishes a review essay titled 'Poems by William Morris' in the *Westminster Review*
1869	Moves to 2 Bradmore Road in Oxford with his sisters Hester and Clara
1873	Pater publishes *Studies in the History of the Renaissance*
1874	W. H. Hardinge scandal; Pater is passed over for a University Proctorship
1876	W. H. Mallock's novel *The New Republic* satirises Pater as Mr Rose
1877	Second edition of *The Renaissance*, for which it is retitled *The Renaissance: Studies in Art and Poetry*. This edition removed the controversial Conclusion, which was restored in the third edition. Meets Oscar Wilde, who is an undergraduate at Magdalen College, Oxford. Travels around Normandy, Brittany and the Loire regions of France in the summer

1878   Withdraws his second volume of essays, 'Dionysus and Other Studies', from production

1878   'The Child in the House', Pater's first 'imaginary portrait' is published in *Macmillan's Magazine*

1882   An extended trip to Rome preparing to write *Marius the Epicurean: His Sensations and Ideas*; correspondence with Violet Paget (Vernon Lee) begins

1883   Resigns Brasenose tutorship but retains his rooms

1885   *Marius the Epicurean* is published. Pater and his sisters move to 12 Earl's Terrace, in West London

1887   *Imaginary Portraits* is published

1888   The third edition of *The Renaissance* is published, reincluding the Conclusion, and with an additional essay, 'The School of Giorgione', which was first published in 1877

1888   *Gaston de Latour* is published in periodical form in *Macmillan's Magazine* between June and October. Pater withdraws it and the novel is left uncompleted

1889   *Appreciations, with an Essay on Style* is published

1891   Following the publication of *The Picture of Dorian Gray*, Pater reviews it for *The Bookman*

1891   Lectures on Plato at Brasenose

1893   *Plato and Platonism* is published, based on Pater's lectures

1893   Pater and his sisters move back to Oxford, 64 St Giles

1894   Pater dies of heart failure at home in Oxford, 30 July

1895   *Greek Studies* is published, edited by Pater's friend Charles Shadwell

1895   *Miscellaneous Studies* is published, edited by Shadwell

1896   *Essays from 'The Guardian'*, edited by Shadwell

CONTRIBUTORS

STEPHEN CHEEKE is a Senior Lecturer in English at the University of Bristol. He is the author of *Byron and Place: History, Translation, Nostalgia* (2003), *Writing For Art: The Aesthetics of Ekphrasis* (2008), *Transfiguration: The Religion of Art in Nineteenth-Century Literature Before Aestheticism* (2016), and *Walter Pater and Persons* (2024).

STEFANO EVANGELISTA is Professor of English and Comparative Literature at the University of Oxford, Fellow of Trinity College, and Einstein Visiting Fellow at the Humboldt University, Berlin (2023-6). He has written widely about aestheticism and decadence, including several articles on Pater and edited collections on Pater, A.C. Swinburne, Oscar Wilde, and Arthur Symons. A former president of the International Walter Pater Society, he is currently one of the editors of the journal *Studies in Walter Pater and Aestheticism*. His monograph, *Literary Cosmopolitanism in the English Fin de Siècle*, came out with Oxford University Press in 2021.

KATE FLINT is Provost Professor of Art History and English at the University of Southern California. She is the author of a number of books and articles on nineteenth-century literary, visual and cultural history, including *The Woman Reader, The Victorians and the Visual Imagination, The Transatlantic Indian*, and *Flash! Photography, Writing, and Surprising Illumination*.

DUSTIN FRIEDMAN is Associate Professor in the Department of Literature at American University. He researches and teaches Victorian and modern literature, aestheticism and decadence, queer theory, and the history and theory of aesthetics. He is the author of *Before Queer Theory: Victorian Aestheticism and the Self* (2019) and co-editor with Kristin Mahoney of *Nineteenth-Century Literature in Transition: The 1890s* (2023). His work has appeared in the journals *Victorian Studies, Victorian Literature and Culture*, and *Modernism/ modernity*, among others, and in several edited collections.

KATE HEXT is Associate Professor of Decadent Literature and the Arts at the University of Exeter and Visiting Professor of English at Ewha Womans University. Her books include *Walter Pater: Individualism and Aesthetic Philosophy* (2013) and *Wilde in the Dream Factory: Decadence and the American Movies* (2024).

LESLEY HIGGINS, Professor of English at York University, is the author of *The Modernist Cult of Ugliness: Aesthetics and Gender Politics* (2002), *Confessing the Flesh: Reading Hopkins in Context* (2025), and co-author, with Marie-Christine Leps, of *Heterotopic World Fiction: Thinking Beyond Biopolitics with Woolf, Foucault, Ondaatje* (2022). She has co-edited *Walter Pater: Transparencies of Desire* (2002) and *Victorian Aesthetic Conditions: Pater Across the Arts* (2010). Together with David Latham, she is the co-general editor of the *Collected Works of Walter Pater* (OUP). As well, she is co-general editor of the *Collected Works of Gerard Manley Hopkins* (OUP), for which she has edited Hopkins's *Diaries* (2015), his *Oxford Essays* (2006), and co-edited the *Dublin Notebook* (2014).

MICHAEL D. HURLEY is Professor of Literature and Theology, and a Fellow of Trinity College, Cambridge. His books include *Angels and Monotheism* (2024), *Faith in Poetry* (2017), *G. K. Chesterton* (2012), and, with Michael O'Neill, *Poetic Form* (2012). He is editor of the Penguin Classics edition of *The Complete Father Brown Stories* and, with Marcus Waithe, co-editor of *Thinking Through Style* (2018).

SARA LYONS is a Senior Lecturer in Victorian Literature at the University of Kent. She is the author of *Algernon Charles Swinburne and Walter Pater: Victorian Aestheticism, Doubt, and Secularisation* (2015) and *Assessing Intelligence: the Bildungsroman and the Politics of Human Potential in England, 1860–1910* (2023).

CATHERINE MAXWELL is Professor of Victorian Literature at Queen Mary University of London, and author of *The Female Sublime from Milton to Swinburne: Bearing Blindness* (2001), *Swinburne* (2006), *Second Sight: The Visionary Imagination in Late Victorian Literature* (2008), and *Scents and Sensibility: Perfume in Victorian Literary Culture* (2017), awarded the 2018 European Society for the Study of English prize for Literatures in English.

LENE ØSTERMARK-JOHANSEN is Professor of English Literature and Art at the University of Copenhagen. She is the author of *Walter Pater and the Language of Sculpture* (2011), of *Walter Pater's European Imagination* (2022), has edited Pater's *Imaginary Portraits* (2019) for the *Oxford Collected Works of Walter Pater* and has most recently edited the volume *Walter Pater and the Beginnings of English Studies* (2023) together with Charles Martindale and Elizabeth

Prettejohn. She has published broadly on word-image relations in the fin de siècle and on the Victorian reception of the Italian Renaissance.

MATTHEW POTOLSKY is Professor of English at the University of Utah. He is the author of *The Decadent Republic of Letters: Taste, Politics, and Cosmopolitan Community from Baudelaire to Beardsley* (2013), and the editor of volume 8 of *The Collected Works of Walter Pater, Classical Studies* (2021).

NICHOLAS SHRIMPTON taught at the Universities of Liverpool and Oxford, where he is now an Emeritus Fellow of Lady Margaret Hall. His new edition of the *Poems of William Blake* was published by Oxford World's Classics in 2019. His publications include 'Dreaming Spires? Arnold's Oxford' (*The New Criterion*, September 2023), 'Charlotte Bronte's *Shirley* and the "Panoramic" Novel' (*Essays in Criticism*, September 2023), and '"To the Queen": Tennyson's Politics' (*Review of English Studies*, February 2024).

JONAH SIEGEL is Distinguished Professor of English at Rutgers University. His books include *Material Inspirations: The Interests of the Art Object in the Nineteenth Century and After* (2020), *and Overlooking Damage: Art, Display, and Loss in Times of Crisis* (2022). Recent articles include 'Artpocalypse: Beauty and Damage on TV' (*Public Books*, August 2023), 'The Handover' (*Los Angeles Review of Books*, August 10, 2023, and 'Killmonger in the Museum: Fantasy, History, Restitution' (*Raritan*, Spring 2023).

GILES WHITELEY is Professor of English Literature at Stockholm University and has published widely on the literature of the long nineteenth century. He is the author of four monographs including, most recently, *The Aesthetics of Space in Nineteenth-Century British Literature, 1843–1907* (2020). He has served as President of the International Walter Pater Society and is editor of *Marius the Epicurean* for Oxford University Press.

JULIANNA K. WILL is an Assistant Professor in the Classics Department at Memorial University of Newfoundland, Canada. Her research focuses on classical reception, especially in relation to sex, gender, and sexuality. She is the author of a forthcoming monograph on the reception of Euripidean tragedy in Victorian England, titled 'The Horror and the Glory: Euripides Among the Victorians'.

KATE HEXT

Introduction
Pater, Now

Walter Pater was an essayist, novelist, critic, short story writer, and teacher. He approached each of these modes with the attitude of a quiet radical, as he gently helped to shape English literature, criticism, and ideas in the late nineteenth century. Pater's career began in a storm of opprobrium. In the climactic Conclusion to his first book, *Studies in the History of the Renaissance* (1873), he declared, 'To burn always with this hard, gem-like flame, to maintain this ecstasy, is success in life.'[1] The 'hard, gem-like flame' in question was desire and passion, and this hedonistic indictment represented a revolution in late nineteenth-century values, albeit one wrapped in a mellifluous metaphor and enclosed in a study that on the surface looked to be about Renaissance art. Amid an ensuing brouhaha, the Conclusion and its author attracted acolytes in Oxford, where Pater was a tutor. For they had captured an emerging zeitgeist and, thus, very soon gained cult status exerting an influence on writers including Oscar Wilde, Vernon Lee, E. M. Forster, and Virgina Woolf. Pater's reputation was to be defined by this forever, for good and bad.

The bad aspect is twofold: first, the moral backlash against Pater and the Conclusion has loomed large in his critical history and so, second, it can be difficult to get beyond it to understand his broader contribution to the history of ideas and literature. In his subsequent publications, he showed himself to be a singularly nuanced thinker, grappling with some of the core issues of his age: the form and capacities of fiction and non-fiction writing, the basis of self-identity and ethics in a secular world, and how it could be possible to imagine beyond the boundaries of normative heterosexuality. To some extent, as discussed later in the present volume, Pater was English literature's Friedrich Nietzsche. They are 'astonishingly similar figures', and Pater's ideas precipitated Nietzsche's impact in Great Britain after 1896, when his work was first translated.[2] At the same time, few Victorian writers are at once so modern in their perspective while being so dense and allusive in their writing as Pater. The difficulties of his work are one of the reasons that it can be challenging to read beyond the Conclusion to address the ideas and style of his wider oeuvre.

The current *Companion* offers ways to understand the full range of Pater's significance. Beyond its address to his work and life, it illustrates that attention to Pater expands our understanding of late-Victorian fiction and the essay form as they come to terms with post-Darwinian sensibility. In doing so, we suggest that Pater challenges how we think today about the relationships between autobiography and criticism, imagination and ideas, the written word and the visual image, and past or imagined lives and the present.

Before turning to the chapters collected here, it would help to consider who Pater was, what made him a misfit in late-Victorian literary studies, the unconventional dynamics between his writing and his contemporary world, and why his work matters today.

Pater in Context

While Pater was a modern, even visionary, thinker he was utterly defined by his historical and cultural moment in Victorian England. He was born in London, in 1839, and died in Oxford, in 1894. It was not a long life, but it was one lived across singularly eventful decades. Queen Victoria ascended to the throne in 1837, and in the course of her reign the British Empire expanded to cover nearly a quarter of the globe, with the colonization of India in 1848 and Kenya from 1885. This was an age of growing social consciousness in Great Britain: a series of Parliamentary Acts slowly began to implement restrictions on factory labour, a system of education for all, and small key improvements in women's rights, while beginning to address the appalling living conditions of the urban population, which was expanding exponentially during Britain's Industrial Revolution. In 1885 the Criminal Law Amendment Act (also known as the Labouchere Amendment) legislated against male homosexuality in England for the first time. A decade later, in 1895, Oscar Wilde became its most high-profile convict. While imprisoned for two years, he was allowed one book per week, and Pater's *Renaissance* was one of his first choices.[3]

As a writer, Pater's attitude toward his period is not straightforward. One of his paradoxes is to epitomize late nineteenth-century sensibility while shying away from any direct response to his society or the vivid events that defined it. For, while the Victorian world was revolving on its axis into its modern state, Pater's writing conjures up a world in words set apart from the immediacies of empire, industry, gender, and sexuality. On typical form, for instance, he portrays Dionysus reborn in medieval France in his story 'Denys L'Auxerrois'; writes an extended impressionistic meditation on Leonardo

DaVinci's *Mona Lisa* in *The Renaissance*; and gives us a literary biographical portrait of a seventeenth-century writer in 'Thomas Browne'. Today his implicit assumption that readers of his works will have a range of highbrow knowledge spanning back to ancient Greece and extending to Italian Renaissance triptychs, and now-forgotten polymaths, may strike us as elitist. While this is not untrue, the more interesting truth is that such departures from reality speak of both Pater's ethos about what literature is and his strategy for living. First let's consider Pater's ethos. His departures from reality have the principle of 'art for its own sake' at their centre. At a time when the future of fiction and criticism were at issue as never before, Pater believed that these are *art forms* not justified by their use in the world or their mirroring of reality but valuable *for their own sake*. This was an ethos that took shape in Oxford and London, where Pater was at the centre of new ideas on literature: Matthew Arnold's 'The Function of Criticism at the Present Time' (1864) and Henry James's 'The Art of Fiction' (1888) steered the discussion in literary circles. Meanwhile, in Oxford, heated ongoing discussions about rebalancing the university curriculum that had till then been almost exclusively focused on the classics curriculum raised the question of whether and how English literature should be studied in universities. In the middle of such discussions, Pater's line on fiction and criticism was radical; realism and social use were often the justification for imaginative writing in public discourse. Instead he proposed an impressionistic and imaginative mode of criticism, and a philosophical mode of fiction.

The second point on strategy is related to Pater's aestheticism. Folded into his jewelled prose style, classical civilization, art history, quasi-fictional portraits, and ekphrastic descriptions are the means by which Pater creates a critical and imaginative distance from the late nineteenth century. While they forsake realism, they refract contemporary issues through fantasised or reanimated historical places and characters. Pater's depiction of Dionysus, then, for example, animates this ancient Greek god of wine and song, into a fictional reflection on masculinity, sensuality, and the ends of pleasure. In this and other stories and essays, Pater seeks to enchant his reader and, in doing so, reflects on current issues while imagining that alternative values are possible.

The nature of Pater's Oxford career tells us both about the character of intellectual life in his period and the kind of academic he was within it. As an undergraduate, between 1858 and 1862, he studied *Literae Humaniores* (or 'Greats') at Queens College, Oxford, and in 1864 he became a fellow at another Oxford college, Brasenose. The city was socially parochial but this was an especially eventful period in its intellectual life, one in which the old certainties – Christian faith, Creation, tradition, and more – were cracking. While Pater tutored in classics his interests were broad: it was his knowledge of newly fashionable German philosophy that helped secure his academic appointment and his first publications were an essay on Samuel Taylor Coleridge and a review, which was to provide the basis for the Conclusion to *The Renaissance*, of poems by William Morris. In the long summer vacations, Pater travelled widely in France, Italy, and Germany, and in essays he refers to landscapes, art works, and authors few English readers would have known. He ventured beyond the arts too, arguing that 'the literary artist' must understand natural sciences and history in order to write well.[4] He was a polymath with wide-ranging enthusiasms and a cosmopolitan mind.

Just as Pater didn't believe that it was possible to restrict thought to a single disciplinary perspective, his writing was not restricted to either non-fiction or fiction. When he resigned his tutorial position in 1883, he began a singularly productive fiction-writing period. His second book was the novel, *Marius the Epicurean* (1885), and it was followed by a collection of short fiction titled *Imaginary Portraits* (1887), then a collection of essays on literature, *Appreciations, with an Essay on Style* (1889), and an essay collection based on his philosophy lectures, *Plato and Platonism* (1893). The range of these works indicates Pater's ambitions: they experiment across fiction and non-fiction, at times fusing and at other times mediating between the two. In a way then Pater was an intellectual butterfly. Or, to use a word that did not then exist, he was *interdisciplinary*. It sometimes makes him difficult to understand and estimate, for his ambitions as a writer – and his belief in reading and writing for its own sake – span beyond the scope of our usual categories and fall in between literary genres.

One of the risks is that Pater's writing lives on in its edited highlights: his ekphrastic description of the *Mona Lisa*, which was excerpted by W.B. Yeats to open the *Oxford Book of Modern Verse* (1936); Marius's epiphany in the eponymous novel; the Dionysian revelries in his 'imaginary portraiture'; and, of course, the Conclusion to *The Renaissance*. There is far more. Reading across Pater's works of fiction, art history, and the history of literature and ideas, as most of the essays in the current volume do, several core concerns emerge. Tracing these we see patterns that help us navigate his works via, say, how he fictionalizes figures from history and the classical world; the way he articulates sensuality; his dramatisation of alternative gendered identities, especially his defection from Victorian gentlemanliness; how eroticism is coded in his figurative language and homoerotic plots; the transition from youth to maturity in his most compelling characters; the fragility of the human body; and unnerving outbreaks of violence in the tranquil worlds he creates. Beyond this nexus of issues related to selfhood, Pater returns again and again to concerns such as the relationships between the arts, in his own word paintings and ekphrasis, and his conviction that '*All art constantly aspires towards the condition of music*';[5] he makes frequent statements on how philosophy could be practised in the modern world; he operates across broad-ranging intellectual contexts and imagines the landscapes of Europe as their stage; he dramatises dichotomies, such as Apollo and Dionysus, fact and fiction, and examines how they break down under analysis.

Pater, 'himself'

In his second novel, *Gaston de Latour* (1888), Pater writes, 'Beyond and above all the various interests upon which the philosopher's mind was ever afloat, there was one subject always in prominence – himself.'[6] Although Pater was not a philosopher in a conventional sense it is a singularly telling insight into his own priorities.

Pater's second paradox is that while the individual – self-identity, personality, psychology – is at the centre of his own writing, he himself is a mystery. The outline facts of his biography are not numerous. These belie a complex emotional and intellectual life of which there is little trace beyond his published works. His few surviving letters are friendly but unrevealing; there are no diaries and few accounts that disturb the impression of a genial but reserved interlocutor. He is, as Henry James wrote approvingly, 'the mask without the face'.[7] The chapters collected in the present volume circle around this inner life as it is glimpsed, suggested, and encoded through his essays and fiction. It would not be quite true to say that Pater hides in his writings. Rather, he uses the expansive, imaginative, unfinished forms of his essays and fiction to explore questions of ethics and aesthetics, understanding that intellectual thought cannot be disengaged from the imagination or the circumstances of lived experience. As he wrote to Vernon Lee (Violet Paget) he endeavoured to make 'intellectual theorems seem like the life's essence of the concrete, sensuous objects, from which they have been abstracted'.[8] And so, Pater's own life – hazy though its details often are – cannot be disengaged from understanding his writing. Reading his works – reading *him*? – challenges us to question how far we can read the author or writer in their texts, and to interrogate how far Pater defines a mode of personal address.

Pater believed that subjective emotions and life circumstances are integral to serious thinking. It would, therefore, in his view, be wishful thinking to be objective about ideas and literature. His main influences include Immanuel Kant, G.W. F. Hegel, David Hume, and Plato. As this range suggests, his was pick-and-mix philosophy of the kind no systematic philosopher would sanction. He could not abide the rigorously abstract forms of philosophical systems and instead explored ideas in the malleable form of the essay. The phrase *to essay* derives from Latin: it means *to try*. As a classicist, Pater would not forget it: his essays try out ideas in sincere attempts to define forms and styles that can give an imaginative, tangible form to abstract questions. They hold within their hesitating voice the possibility that their writer may be wrong, or that the balance of his thinking may alter in the future. They invite their readers to engage in the endeavour towards truths that are not final but know themselves to be conditional, provisional. Accordingly, Pater is, as several of the following chapters note, an author who constantly revised himself, making numerous alterations between periodical and book publication of the same works, as if in ceaseless dialogue with himself.

Pater's singularly personal writing endeavours toward, in his own words, 'transparency in language – the control of a style which did but obediently shift and shape itself to the mental motion, as a well-trained hand can follow on the tracing-paper the outline of a drawing below it'.[9] After all, he believed that nothing can be known except 'under conditions'.[10] In an essay on Charles Lamb (1878) he sets out his ethos based in empiricism, which is the philosophical position that ideas are developed from observations and experiences in the world:

> And, working ever close to the concrete, to the details, great or small, of actual things, books, persons, and with no part of them blurred to his vision by the intervention of mere abstract theories, he has reached an enduring moral effect also, in a sort of boundless sympathy.[11]

This is a writer reckoning with the modern world. In doing so, he expands the scope of our understanding of modern identity. For him, empirical observation of the modern world creates a sympathetic subject. He also aims to redefine literature: 'Oh!' he exclaims, 'for a literature set free, conterminous with the interests of life itself.'[12] His is a firm belief in the central importance of imaginative literature; one defined on very different terms to, say, Henry James or George Eliot. Still, one with ethics at its centre.

Pater Today

Pater's place in literary studies today is singular, complicated, and vital. His work does not map onto popular or canonical forms of Victorian fiction or criticism. It does not illustrate the critical and cultural current that adopted him, the decadent movement. Neither does Pater neatly reflect his period. These things make him and his works prone to misinterpretation, narrow interpretation, or outright omission. Yet, English literature and art history in the final quarter of the nineteenth century make no sense without Pater: the way in which he addressed difficult questions about the future of literature and philosophy, personal identity when religious faith, the value of fiction and style, subjectivity in criticism, and queer masculinity make him a deeply important and influential writer. With these issues, his works also raise questions that resonate today about the relationship between literature, criticism, and how we should live.

Pater's critical reputation continued to be chequered after *The Renaissance*. He was never the kind of person to announce himself as an Important Thinker. Unsystematic as he chose to be, he was often overlooked or subjected to moralising tendencies. Since his early *succès de scandale*, his critical reception reads like an effort to illustrate his seriousness. Ruth C. Child's *The Aesthetic of Walter Pater* (1940) and Rene Welleck's 'Walter Pater's Literary Theory and Criticism' (1957) were among the first to pay serious, sustained attention to his interventions in literature and ideas.[13] Billie Andrew Inman's work in the mid-twentieth century uncovered the innumerable philosophical influences and allusions enfolded unreferenced within Pater's writings, showing just how deeply his work was engaged in critical dialogue with the history of ideas.[14] The advent of queer theory and gay studies from 1990 combined with new interest in Oscar Wilde following Richard Ellmann's biography (1987), to put the life back into Pater. Inman's discovery of evidence that Pater had been reprimanded by Benjamin Jowett for a flirtation with an undergraduate student,[15] alongside Richard Dellamora's *Masculine Desire: The Sexual Politics of Victorian Aestheticism* (1990) and James Eli Adams's *Dandies and Desert Saints: Styles of Victorian Masculinity* (1995), showed that Pater's attention to sexual difference, sublimated desire, and queer styles of masculinity are integral not only to his characters and their lives but also to his philosophical position on pleasure.

Pater no longer requires rescuing from moral opprobrium. He is a writer who stands on the cusp of modernity, hesitatingly so. He is in many ways peculiar, not exemplifying the stories we usually like to tell about Victorian literary trends, personalities, or cultural movements. He shows us how literary reputations are ambivalently made by prevailing prejudices and priorities. While in some ways his quintessentially Victorian conservativism and shyness cannot be underestimated, his articulation of new conditions in modern thought make him a progenitor of core features of twentieth- and twenty-first-century literature and ideas. The chapters in the current volume suggest ways of appreciating Pater's contributions to literary criticism, philosophy, art history, and fiction-writing, in contexts that assist with understanding the range of his intertextual references and his contemporary culture. These are organised around three key aspects. The first three chapters focus on the place of Pater and his works in the intellectual and social contexts of Oxford and London. The next chapters turn to specific works and forms, close reading texts in the context of their publication histories and culture. The last three chapters address Pater's intellectual influences on modernism and new critical contexts.

Pater's belief in 'art for its own sake' and his creation of new literary forms in which to grapple with the multifarious questions modernity posed to self-identity are an abiding concern in these chapters. As they illustrate the integral relationship between Pater's biography, including its silences, and his peculiar mode of criticism they identify new dialogues with present criticism.

Notes

1. Walter Pater, *The Renaissance: Studies in Art and Poetry*, ed. Hilary Fraser (Oxford: Oxford University Press, 2025), 199.
2. Patrick Bridgwater, *Anglo-German Interactions in the Literature of the 1890s* (Oxford: Legenda, 1999), 11, 240–1. Nietzsche was first translated in 1896.
3. Sturgis, Matthew, *Oscar: A Life* (London: Head of Zeus, 2018), 591, 597.
4. Walter Pater, *Appreciations, with an Essay on Style* (Evanson, Il: Northwestern University Press, 1987), 16.
5. Pater, *Renaissance*, 145.
6. Walter Pater, *Gaston de Latour*, vol 4, *Complete Works of Walter Pater* (Oxford: Oxford University Press, 2019), 92.
7. Henry James to Edmund Gosse, *13 December 1894, Letters, 1883–1895*, Leon Edel, ed., vol. 4 (London: Macmillan, 1980), 492.
8. Letter to Violet Paget, *4 June 1884, Letters of Walter Pater*, ed. Lawrence Evans (Clarendon Press, 1970), 54.
9. Pater, *Appreciations*, 206.
10. Pater, *Renaissance*, 180.
11. Pater, *Appreciations*, 109.
12. Walter Pater, *Imaginary Portraits* (New York: Allworth Press, 1997), 89.
13. René Wellek, 'Walter Pater's Literary Theory and Criticism', *Victorian Studies* 1, no. 1 (September 1957): 29–46.
14. For a fuller account of Pater's critical history, see Kate Hext, 'Recent Scholarship on Walter Pater: "Antithetical Scholar of Understanding's End"', *Literature Compass* 5 (2008): 407–423, https://doi.org/10.1111/j.1741-4113.2008.00522.x
15. See Billie Andrew Inman, 'Estrangement and Connection: Walter Pater, Benjamin Jowett, and William M. Hardinge', in *Pater in the 1990s*, ed. Laurel Brake and Ian Small (Greensboro, NC: ELT Press, 1991), 1–20.

I

SARA LYONS

Pater as Public Intellectual

In his often-unreliable 1907 biography of Walter Pater, Thomas Wright relates a suggestive anecdote about Pater's public persona. At an unspecified date and on an unknown topic, Pater lectured in his customary low-speaking voice to a select audience at the Literary Institute on Albemarle Street in Mayfair, London. Pater was also notorious for avoiding eye contact with his audience while lecturing. Oscar Wilde was among the attendees, and afterwards Pater whispered to him, 'I hope you heard me, Mr. Wilde'. 'We overheard you', Wilde quipped. 'Really, Mr. Wilde', Pater replied, 'you have a phrase for everything'.[1]

Wilde's remark suggests that Pater's introversion could generate a sense of intimacy with him: his refusal, or inability, to project his voice properly could make his audience feel as if they were in on a secret. Wilde's remark also seems to hint at a certain theatricality in Pater's reticence, though this may be Wilde's projection. Pater's image, for both Victorian and modern audiences, has been coloured by Wilde's discipleship in ways that are difficult to filter out. The admiration does not seem to have been entirely mutual: although Pater was cordial to Wilde, he apparently disliked him and was discomfited by Wilde's appropriations of his work (Wright, 2:125–127).[2] In particular, Pater seems to have been discomfited by Wilde's determination to say the quiet part out loud and clarify for the Victorian public that his own *Studies in the History of the Renaissance* (1873) was a 'golden book' of queer hedonism Pater died a few months before Wilde's trials in 1895, but Wilde ensured that Pater's name was linked with the scandal over his own homosexuality by declaring Pater 'the only critic of the century whose opinion I set high' under cross-examination at the first trial.[3] Pater's immediate posthumous reputation was determined by the atmosphere of homophobic panic that followed in the wake of Wilde's trials and which infused the culture of literary modernism.[4] Down to the present, critical views of Pater often turn on the degree to which one considers Wilde an insightful interpreter of Pater: whether Wilde 'overheard' Pater correctly, or just heard what he wanted to hear. Wright's anecdote hints that Wilde was Pater's ideal auditor: the phrase 'I hope you heard me, Mr Wilde' can be interpreted to mean that Pater wanted to be understood by Wilde in particular. However, this fits so well with Wilde's fantasy of being Pater's star protégé that one suspects that the anecdote is Wilde's invention, or at least that it has been somehow improved by Wilde.

Pater was not always a diffident public speaker. As an undergraduate and then a junior Fellow at the University of Oxford, he had a reputation as a 'brilliant and paradoxical talker' who had a 'new and daring philosophy of his own' and made no secret of his hostility to Christianity (Wright, 1:203–204).[5] This reputation seems to have cost him professional advancement: Pater's old school friend and fellow Oxford student, John Rainer McQueen, wrote to the Bishop of London to prevent his ordination in the Church of England, and he twice failed to gain clerical fellowships at the university (though this may have been at least in part because he had graduated with a disappointing second-class degree [Wright, 207–209]). The fact that Pater contemplated ordination despite his apparently outspoken atheism captures the contradictions of the transitional moment at which he began his academic career. The University of Oxford was undergoing a process of secularisation, and the extent to which it was possible for a clerical don to be critical of Christian orthodoxy was a burning question. Pater's background motivation for pursuing a clerical career was surely financial – he needed to support himself and his two unmarried sisters – and the clerisy was still a conventional path for scholarly young men without much money. In the event, Pater would become the first non-clerical fellow of Brasenose College, Oxford, in 1864, but the University Test Acts – the requirement that university staff subscribe to the Thirty-Nine Articles of the Church of England – were not abolished until 1871 (the tests had been abolished for students taking BA degrees in 1854). Pater's turbulent career at Oxford was produced in part by an atmosphere of conflict and confusion over the extent to which it was permissible for a university teacher to be a secular thinker.

Just after he finished his undergraduate degree and while applying for university posts, Pater was elected to the Old Mortality Society at Oxford, a discussion club made up of undergraduates and junior fellows. The Old Mortality had a self-consciously liberal sensibility, but Pater – perhaps inadvertently – exposed the limits of its commitment to the free play of ideas. In 1864, two weeks after he had been elected a Fellow of Brasenose, Pater delivered a paper to the Society on Johann Gottlieb Fichte's ideal of a scholar and the concept of 'subjective immortality'.[6] No copy of the paper survives, but it sparked a furore because it seemed to romanticise atheism as the royal road to heightened aesthetic experience. S. R. Brooke, a conservative member of the Society, condemned it as one of 'the most thoroughly infidel productions' he had ever heard and complained that Pater

> advocated 'self-culture' upon eminently selfish principles, and for what to us appeared, a most unsatisfactory end. To sit in one's study all [day] and contemplate the beautiful is not a useful even if it is an agreeable occupation, but if it were both useful and agreeable, it could hardly be worthwhile to send so much trouble upon what may at any time be wrested from you. If a future existence is to be disbelieved the motto 'Let us eat and drink for tomorrow we die', is infinitely preferable.   (Brooke qtd. in Monsman, 30)

Brooke's reaction makes clear that the lost essay contained the germs of the Conclusion to *Studies in the History of the Renaissance,* which would also scandalise many because it seemed to celebrate modern secularisation as a chance to revive the ancient philosophy of hedonism, or Epicureanism. As with the later scandal over the Conclusion, the offence caused by Pater's Fichte essay is likely to elude modern readers: advocating 'sit[ting] in one's study all [day]' and contemplating the beautiful scarcely seems like revolutionary counsel to a group of students and fellows. Yet Brooke clearly found that element of the essay particularly inflammatory – indeed, he claims that he would have found it *preferable* if Pater had frankly advocated sensual self-indulgence. It is possible that Brooke detected a homoerotic subtext in Pater's ideal of the scholar's life (another essay Pater delivered to the Society, 'Diaphanèitè', is vaguely homoerotic in its vision of the ideal aesthetic personality, and the Fichte essay may have been so too). But it is noteworthy that Pater's vision of the scholar as one who contemplates the beautiful without any moral or utilitarian purpose in view – not even a theological excuse for it – was found disturbingly radical. As Stefani Collini has observed, Victorian public intellectuals – 'public moralists', in his influential formula – generally 'exhibited an obsessive antipathy to selfishness, and consequently their reflections were structured by a sharp and sometimes exhaustive polarity between egoism and altruism' (Collini, 65). The onus upon public intellectuals to champion the virtues of duty and self-sacrifice weighed particularly heavily if they were known to be at all sceptical of religious orthodoxy. From the start, Pater's notion of the scholar-aesthete was, in contrast, at once quasi-aristocratic and Romantic in its emphasis upon unproductive pleasure and the cultivation of a rich, sensuous individuality. And Brooke would not be alone in taking offence: Pater's essay motivated a group of students to form a Christian counter-society, the Hexameron (Monsman, 31). Thus, within two weeks of taking up his fellowship, Pater had united a conservative faction against him at Oxford.

Was the young Pater trying to gain a reputation as a campus radical? Accounts of Pater often distinguish between a young firebrand Pater and a penitent or at least more prudent older Pater. But the distinction between the two tends to assume that the proper boundaries of intellectual enquiry were obvious to Pater and that the penalties – and rewards – of transgression were easy for him to calculate. Pater's contradictory public image as the Pied Piper of aestheticism and corrupter of youth, on the one hand, and as a timid and ascetic scholar on the other, is partly attributable to contradictions within the culture of Victorian Oxford and to the fact that the role and status of the don were in flux. They are also attributable to the fact that Pater tried to combine his life as a university don with a career as a literary journalist.

While still a junior Fellow at Oxford, Pater sought to establish himself as a journalist in serious periodicals with liberal and radical affiliations: the *Fortnightly Review* and the *Westminster Review*, respectively. In this context, it was necessary for him to demonstrate a certain intellectual and stylistic brio to make his mark as a critic. And where Oxford broadly demanded deference to religious and intellectual tradition, publications like the *Westminster* and the *Fortnightly* valued the interrogation of received ideas and the forceful expression of opinion. Pater first published three articles: 'Coleridge's Writings' (1866), 'Winckelmann' (1867), and 'Poems by William Morris' (1868) in the *Westminster*. In different ways, these essays crystallised the iconoclastic elements of his aestheticism: 'Coleridge's Writings' clarified its anti-theological bent; 'Winckelmann' its homoerotic Hellenism; and 'Poems by William Morris' its equation of secularism, paganism, and sensuality. However, these articles were published anonymously – a practice that was still conventional but passing out of favour. As Laurel Brake points out, Pater could also take refuge in the review format: although all three essays are strikingly polemical in places, Pater could blur the distinction between polemic and disinterested exposition and write as if he were merely offering a sympathetic appraisal of Winckelmann or attempting to capture the mood conjured by Morris's poetry (Brake, 189–190). Pater also used this technique of sympathetic, elusively polemical exposition in a series of articles on Renaissance figures published in the *Fortnightly Review*: 'Notes on Leonardo da Vinci' (1869), 'A Fragment on Sandro Botticelli' (1870), 'The Poetry of Michelangelo' (1871), and 'Pico della Mirandola' (1871). These essays also articulate Pater's investment in homoeroticism ('Leonardo da Vinci' and 'Michelangelo') and his anti-theological ideal of paganism ('Sandro Botticelli'), but they do so somewhat more delicately, perhaps because they were published under his signature. However, when Pater decided to republish the *Fortnightly* essays alongside 'Winckelmann' and an excerpt of 'Poems by William Morris' under his own name and the title *Studies in the History of the Renaissance* in 1873, he lost the protections afforded him by Victorian periodical culture (the volume also included three new essays and a Preface). Read together, the subtle provocations of individual essays no longer seemed subtle, and it became clear Pater's aestheticism was not just a heady passage provoked by particular lines of Morris's poetry or a Botticelli painting: it was, or at least aspired to be, a coherent philosophy. And that philosophy did not confine itself to the realm of Renaissance art or even aesthetics more broadly but made claims about how best to live in the here and now. Shorn of its original context of literary criticism and elevated to the status of a 'conclusion', 'Poems by William Morris' resonated as a seductive neo-pagan manifesto.

Studies in the History of the Renaissance garnered admiring – or at least partly admiring – reviews from John Morley, John Addington Symonds, Sidney Colvin, Frederick G. Stephens, and Emilia Dilke.[7] But it ignited a scandal within the still essentially ecclesiastical world of Oxford. The book was condemned from the pulpit by John Mackarness, Bishop of Oxford, as representative of the 'current school of unbelief'. 'Can we wonder that some who played an honourable part in Oxford life a generation since, refuse to let their sons imbibe lessons so alien from the lore they learned?' he asked his congregation. 'Can you wonder that to young men who have imbibed this teaching the Cross is an offence, and the notion of a vocation to teach it an unintelligible craze?' (Seiler, 96). The Reverend W. Wolf Capes, Pater's former tutor and a 'select preacher' to the University of Oxford, gave a University sermon on 'humanitarian culture' and modern hedonism that was plainly an attack on Pater (Capes qtd. in Donoghue 1995, 58). John Wordsworth, Chaplain and Tutor at Brasenose and one of Pater's former students, wrote to Pater that he ought to have suppressed the book: its atheism and philosophical relativism endangered impressionable minds, and he henceforth regarded it as his 'duty' to 'oppose' Pater (Seiler, 63).

There were denunciations from conservative critics beyond Oxford as well. In *Blackwood's Magazine*, Margaret Oliphant derided the book's 'elegant materialism', deeming it the product of an overrefined Oxford mind (Oliphant 1873, 608). W. J. Courthope identified Pater as the archetype of an 'epicene' form of 'literary Liberalism', which sacrificed common sense on the altar of solipsism (Courthope 1874, 409). And in 1876, Courthope used the occasion of reviewing a new edition of William Wordsworth's poetry to attack Pater again, deploring in passing 'the effeminate desires which Mr. Pater, the mouthpiece of our "artistic culture", would encourage in society' (Courthope 1876, 136). As this suggests, the tendency for conservative critics to identify Pater as a symptom of a degenerate strain in modern culture – whether the precise diagnosis was individualism, liberalism, unbelief, scientific materialism, hedonism, effeminacy, 'the Greek spirit', or some hybrid of these – persisted long after the outcry over the book's initial publication. For example, in 1879, W.S. Lilly claimed that Pater was an 'evangelist' for a 'sentimental materialism' that destroyed any notion of human dignity: 'the *man* vanishes, and you have instead a "creature more subtle than any beast of the field, but likewise cursed above any beast of the field"' (Lilly, 175).

To modern readers, the fact that so much of the scandal surrounding *The Renaissance* centred on the corruption of young men seems telling and registers as evidence that Pater's homosexuality was something like common knowledge. It is certainly possible to detect a strain of homophobia in critiques of Pater, which were – ironically – often rather florid, as if his critics were attempting to contain the charisma of his style by parody: his aestheticism is variously attacked for its 'scepticism and sensuality, the luxurious effeminacy of its thought, the foppish singularity of its diction'; for its 'Circean spells, its deification of the flesh, its mawkish and unwholesome jargon of aestheticism'; and its 'rococo' effort to 'deck [...] dim altars with [...] the ephemeral wreaths of evanescent flowers'.[8] In 1876, W. H. Mallock's roman à clef, *The New Republic: Or, Culture, Faith and Philosophy in an English Country House,* began to be serialised in *Belgravia* magazine, and it perhaps put the secret of Pater's homosexuality into wider circulation. The novel contains an unmistakable portrait of Pater in the figure of Mr. Rose, a grandiloquent aesthete who 'always seems to talk of everybody as if they had no clothes on' (Mallock, 278). Mallock's parody contained allusions to Pater's sexuality: for example, Mr. Rose speaks of decorating the chamber of the 'woman *or the youth* that we love' [my italics] and reads aloud a homoerotic sonnet written by a youth of eighteen whose 'education' he is 'direct[ing]' (Mallock, 27; 271–272). This last detail actually has its origins in reality, or at least in rumours about Pater. In or around 1874, Pater was supposed to have had an intimate relationship with a Balliol undergraduate, William Hardinge Money, who wrote homoerotic poems and was so generally indiscreet about his homosexual desires that he earned the nickname 'the Balliol Bugger'.[9] Other students aired their concerns about Hardinge to Jowett in his capacity as Master of Balliol, and Jowett rusticated Hardinge for a term.

The Hardinge episode seems to have had more serious consequences for Pater. It appears that Jowett debarred Pater's promotion on account of it: in 1874, Pater was denied a University Proctorship that was all but earmarked for him following an interview with Jowett. The nature of Pater's relationship with Hardinge, the extent to which rumours of the scandal leaked beyond Oxford and certain literary circles, and its impact on Pater's career are all matters of conjecture. Nonetheless, it is reasonable to infer that the Hardinge affair, coupled with the scandal over *The Renaissance*, pushed Pater into a defensive posture and made him anxious about his public reputation. It surely played a part in Pater's self-censorship: he suppressed the Conclusion in the second edition of *The Renaissance* because it 'might mislead some of those young men into whose hands it might fall' and toned down some of the more incendiary passages throughout the volume; he restored the Conclusion in the 1888 edition of *The Renaissance*, but with some amendments that rendered it more hospitable to Christianity.[10] After *The Renaissance*, Pater's work is generally more affirmative of Christianity, which is increasingly posited as a complement rather than an antagonist to his ideal of aestheticism. Nonetheless, the extent to which Pater's revisions of his early work amount to a retraction of his original ideas remains a matter of critical debate.[11]

If *The Renaissance* offended some readers, it enchanted others. Pater's friend Mrs Humphry Ward recalled how 'the strange and poignant sense of beauty expressed in it, its entire aloofness [...] from the Christian tradition, its glorification of the higher and intenser forms of pleasure [...] both stirred and scandalised Oxford [...] There was a cry of "Neo-Paganism"' (Ward qtd. in Seiler, 19). Pater acquired many avowed acolytes and protégés – 'Michael Field' (the shared pseudonym of Katharine Bradley and Edith Cooper), Lionel Johnson, Vernon Lee, George Moore, Arthur Symons, and of course Wilde, to name only some of the more notable ones – and would come to be both hailed and reviled as a pioneer of an aesthetic 'cult', 'craze', or 'movement'. Pater was one of the recognisable inspirations for the aesthetic poet Bunthorne in W. S. Gilbert and Arthur Sullivan's 1881 comic opera *Patience*, which served both to glamorise and to discredit aestheticism in the popular imagination. Meanwhile, Paterian aestheticism evolved into something like an undergraduate subculture at Oxford. The poet Richard Le Gallienne recalled in his autobiographical book *The Romantic 90s* that 'in those days we were all going around quoting [Pater's] famous description, or rather re-creation, of the Mona Lisa [...] and we were all exhorting each other to maintain that ecstasy which is the true success in life' (Le Gallienne, 117).

Pater's capacity to attract young acolytes was inseparable from his notoriety. Contemporaries often imagined Pater as a sinister pedagogue who exercised overwhelming influence over young men: he was a 'demoralising moraliser', in Benjamin Jowett's damning judgment (Jowett qtd. in Monsman, 64). This preoccupation with Pater's sway over the young stemmed in part from the fact that the identity of the university don was conceived in pastoral terms: the duty of the don was to forge close relationships with students and provide Christian mentorship. The tutorial system at Oxford was designed to facilitate this type of pastoral care: the college tutor was a non-specialist who supervised the totality of his students' educations so that he could minister to their spiritual as well as intellectual development. The primacy of the tutorial system had been diluted by the introduction of inter-collegiate lectures in the mid-1860s, which enabled the provision of more specialist instruction.[12] Nonetheless, the pastoral ideal persisted and underpinned Pater's reputation as a kind of decadent Socrates, leading youth astray with his riddling philosophy. Pater's work sometimes evokes the ancient Greek tradition of *paiderastia* – erotic love between a male teacher and his younger male student – in vague, idealistic terms, and the alarm over Pater's influence may be because some suspected that he conflated the pastoral ideal with a 'Greek' model of pedagogy.[13] It also reflected underlying disquiet at Oxford over whether a lay tutor – let alone a known religious sceptic – could fulfil this traditionally sacerdotal role. When John Wordsworth wrote to reproach Pater, he invoked the pastoral ideal and suggested Pater's public atheism had made him unfit to fulfil it: how could he oversee students' divinity examinations after publishing *The Renaissance*? Wordsworth acknowledged that Pater was free to 'publish whatever [he] pleased' because of the abolition of the University Test Acts but implored him to prioritise his higher duties to 'minds weaker than [his] own' at Oxford – implicitly, the minds of his students (Wordsworth qtd. in Seiler, 62).

Accounts of Pater's actual conduct and style as a university teacher are somewhat contradictory. Arthur Benson, Pater's friend and biographer, asserts that Pater did not 'consider himself a professional educator' and relates anecdotes which suggest that Pater was a fairly lackadaisical don (Benson, 23). Some of these are comic, as if Pater were performing aesthetic idealism as a mode of camp (or a means of shirking academic duties): for example, Pater once apparently lost the mark sheet associated with a bundle of essays he had been examining as part of a scholarship competition. When the list of names was read out to him in the hopes of jogging his memory about the marks he had allocated, Pater was unable to recall anything until the surname 'Sanctuary' was reached. 'Ah!' said Pater, 'I remember him – it was such a beautiful name' (Benson, 191–192). Pater could be cynical about his educational duties: he reportedly said:

> Most [Brasenose students] are fairly well-to-do, and it is not necessary that they should learn very much. At some Colleges I am told that certain of the young men have a genuine love for learning; if that were so [at Brasenose] it would be quite too dreadful. (Benson, 193)

Yet Humphry Ward recalls Pater being exacting in his feedback on student essays: 'he was severe on confusions of thought, and still more so on any kind of rhetoric. An emphatic word epithet was sure to be underscored, and the absolutely right phrase suggested' (Ward qtd. in Benson, 25). There are numerous anecdotes which attest to Pater's awkwardness as a university lecturer, as well as to the fact that his lectures and tutorials were not pitched to be accessible to an undergraduate audience, still less designed to help students pass their examinations (Benson, 20, 159; Wright, 2:118–119; Donoghue, 35). Yet these anecdotes arguably point toward Pater's high intellectual standards rather than his laxity as a teacher. According to Ward, Pater prided himself on being a modern lecturer who ensured that his lectures were 'crammed with thought' and composed with utmost care, in contrast to the perfunctory lectures of prior generations of Oxford dons (Ward qtd. in Benson, 84). And the same teaching style that alienated some students evidently entranced others. One of his former students, Lewis Campbell, said that Pater was 'worshi[pped]' by undergraduates and his 'conversation and his philosophy magnetised' them. However, 'the knowledge obtained in that way was not, as his pupils were to discover, the "sort that paid"'; apparently one student got 'only a Fourth' (that is, the worst kind of pass degree) because he wrote so 'gushingly' under Pater's influence (Campbell qtd. in Wright, 1:206).

As William Shuter has pointed out, Pater may have owed his position as a lay tutor at Oxford to modernising forces within the university, but his sensibility and work ran against the grain of modernising Oxford in crucial respects (Shuter 1997, 80–81). Pater reportedly made this picturesque intervention in a debate about university reform in the common room at Brasenose: 'I do not know what your object is. At present the undergraduate is a child of nature; he grows up like a wild rose in a country lane; you want to turn him into a turnip, rob him of all grace, and plant him out in rows' (Pater qtd. in Wright, 2:119). Pater was hostile to the increasing emphasis upon examinations and the development of a culture of meritocratic competition within the university.[14] This attitude was probably one source of Pater's estrangement from Jowett, who saw Oxford as an incubator for the nation's governing elite and thought that a university degree ought to be strenuous preparation for a life of public service.[15] To this end, reformers like Jowett also wanted to make Oxford more open to middle-class men of talent, and less like a private club for the sons of aristocrats. The new centrality of examinations was considered an engine of this more modern, meritocratic vision of Oxford. In this context, Pater's aestheticism could seem like a form of Luddism: how could the worship of beauty prepare young men to rule a nation and an empire? And it smelled vaguely of *ancien régime* Oxford: wasn't Pater preaching a fantasy of aristocratic dilettantism in an institution adapting, however slowly, to the modern world? Benson reflects on Pater's anachronistic quality in relation to Victorian Oxford:

> It is fair to say that the air of the Universities is not at the present moment favourable to the pursuit of *belles lettres* and artistic philosophies. The praise of academical circles is reserved [...] for people of brisk bursarial and business qualifications, for men of high technical accomplishment, for exact researchers, for effective teachers of prescribed subjects, for men of acute and practical minds, rather than men of imaginative qualities. (Benson, 181–182)

Pater's failure to be an 'exact researcher' is especially telling here. From the 1860s, dons such as Mark Pattison and Henry Halford Vaughan had argued that Oxford ought to be transformed into a university on the 'German' model: that is, after the pattern of the research universities developed in Germany in accordance with the ideals of Wilhelm von Humboldt. Proponents of the research ideal thought that the pursuit of advanced knowledge should be part of the vocation of the university teacher, and that students should be taught cutting-edge research by specialists rather than a fixed curriculum by generalists. Pattison was Pater's friend and Pater's own intellectual ideals have affinities with his: like Pattison, Pater was influenced by the Germanic humanist ideal of *bildung,* which emphasises that the young ought to pursue many-sided personal development and that education is valuable as an end in itself.[16] However, advocates of the 'Germanisation' of the university tended to emphasise disciplinary specialism and the production of new knowledge. They also favoured the broadening of curricula and the creation of new disciplines and fields of research.[17] Pater appears to have been resistant to such innovations. In his only public intervention in a contemporary debate, he expressed scepticism about the development of English literature as a university subject. He feared it would detract from the study of classics, which he regarded as the bedrock of a humanities education.[18] And while Pater may have won his Fellowship on the strength of his expertise in German philosophy, he did not ultimately measure up to the new ideal of the 'specialist' scholar. His body of work is markedly eclectic in form and content and draws upon many disciplines: history, art history, philosophy, theology, literary criticism, anthropology, archaeology, and philology. As this disciplinary range suggests, Pater was really an inspired synthesiser of the work of others rather than a scholar who could lay claim to original research discoveries. He also valued subjective impressions and an 'imaginative sense of fact' over scholarly rigour (Pater 1889, 4), notoriously playing fast and loose with textual and historical evidence to blur the distinction between his own subjectivity and his objects of analysis. Emilia Dilke had rebuked him for this in her review of *The Renaissance*:

> Instead of approaching his subject, whether Art or Literature, by the true scientific method, through the life of the time of which it is was an outcome, Mr Pater prefers in each instance to detach it from its surroundings, to suspend it isolated before him, as if indeed it were a kind of air-plant independent of ordinary sources of nourishment [...] We [...] feel as if we were wandering in a world of unsubstantial dreams.   (Dilke, 693)

As Ian Small has pointed out, Pater's celebration of the individual's subjective impressions has often been considered a sign of his modernity, even his radicalism, but it may also be understood as conservative in an important respect (Small, 95–96). Pater harkened back to the tradition of Victorian sage writers like Matthew Arnold, Thomas Carlyle, and John Ruskin, wherein critical authority rested upon a writer's compelling style and breadth of erudition (even if Pater rebelled against the heavy moralism of that tradition). In his reliance upon the magic of his own critical persona, Pater could seem out of date, a holdout against modern academic standards and modes of authority.

Although Pater was apparently determined to avoid further scandal in the wake of *The Renaissance* and the Hardinge affair, he still sought recognition and professional advancement within Oxford. In 1877, he put himself forward as a candidate for the position of Oxford Professor of Poetry, formerly held by Matthew Arnold. The position was elected by the Congregation, which meant that all MA students then resident at the university could vote on the candidates (though the candidate list itself was vetted by the University's Council, the controlling body of the university). This meant the election entailed public campaigns by the candidates, and the contest was followed avidly by Oxford students and the press. Pater withdrew his candidacy after Richard Tyrwhitt, rector of St. Mary Magdalen, Oxford, published an article entitled 'The Greek Spirit in Modern Literature' in the *Contemporary Review*. Tyrwhitt decried the modern literary tendency to use Hellenism to legitimise agnosticism and moral relativism, especially in relation to homosexuality. John Addington Symonds, another candidate for the Poetry Professorship, was the explicit target of Tyrwhitt's critique, but Pater understandably felt indicted too, and both men bowed out of the race.[19] Three years later, in 1880, Pater resigned his tutorship at Brasenose (though retained his Fellowship) and took lodgings with his sisters in Kensington, London. This entailed a significant loss of income but allowed Pater to focus more intently on completing his first novel, *Marius the Epicurean* (Benson, 83). It also allowed him regular escape from the surveillance of Oxford and enabled him to spend more time socialising in London literary and artistic circles, some of which were notably bohemian and queer.[20]

Benson suggests Pater was hurt that his resignation from his tutorship was accepted so readily at Brasenose (Benson, 83). Pater did not entirely abandon hope of a prestigious position at Oxford: in 1885, he put his name forward to succeed John Ruskin as the Slade Professor of Fine Art, though he was passed over for the post. Pater's withdrawal from the Poetry Professorship contest and his failure to win the Slade Professorship suggest that an aura of disrepute still clung to him. Yet these episodes also attest to his ambition: although he is almost always characterised by friends and acquaintances as extremely modest and unworldly, he clearly aspired to a high position at Oxford and to the kind of magisterial cultural authority possessed by Arnold and Ruskin. When the University of Glasgow awarded Pater an honorary degree in 1894, Pater duly travelled to Glasgow to accept it but he apparently felt that it would have been more fitting if such acknowledgment came from Oxford (Wright, 2: 207–208). As Billie Inman has suggested, additions Pater made to his discussion of the medieval scholar Peter Abelard in the 1877 edition of The Renaissance may be taken to encode his own Romantic self-image as a thinker, as well as his bitterness about his career at Oxford (Inman, 18–19). Pater constructs Abelard as a tragic standard-bearer of the humanist tradition, persecuted by lesser men for the beauty of his ideas:

> The opposition into which Abelard is thrown, which gives colour to his career, which breaks his soul to pieces, is a no less subtle opposition than that between the merely professional, official, hireling ministers of that system, with their ignorant worship of system for its own sake, and true child of the light, the humanist, with reason and heart and senses quick, while theirs were almost dead. (Pater, TR 80)

The publication of Marius the Epicurean in 1885 partly rehabilitated Pater's reputation. The protagonist's ambiguous journey from Epicureanism to Christianity was open to being read as a semi-autobiographical conversion narrative and seemed to herald a new moral seriousness in Pater.[21] Readers 'alarmed' by The Renaissance will be 'reassured' by Marius, noted the anonymous reviewer in the Pall Mall Gazette; '[Marius] should be wholly inoffensive to any reasonable person'.[22] After Marius and in the final decade of his life, Pater attained greater public renown and, with it, a qualified respectability: although he was frequently acclaimed as a stylist and acknowledged as a distinguished man of letters, reviewers still often suggested that there remained something dubious about his writing. Such critical misgivings tended to focus more on Pater's style than upon the philosophies he was thought to espouse. Indeed, it became customary for Pater's reviewers to articulate intense ambivalence about his style, often by turns extolling and disparaging its refinement over the course of a review.²³ And ardent fans of *The Renaissance* could feel betrayed by Pater's seeming capitulation to his detractors. For example, Katherine Bradley, one half of the poetic couple 'Michael Field', wrote in her diary in 1890: '[Pater] had struck out the Essay on Aesthetic Poetry in *Appreciations* [for the second edition] because it gave offence to some pious person – he is getting hopelessly prudish in literature & defers to the moral weakness of everybody. Deplorable!' (Bradley qtd. in Seiler, 10). On the whole, however, the self-consciously aesthetic and decadent writers of the fin de siècle were not deterred by Pater's apparent conservative turn and continued to pay homage to him. In 1893, Symons celebrated Pater as one of the pioneers of literary decadence in England, identifying not only *The Renaissance* but *Marius the Epicurean* and *Imaginary Portraits* as epitomising the 'morbid subtlety of analysis' and 'morbid curiosity of form' that defined the *avant-garde* literature of the 1890s (Symons, 858–9). In this way, Pater was reborn as a 'decadent' writer in the 1890s even as he seemed to disavow the aestheticism that had made him famous twenty years earlier.

Pater's efforts to distance himself from the scandalous success of *The Renaissance* and his growing eminence in the literary world do not seem to have remedied his outsider status at Oxford. Pater's failure to attend the Shelley Memorial held at Oxford in 1892 suggests his enduring marginality within the university. To mark Percy Bysshe Shelley's centenary, Shelley's daughter-in-law, Lady Jane Shelley donated a famous statue of the dead Shelley by Onslow Ford to University College, Oxford. The presentation of the statue was a significant event at Oxford, and 'all men of distinction' at the university were invited (Wright, 2:193). Pater's friend Edmund Gosse later asked him about his absence. 'I was not asked', Pater reportedly said (Wright, 2:193). Pater's exclusion feels especially poignant given that it is hard to imagine an Oxford eminence who would have appreciated the sculpture or commemorated the legacy of Shelley more sincerely than him. He might nonetheless have consoled himself with the irony that Oxford's reclamation of Shelley – who had been expelled from the University in 1811 because of his pamphlet on the 'Necessity of Atheism' – should be a yardstick of his own institutional rejection. As Wright remarks in relation to the episode, 'the owlet, the sparrow, the wren, the bat, and even the gnat had been invited, but the bird of paradise was passed over' (Wright, 2:194).

Pater gave public lectures intermittently in the final decade of his life. This was a conventional means for writers to supplement their incomes, and the speaking fees were surely part of Pater's motivation. Pater's growing celebrity meant that he sometimes attracted large audiences, but he apparently made as few concessions to the general public as he did to undergraduates: his topics were often esoteric, the arguments hard to follow, and his style of delivery painful (Benson, 159 and Wright, 2: 47–49). Some of these lectures were at institutions that aimed to uplift working- and lower-middle-class audiences: for example, he delivered a lecture on 'Demeter and Persephone' at the Birmingham and Midland Institute; in 1890, he delivered a lecture on humanism at Toynbee Hall (Wright, 1:46–47). Pater's underwhelming performances at such events are sometimes taken as evidence of the essentially elitist and hermetic nature of his aestheticism.[24] This is not a fair surmise. The fact that Pater possessed 'the charisma of the coterie' (at least in some measure) rather than 'the charisma of the masses' does not necessarily mean his efforts to communicate to a general audience were made in bad faith.[25] Pater's acceptance of speaking invitations to places like Toynbee Hall and the Birmingham and Midland Institute suggests he had at least-theoretical sympathy with the impulses of John Ruskin and William Morris to democratise aesthetic experience. As Linda Dowling has argued, the conservative hostility to Pater's work hinged partly on a recognition that his exaltation of aesthetic experience had a dangerously egalitarian undercurrent: although seemingly intended for a coterie of Oxford students and connoisseurs, its emphasis upon the authority of the individual's sensory perceptions implied the subversion of hierarchies of knowledge and taste (Dowling 1994, 76–89). And Pater's defects as a public speaker were not ultimately a barrier to the popularisation of his ideas, even if that popularisation had to be mediated by his many acolytes and admirers. In his obituary notice for Pater, Le Gallienne suggested that the cultural impact of Pater's work was incalculable because he had kindled the creativity of so many other writers. The future of modern literature would therefore be Paterian, however covertly or unconsciously:

> The man in the street knows nothing of the 'Studies in the Renaissance' [...] yet in subtle indirect fashion these books will influence his children's children [...] [Pater] is one of those writer's writers who reach what we call the general public at second or perhaps tenth hand. He is one of those literary springs, 'occult, withdrawn', at which the best young writers have secretly drunk. He is like the unseen hand in Bunyan pouring unacknowledged oil upon the flames of their various talents.   (Le Gallienne qtd. in Seiler, 280)

Notes

1. Wright, Thomas, *The Life of Walter Pater*. 2 vols. (London: Everett, 1907). Hereafter cited parenthetically. Despite its unreliability, Wright's biography is

still an important source of contemporary anecdotes and opinions about Pater, and useful for gaining an impression of his Victorian reputation. For analysis of the veracity of Wright's biography, see Laurel Brake, 'Judas and the Widow: Thomas Wright and A. C. Benson as Biographers of Walter Pater', in *Walter Pater: An Imaginative Sense of Fact*, ed. Phillip Dodd (London: Routledge, 1981), 39–54.

2. See also Denis Donoghue, *Walter Pater: Lover of Strange Souls* (New York: Alfred A. Knopf, 1995), 80–85. Hereafter cited parenthetically.

3. Qtd in Robert M. Seiler (ed.), *Walter Pater: The Critical Heritage* (London: Routledge, 1995), 162. Seiler is cited parenthetically hereafter.

4. Stefano Evangelista, *British Aestheticism and Ancient Greece: Hellenism, Reception, Gods in Exile* (Basingstoke: Palgrave Macmillan, 2009), 158–165; Lesley Higgins, 'No Time for Pater: The Silenced Other of Masculinist Modernism', In *Walter Pater: Transparencies of Desire*, eds. Laurel Brake, Lesley Higgins, and Carolyn Williams (Greensboro: ELT Press, 2002), 37–54.

5. Arthur C. Benson, *Walter Pater* (London: Macmillan, 1906), 20, 32. Hereafter cited in text.

6. For full details of the controversy over the Fichte essay, see Gerald Monsman, *Walter Pater* (Boston, MA: Twayne, 1977), 29–35. Monsman is cited hereafter parenthetically.

7. Seiler, *Critical Heritage*, 1995, 71, 57–61, 47–54, 78–81, 71–73.

8. See William John Courthope, 'The Prose Works of William Wordsworth'. *Quarterly Review* 141 (January 1876), 136; W. S. Lilly, 'The New Gospel'. *Time* 1 (1879), 169–175; 175; and Margaret Oliphant, 'New Books'. *Blackwood's Magazine* 114 (November 1873), 596–617; 608–609.

9. For a full account of the episode, see Billie Inman, 'Estrangement and Connection: Walter Pater, Benjamin Jowett and William M. Hardinge'. *Walter Pater in the 1990s*, eds. Laurel Brake and Ian Small (Greensboro, NC: ELT Press, 1991), 1–20.

10. Walter Pater, *The Renaissance: Studies in Art and Poetry*, ed. Hilary Fraser (Oxford: Oxford University Press, 2025), 197. Hereafter, cited parenthetically as *TR*.

11. For illuminating analysis of the distinction between 'early' and 'late' Pater, see Carolyn Williams, 'On Pater's Late Style'. *Nineteenth Century Prose* 24 (1997), 143–158.

12. William Shuter, *Reading Walter Pater* (Cambridge: Cambridge University Press, 1997), 80. Hereafter cited parenthetically.

13. See Linda Dowling, *Hellenism and Homosexuality in Victorian Oxford* (Ithaca: Cornell University Press, 1994), 81–85, 92–103.

14. Pater's aversion to the 'pedantic, mechanical discipline' he associated with examination culture was the reason he gave for his resistance to the introduction of English Literature to the Oxford curriculum. See Pater, 'To *The Pall Mall Gazette*' (27 November 1886), in Lawrence Evans (ed.), *Letters of Walter Pater* (Oxford: Clarendon Press, 1970), 102.

15. See Adrian Wooldridge, *The Aristocracy of Talent: How Meritocracy Made the Modern World* (London: Penguin, 2021), 158, 164.

16. See Hugh Stuart Jones, *Intellect and Character in Victorian England: Mark Pattison and the Invention of the Don* (Cambridge: Cambridge University Press, 2007), 164.

17. See Jones, *Intellect and Character in Victorian England*, 258; and Michael Sanderson, *Education, Economic Change and Society in England 1780–1870* (Cambridge: Cambridge University Press, 1995), 41–42.

18. In 1886, the *Pall Mall Gazette* solicited Pater's opinion on the introduction of English literature to the curricula of Oxford and Cambridge Universities, and he wrote a letter in response. See Evans, 1970, 101–102.

19. For a full account of the contest for the Poetry Professorship as a symbolic 'referendum' on Oxford liberalism and its capacity to tolerate agnosticism and homosexuality, see Dowling, 1994, 89–82 and 112–113.

20. See Laurel Brake, *Writers and Their Work: Walter Pater* (Tavistock: Northcote House, 1994), 83.

21. Some contemporaries who knew Pater interpreted *Marius* as an allegory of Pater's own return to Christianity. See for example William Sharp, *Papers Critical and Reminiscent* (New York: Duffield & Company, 1912), 221, and Mrs Humphry Ward's review in Seiler's *Walter Pater*, 138.

22. Quotation from anonymous reviewer, 'Marius the Epicurean', *Pall Mall Gazette*, 18 March, 1885, 5.

23. See for example the following reviews of Pater's *Appreciations* collected in Seiler's *Critical Heritage*: Oliphant, 214–219; C.L. Graves, 209–214; William Watson, 205–209; 'Unsigned Review', *Pall Mall Gazette* 198–200; Agnes Repplier, 232; and Courthope, 658–662.

24. See Diana Maltz, *British Aestheticism and the Urban Working Classes, 1870–1900: Beauty for the People* (Basingstoke: Palgrave Macmillan, 2006), 8–9.

25. I borrow the distinction between the charisma of the coterie versus the charisma of the masses from Clark, who is drawing upon Roger Eatwell's 'The Concept and Theory of Charismatic Leadership', *Totalitarian Movements and Political Religions* 7/2 (2006): 141–156.

2

STEPHEN CHEEKE

The Private Pater

Reading others, we are likely to encounter our own 'elusive inscrutable mistakable self', in Walter Pater's phrase.[1] We are 'mistakable' to others, as well as to ourselves. What is most private about the self is especially prone to be mistaken because it will be constituted, in part, by secrets. And yet when we respond to the work of artists and writers with real intensity, we recognise what Pater called the 'intimate impress of an indwelling soul'.[2] We enter into a private or personal intimacy, which seems immediately unmistakeable. Two half-truths have been told about the private life, or the secret intimacy, of Walter Pater. The first is that this was especially and peculiarly invisible; that both in his life and in his art, Pater was successful in concealing himself from his contemporaries, as well as for posterity. The second is that, in fact, he was an especially, peculiarly autobiographical writer, whose private or personal sensibility is laid bare in very conspicuous ways, for those able to see it. These two perspectives contrast with, rather than contradict each other, and they are intertwined in Pater's writings.

Persons who had some claim to friendship with Pater but with whom he was never really intimate complained that he was incapable of real intimacy. 'I pondered on the great military moustache that had seemed at first a discrepancy', wrote George Moore, 'but which had now begun to seem an essential part of him who wished above all things to preserve his real self for himself and to present to the world, even to his friends, a carefully prepared aspect – a mask'.[3] '[H]e could be kind, courteous, considerate, and sincere', wrote his early biographer, A.C. Benson, 'but he could not be intimate; he always guarded his innermost heart'.[4] For many Pater could seem frustratingly remote, evasive, even on occasions 'buttoned up'.[5] Those with whom he was intimate, such as Edmund Gosse, would also attest to a certain reserve. 'He was an assiduous host, a gracious listener; but who could tell what was passing behind those half-shut, dark-grey eyes, that courteous and gentle mask?'[6] Having observed him at the London Institute in November 1890, where Pater was lecturing on the French writer Prosper

Mérimée, Edith Cooper noted in her journal: 'I always feel that, like every Epicurean, his courteous exterior hides a strong nature, not innocent of barbarism.' 'Would'nt [sic] one give much to surprise The Bacchant in Walter Pater!'[7]

Perhaps no one had that good fortune – we don't really know. Cooper was right, however, to discern a darker side to Pater's imagination, one that is apparent in many of his writings, especially in the essays on Greek myth of 1876, in the violence of some of the *Imaginary Portraits* (1887), or in the study of 'The *Bacchanals* of Euripides', published in 1889. Her urge was to unmask a private self that would surely contrast with – contradict even – the imperturbable exterior. It is a strikingly recurrent theme in the reception of Pater's writings among his contemporaries, and one working on several levels. Is there a discrepancy between appearance and reality, a mask or disguise? Is some vital element being carefully hidden? What is partly at issue are the terms of the relationship between the private life and the work, which for various reasons are especially complex in Pater's case – 'for he was a *case* if ever there was one!', as Henry James observed.[8] One factor in calibrating these terms is just how uneventful Pater's life appears to have been, on the surface at least. Anyone tempted to write his biography would need to be stimulated by the fact that much of what we would think of as constituting incident and colour seems either not to have occurred at all or to have escaped notice. 'The reader who looks for desperate adventures will be grievously disappointed', warned Thomas Wright, rather inauspiciously, as this was in the opening pages of his biography. 'Pater slew neither lion nor centaur nor ferocious sow.'[9] Although not averse to arranging favourable notices of his books, Pater was essentially shy of publicity; he disliked public lecturing and seems to have especially disliked letter-writing. Compared to other major Victorian prose writers, who tended to prolixity both on the printed page and in private correspondence, he has left a very thin paper-trail. Writing to Thomas Wright in January 1900, and hoping to put him off his attempt at biography, Pater's sister Hester hinted:

> My brother's life was very uneventful – his inner life is best known from his books. He was very reticent even with those nearest to him and wrote few letters.[10]

'Pater, as a human being, illustrated by no letter, by no diaries, by no impulsive unburdenings of himself to associates, will grow more and more shadowy', noted Gosse.[11] 'He wrote letters with distaste, never really well, and always with excuses or regrets in them.'[12] Laurence Evans (the first editor of Pater's letters) observed that 'a strategy of studied blandness is visible in the correspondence'.[13] There are gaps in the biographical record too, 'weeks or even months in which he seems to have taken literally his favourite motif of evanescence and drifted away'.[14]

One way of becoming an enigma is to do nothing. Pater 'cultivated a substantial social life' among a 'small circle of friends', but at the same time, he seems to have positively avoided forming even an acquaintanceship with some of the most obvious names among his peers (John Ruskin, who was the first Slade Professor of Fine Art in Oxford 1869–1878, and held the post again in 1883–1885, being the most obvious).[15] Although often sought out by writers of a younger generation, in person he was not what they expected to encounter at all. 'He is very plain & heavy & dull, but agreeable', Vernon Lee recorded on her first meeting: 'Quite unaffected, & not at all like Mr. Rose.'[16] Mr. Rose was the character based upon Pater in W.H. Mallock's parody of late nineteenth-century literary culture, *The New Republic* (1877), a stereotype of the aesthete which would eventually merge in the popular imagination with the figure of Oscar Wilde. When Richard Le Gallienne was about to pay Pater a visit in Oxford, Wilde offered a warning:

> But I must tell you one thing about him, to save you from disappointment. You must not expect him to talk like his prose. Of course, no true artist ever does that. But, besides that, he never talks about anything that interests him. He will not breathe one golden word about the Renaissance. No! he will probably say something like this: 'So you wear cork soles in your shoes? Is that really true? And do you find them comfortable? . . . How extremely interesting!'

'Here indeed was no exquisite languishing "aesthete," such as his work might have misled one into fearing', Le Gallienne noted when the meeting took place.[17] Was this because the image itself was a false deduction from the work, or because the work was not like the private man at all? Or was Pater simply dissembling? In an unfinished manuscript essay titled 'The Aesthetic Life', dating from around 1893, Pater wrote of the typical aesthete: 'It is part of his tact, his finely educated sense of fitness, to dissimulate his interests, to say less than he really feels, to carry about with him in self-defence through a vulgar age a habit of reserve, of irony it may be, this again becoming in its turn but an added means of expression.'[18] This may be a covert defence of Oscar Wilde, but how far does it apply to Pater himself as an 'aesthete', one wonders? 'Everything Oscar does is a deliberate trap for the literalist', Henry James wrote.[19] And yet Wilde was himself something of a conscious literalist, or ironist, when it came to reading Walter Pater. When Pater reinstated a revised Conclusion to the 1888 edition of *The Renaissance*, he explained that he had omitted it from the 1877 edition because 'I conceived it might possibly mislead some of those young men into whose hands it might fall'

(197). It is perhaps the most-discussed footnote of the entire century. In fact, the whole question of when and how Pater's work was misleading, and of who exactly had been misled by it (having perhaps taken the Conclusion too literally), would be central to his reception. It is also one of Pater's own subjects: how the axioms of philosophical wisdom may be compromised or corrupted in lived experience. How philosophy (like the self) is also always 'mistakeable'.

An idea established itself, then, of a strict division between the private life (which had been dull and uneventful) and the writings (extraordinary). What seemed to be a kind of alchemy offered obvious temptations to a would-be biographer, the chief of which would be the assumption that if Pater had 'put whatever life he had into his work, it should be possible even now to thwart him and remove the concealed life from the work by biographical deduction'.[20] The trap had thus been set for reading him as autobiographical in everything he wrote (sometimes in a highly coded form), even as he wrote almost nothing of what we might call pure autobiography.

And yet those who knew his work well insisted that this autobiographical dimension was a real one. William Sharp:

> There are few more autobiographical writers, though almost nowhere does he openly limn autobiographical details. Only those lovers of his work who have read, and read closely, lovingly, and intimately, all he has written, can under-stand the man. He is one of those authors of whom there can never be any biography away from his writings.

Sharp concluded that 'the inner life of Walter Pater is written throughout each of his books'.[21] 'Everything in Pater was in harmony', Arthur Symons wrote, 'when you got used to its particular forms of expression'.[22] The terms are those of initiates. You must get used to something – a code? – or be an intimate, to understand him. The greater a reader's familiarity with the work, the clearer the code becomes. 'It is all, the criticism, and the stories, and the writing about pictures and places, a confession, the *vraie verité* (as he was fond of saying) about the world in which he lived.' But he added: 'It was a world into which we can only look, not enter, for none of us have his secret.'[23]

The confession that does not give away its secret seems paradoxical. It highlights the distinction between two ways of thinking about the private or personal, which may offer us a distinction, too, between the 'inner' and the 'outer' life. On the one hand, Pater's writings are always self-reflexive. They have a pronounced autobiographical dimension, in the sense in which the 'desire of self-portraiture', as Pater wrote of Charles Lamb and of Michel de Montaigne, often seems to be 'the real motive in writing at all'.[24] Both

Marius the Epicurean (1885) and *Gaston de Latour* (1888) are spiritual and intellectual biographies of their author – of the thinker as a young man. A third novel was planned in the series, in which the protagonist would be discovered in late eighteenth-century England. Pater would have had the distinction among nineteenth-century English writers in having written a trilogy of historical *Bildungsroman*. He is self-reflexive, too, in the sense that all his essays on other writers, artists and thinkers are expressions of Pater's own sensibility and personality; indeed, these essays refract other figures, sometimes creatively reinventing them, through a personal perspective. His *Imaginary Portraits* are in some ways close to what we might now call autobiografiction, and 'The Child in the House' (1878), which Pater described as 'the germinating, original, source, specimen, of all my *imaginative* work', is a form of life-writing based upon his own boyhood.[25]

On the other hand, this is not quite the same thing as discovering clues to facts about the biography or reading the work as an exposure of the private life. This was the fate Henry James believed Pater to have had the luck to have escaped. Writing to Edmund Gosse in December 1894, James expressed his envy:

> ... how curiously negative and faintly-grey he, after all telling, remains! I think he has had – will have had – the most exquisite literary fortune: i.e. to have taken it all out, wholly, exclusively, with the pen (the style, the genius,) and absolutely not at all with the person. He is the mask without the face, and there isn't in his total superficies a tiny point of vantage for the newspaper to flap his wings on.[26]

Taking 'it all out' with the pen suggests the disappearance of the personal life in the sublimation of the writing process, and the covert aggression upon 'life' such a process entails. Neither newspaper columnist nor biographical gossip would find anything to go on. The suggestion of a sexual metaphor is one of masturbation – the solitary and, in a sense, the non-active ideal of a hieratic devotion to Art. 'How to write the biography of a celibate?' – James seems to be asking, perhaps self-interestedly.

This enviable invisibility is partly (but only partly) about Pater's sexuality and sexual history. His writings have a homoerotic or homophilic dimension which has long been recognised, even if it was not always valued, a dissident and potentially subversive element in relation to Victorian culture. In Oxford circles, Pater is associated with the development of a particular kind and temper of Hellenism in which love between men is privileged. Benjamin Jowett's translations of Plato's dialogues (1871), and the influence of his teaching upon Oxford Hellenism more generally, although Christianised and homophobic in their interpretation of the institution of Greek *paederastia* (the love of an older man for a younger pupil), nevertheless had what Linda Dowling calls the 'unintended consequence' of giving writers such as Pater, John Addington Symonds, and Wilde a 'glimpse in Plato's defence of transcendental, "Uranian" love a vocabulary adequate to their own inmost hopes, and to see in "Greek love" itself the promise of a Hellenic individuality and diversity with the most positive implications for Victorian civilization'.[27] This is an important movement within Victorian culture in the latter half of the century. But the issue of Pater's sex life is another matter. The William Money Hardinge affair, in which supposedly intimate and compromising letters from Pater to the Oxford undergraduate Hardinge were passed on to Benjamin Jowett in 1874, is certainly a 'point of vantage' to have emerged in modern times for the literary gossip, but it is deeply ambiguous and uncertain in all of its details. On the spectrum of what we would now call homosexual practice, Pater may have been active or not, we do not know. The question of when, how, or even *if* the male spiritual procreancy celebrated by Oxford Hellenists becomes practice – and the range of practice – is central to the Wilde trials, which came soon after Pater's death. At what point does the Socratic *eros* of the tutorial relationship – the intimate and loving friendship of an older man and a younger pupil – become actively sexual, and what would this mean – would it be a consummation or a betrayal of that relationship? 'Death spared him the tragedy of Wilde's trial, a tragedy we can conceive only as the sacrifice of male homosexuality to male homophobia. But Pater's homoeroticism cannot be represented in the terms of such a discourse', writes William Shuter.[28] Very often the narrative has been told of Pater's writing life as a change from an early aesthetic individualism (radical, pagan, sexually dissident) to a later *rapprochement*, both with the Christian Church and with conventional mores, in which the movement from aesthete to moralist is presented as a transformation from one thing into its opposite, rather than as a development, or even (as Pater sought to convince us), a prolonged clarification. For Pater it is certain that the aesthete and the moralist were not discrete *personae* in his personality separated by time and determined by scandalous life-events.

These are the main obstacles, then, to discovering a 'private' Walter Pater. Even though assumptions about his personal life were very much bound up with the reception of his work, almost nothing is known about what is most private in any life – the sex life. Pater scholars would give much to surprise the Bacchant in their biographical subject, but there is no such satisfaction to be had. There are gaps and *lacunae* in the biography more broadly too; missing dates; an evasive and bland correspondence; two unmarried sisters devoted to protecting his reputation; no memoir. Such a little imprint, in a writer who was himself drawn to littleness, to the unheroic or small-scale: 'that littleness in which there is much of the whole woeful heart of things', as Pater says in his 1878 essay on Charles Lamb.[29] What is remarkable is just how often this general faintness of impression, uneventfulness, and near invisibility are reflected in the work itself, indeed are often Pater's subject. 'In an age when the lives of artists were full of adventure, [Sandro Botticelli's] life is almost colourless', Pater wrote with approbation. 'Only two things happened to him' (39–40). The same observation may be found in biographies of Pater. The colourlessness in Botticelli's life is connected to the principle of moral neutrality, exemplified by Dante's rebel angels who stood apart or refused to take sides in the war in heaven, being 'neither for Jehovah nor for His enemies' (44). Dante condemned them to Hell for this abstention, but Pater sympathises with what he took to be Botticelli's sympathy for them. Clearly, the moral value of neutrality or indifference – that 'recurring liberal ideal, the neutral subject position' – is something that can never be taken for granted and is a major site of contestation throughout nineteenth-century culture.[30] Pater's own life and work have often been taken to exemplify an admirable neutrality, a resistance to various forms of cultural authority. In this light, Pater is claiming a real value in living 'without disgrace and without praise' (in Dante's phrase), of escaping the world's report. In his final, unfinished novel, *Gaston de Latour* (1888, 1894), he observes of Montaigne:

> The natural second-best, the intermediate and unheroic virtue (even the Church, as we know, by no means *requiring* 'heroic' virtue), was perhaps actually the best, better than any kind of heroism, in an age whose very virtues were apt to become insane. [...] In that age it was a great thing to be just blameless.[31]

Pater is writing about sixteenth-century France and its religious wars, but this is also a nineteenth-century virtue at odds with many of the central Victorian assumptions about action and heroism. Towards the beginning of his writing life, in his essay 'On Wordsworth' (1874), first published in the *Fortnightly Review* and later revised for *Appreciations, with an Essay on Style* (1889), Pater had observed: '[Wordsworth's] life is not divided by profoundly felt incidents; its changes are almost wholly inward, and it falls into broad, untroubled spaces.' This inwardness reflected a more general principle:

> That the end of life is not action but contemplation – *being* as distinct from *doing* – a certain disposition of the mind: is, in some shape or other, the principle of all the higher morality. In poetry, in art, if you enter into their true spirit at all, you touch this principle, in a measure: these, by their very

sterility, are a type of beholding for the mere joy of beholding. To treat life in the spirit of art, is to make life a thing in which means and ends are identified: to encourage such treatment, the true moral significance of art and poetry. Wordsworth, and other poets who have been like him in ancient or more recent times, are the masters, the experts, in this art of impassioned contemplation.[32]

Aristotle's twin notions of *enargeia* (acute mental activity) and *theoria* (divine-like attention) as expounded in the *Ethics*, one of the texts Pater taught at Oxford, stand behind this ideal of 'impassioned contemplation'. The latter had been Christianised by John Ruskin in the second volume of *Modern Painters* (1846), so that it would stand for reverent contemplation of divinity in the natural world. This is perhaps closer to the truth of Wordsworth's vision than Pater's idea of an absolutely disinterested form of 'beholding', detached from any theological grounds. In Pater's vision, however, we see an outline of the substitution of art for religion, one of the larger cultural processes underpinning the nineteenth century. T.S. Eliot called the process a 'degradation' of religion, for which he blamed Pater and Matthew Arnold.[33] For others, however, this was an emancipation. In his chapter of *The Renaissance*, 'Two Early French Stories', Pater connects the 'antinomianism' of the French renaissance of the late twelfth century with the writings of Joachim de Fiore (c.1135–1202), a medieval Italian theologian and mystic who had heralded a coming age which would see the 'third and final dispensation of a "spirit of freedom"' (89), a freedom of contemplation unbounded by the prevailing moral law. This idea appealed not only to aesthetes like Wilde, who were in open battle with the moral law, but to those seeking to subordinate religion to art at the turn of the century, such as W.B. Yeats when he came to edit the work of William Blake, and to discover the thought of Friedrich Nietzsche.

Few things are so elusive as the 'spirit of freedom', sovereign index of the private liberal individual, and another form of invisibility, or secrecy. Even before such a notion began to wind itself around his own reputation, however, Pater seemed drawn to artists and philosophers of the Renaissance whose lives and works contained this element. In the essay added to the third edition of *The Renaissance* in 1888, titled 'The School of Giorgione', Pater noted that 'something fabulous and illusive has always mingled itself in the brilliancy of Giorgione's fame' (149). J.A. Crowe's and G.B. Cavalcaselle's *A History of Painting in North Italy* (1871) may have drastically limited the number of authentic works by the master, but Pater was interested in something else:

But, although the number of Giorgione's extant works has thus been limited by recent criticism, all is not done when the real and the traditional elements in what concerns him have been discriminated; for, in what is connected with a great name, much that is not real is often very stimulating. For the aesthetic philosopher, therefore, over and above the real Giorgione and his authentic extant works, there remains the *Giorgionesque* also – an influence, a spirit or type in art, active in men so different as those to whom many of his supposed works are really assignable. A veritable school, in fact, grew together out of all those fascinating works rightly or wrongly attributed to him; out of many copies from, or variations on him, by unknown or uncertain workmen, whose drawings and designs were, for various reasons, prized as his; out of the immediate impression he made upon his contemporaries, and with which he continued in men's minds; out of many traditions of subject and treatment, which really descend from him to our own time, and by tracing which we fill out the original image. Giorgione thus becomes a sort of impersonation of Venice itself, its projected reflex or ideal, all that was intense or desirable crystallising about the memory of this wonderful young man.   (152)

To 'become a sort of impersonation of something' is a wonderfully suggestive phrase, making the actor passive in his impersonation, personalised and depersonalised at once in the absorption of a city's 'reflex': the *Giorgionesque*. One of Pater's favourite metaphors of chemical process (crystallisation) might make us ponder the idea of the *Pateresque* in Pater too: 'an influence, a spirit or type', a 'school' active in men of widely different temperaments to him, such as Moore, or Wilde, or Symons.

Carolyn Williams describes the methodology of the Giorgione chapter as 'an early version of reception-aesthetics, in which [Pater] accepts and analyses "received" views, implicitly defining them as "data" simply because they are historically "given".'[34] In other words, you can choose to be credulous about legends because they help us to understand the subject around whom they have grown. It is a generous and fructifying critical principle, but it is also a risky one, which should be borne in mind when thinking about Pater himself. In the chapter of *The Renaissance* on Leonardo da Vinci, he writes that Leonardo's '*legend*, as the French say, with the anecdotes which every one remembers, is one of the most brilliant chapters of Vasari' (127) (the biographer of Renaissance artists).[35] This *legend* has been corrected by antiquarians, but 'a lover of strange souls may still analyse for himself the impression made on him' (128) by the stories told of Leonardo. 'Vasari's story of an earlier Medusa, painted on a wooden shield, is perhaps an invention; and yet, properly told, has more of the air of truth about it than anything else in the whole legend' (130). Again, this is a thought with large implications. Throughout the chapter on Leonardo, Pater plays upon the idea of the legend and the secret:

His type of beauty is so exotic that it fascinates a larger number than it delights, and seems more than that of any other artist to reflect ideas and views and some scheme of the world within; so that he seemed to his contemporaries to be the possessor of some unsanctified and secret wisdom.   (127)

We read of 'the secret places of his nature' (129); that Leonardo seemed to be something like 'the sorcerer or the magician, possessed of curious secrets and a hidden knowledge, living in a world of which he alone possessed the key' (131); that he seemed like someone going about a 'secret errand' (127); that he had offered to sell 'strange secrets in the art of war' (132) to Ludovico Sforza, Duke of Milan. There were 'men with just enough genius to be capable of initiation into his secret' (136). He 'penetrated into the most secret parts of nature' (133). His masterpieces emerged out of 'the secret places of a unique temperament' (136). The *Mona Lisa* had learned the 'secrets of the grave' (140). 'Secrecy' proliferates in and of itself, as a primary effect, without the disclosure of what these secrets might be in any particularity. The 'secret' is matched with another important word for Pater: 'strange' (which occurs twenty times in the Leonardo chapter alone). The process of *making strange* (partly rooted in the repetition of key words) is an imaginative one at the heart of Pater's writings. In an essay of 1876 he defined Romanticism as the 'addition of strangeness to beauty', which suggests defamiliarisation.[36] But it is also an openness to strangeness, to the stranger, and is therefore a principle of curiosity and hospitality. ('Strange' also points towards the category of the 'weird' which has recently become central to thinking about the Gothic.) For Pater, Leonardo had exemplified the 'art of going deep, of tracking the sources of expression to their subtlest retreats, the power of an intimate presence in the things he handled' (130). Going deep evokes the activity of deep-sea diving that he attributed to the *Mona Lisa*, and 'tracking' seems close to 'trafficking': '[she has] trafficked for strange webs with Eastern merchants' (140). But this 'art' – of going deep and tracking or trafficking in the strange – is also Pater's own method, and the discovery of 'intimate presence' is at the core of his aesthetic vision. What is 'strange' – what is most private – is also potentially something most intimately present. Premonitions and omens, auguries and divinations, presentiments, intimations, are all necessary elements of this traffic. 'The science of that age [the fifteenth century] was all divination, clairvoyance, unsubjected to our exact modern formulas', Pater wrote, 'seeking in an instant of vision to concentrate a thousand experiences' (131). This is not a criticism of Renaissance science but an appropriation of its supposed methods for his own writings, and a precise description of Pater's vision of the *Mona Lisa*, 'the seventh heaven of symbolical expression' (139). The passage on the

Mona Lisa is the prose piece for which Pater is most famous, one Yeats described as having 'dominated a generation, a domination so great that all over Europe from that day to this men shrink from Leonardo's masterpiece as from an over-flattered woman'. 'Only by printing it in *vers libre*', Yeats wrote, 'can one show its revolutionary importance'.[37] Part of what Yeats meant was that Pater's prose seeded a rhythm for early modernist poetry. (Yeats's 1936 anthology of modern poetry opens with his rendering of the passage as free verse.) But he also meant that its symbolic expression anticipated the revolutionary methods of Symbolism, which Arthur Symons had celebrated in nineteenth-century French and Belgian literature and which Yeats had again connected to William Blake.

The method is further defined in the passage in which Pater describes a series of drawings in which we see Leonardo's 'type of womanly beauty':

> They are the clairvoyants, through whom, as through delicate instruments, one becomes aware of the subtler forces of nature, and the modes of their action, all that is magnetic in it, all those finer conditions wherein material things rise to that subtlety of operation which constitutes them spiritual, where only the finer nerve and the keener touch can follow. It is as if in certain significant examples we actually saw those forces at their work on human flesh. Nervous, electric, faint always with some inexplicable faintness, these people seem to be subject to exceptional conditions, to feel powers at work in the common air unfelt by others, to become, as it were, the receptacle of them, and pass them on to us in a chain of secret influences.　　　　　　　　　　　　　(135–36)

There are many such passages in Pater's writings which could be detached to stand as figurative commentaries upon his own method – a further, deeper kind of self-reflexivity. The 'strange web' (one of his master-metaphors) has become visible in these women as if an x-ray has revealed its presence in the nervous, electric body, in an instant of vision. They are the instruments of its apparitional power. Near invisibility, inexplicable faintness, and nervous delicacy have become the instruments of a finer sensibility attuned to powers unfelt by others, able to pass these on in a chain of secret influences by a kind of clairvoyance. The metaphor here is itself the double, like a photographic negative, of a figure Pater uses later in the same chapter. The fading of Leonardo's *The Last Supper*, decaying rapidly on the plastered walls of the Dominican church in Milan because it was painted not in fresco but in oils, produced an effect in which the figures seem to be 'ghosts through which you see the wall, faint as the shadow of leaves upon the wall on autumn afternoons' (95). They are silhouettes: a quintessentially *Pateresque* figure, in which private shadows obtain a public outline.

Notes

1. 'The History of Philosophy' (c.1880), Houghton manuscript, Harvard University, bMS, Eng 1150 (2).
2. Walter Pater, *The Renaissance: Studies in Art and Poetry*, ed. Hilary Fraser (Oxford: Oxford University Press, 2025), 107. Hereafter, *The Renaissance*, citations intext.
3. George Moore, *Avowals* (London: Heinemann, 1924), 180.
4. Arthur Christopher Benson, *Walter Pater* (London: Macmillan, 1906), 185.
5. Frank Harris, 'Walter Pater', *Contemporary Portraits* (New York, 1919), 203–226; in Robert Morris Seiler (ed.), *Walter Pater: A Life Remembered* (Calgary: University of Calgary Press, 1987), 135. Hereafter, Seiler.
6. Edmund Gosse, *Critical Kit-Kats* (London: Heinemann, 1896), 266.
7. Lecture on 'Prosper Mérimée', 24 November 1890. Michael Field, *The Poet: Published and Manuscript Materials* ed. Marion Thain and Ana Parejo Vadillo (Plymouth: Broadview Editions, 2009), 242–3.
8. From a letter from Henry James to A. C. Benson, 31 May 1906, in Seiler, 260.
9. Thomas Wright, *The Life of Walter Pater* 2 vols (London: Everett & Co., 1907), I, xviii
10. Letter dated 31 January 1900, Seiler, 253.
11. Gosse, *Critical Kit-Kats*, 271.
12. Symons, in Seiler, 127.
13. Lawrence Evans, ed. *Letters of Walter Pater* (Oxford: Clarendon Press, 1970), xxiv. Robert M., 'Seiler Also Notes a 'Defensiveness' and 'Diffidence' in the Correspondence'. In *Collected Works of Walter Pater: Volume IX: Correspondence*, ed. Robert M. Seiler (Oxford: Oxford University Press, 2023), 25. [Hereafter, *CWWP IX*]
14. Denis Donoghue, *Walter Pater: Lover of Strange Souls* (New York: Alfred Knopf, 1995), 23.
15. *CWWP: IX*, 25;27.
16. Cited in Evans, *Letters*, xxxvi.
17. Richard Le Gallienne, *The Romantic '90s* (1926; London: Putnam, 1951), 56–57.
18. Pater, 'The Aesthetic Life' (c.1893), bMS Eng 1150 (7), Houghton Library, Harvard University.
19. Henry James, *Henry James: A Life in Letters*, ed. Philip Horne (London: Allen Lane, 1999), 246.
20. Donoghue, *Walter Pater*, 9.
21. William Sharp, 'Some Personal Reminiscences of Walter Pater', *Atlantic Monthly*, 74 (December 1894), 801–814; in Seiler, 93.
22. Arthur Symons, *A Study of Walter Pater* (London: Charles J. Sawyer, 1932), 5.
23. Arthur Symons, 'Walter Pater', *Monthly Review* 24 (September 1906), 14–24; Seiler, 124.
24. Pater, 'Charles Lamb', *Appreciations*, WWP, 117.
25. Pater, Harvard manuscript, cited in Evans, *Letters*, xxix.
26. Pater, Letter of December 13 1894, cited in Seiler, 200.
27. Linda Dowling, *Hellenism and Homosexuality in Victorian Oxford* (London: Cornell University Press, 1994), 66.

28. William F. Shuter, 'The "Outing" of Walter Pater', *Nineteenth-Century Literature* 48:4 (March 1994), 480–506. 'The "Outing" of Walter Pater', 480–506 (506).

29. 'Charles Lamb', *Appreciations*, WWP, V, 110.

30. David Russell, *Tact: Aesthetic Liberalism and the Essay Form in Nineteenth-Century Britain* (Princeton: Princeton University Press, 2018), 119.

31. Pater, *Gaston de Latour*, WWP, IV, 93–4.

32. Pater, *Appreciations: With an Essay on Style*, WWP, V, 44; 62.

33. Thomas Stearns Eliot, 'Arnold and Pater', in *The Complete Prose of T. S. Eliot: The Critical Edition: English Lion, 1930–1933* (Baltimore: Johns Hopkins University Press, 2015), ed. Jason Harding and Ronald Schuchard, IV, 'Arnold and Pater' (1930), 178–187 (185).

34. Carolyn Williams, *Transfigured World: Walter Pater's Aesthetic Historicism* (Ithaca, NY: Cornell University Press, 1989), 84.

35. In French, 'legend' has more of a sense of the merely historical or written record, rather than myth.

36. 'Romanticism', *Macmillan's Magazine* 35, no. 205 (November, 1876), 64–70 (65). The thought originates in Francis Bacon's essay 'Of Beauty' (1612) and is recycled in the nineteenth century by Charles Baudelaire and Edgar Allan Poe.

37. William Butler Yeats, *The Oxford Book of Modern Verse* (Oxford: Oxford University Press, 1936), vii.

3

CATHERINE MAXWELL

Pater and Style

'As the painter in his picture, so the artist in his book, aims at the production by honourable artifice of a peculiar atmosphere', writes Pater in his famous 1888 essay 'Style'.[1] It is noticeable how Pater's early critics, many of them friends or associates, commented on his atmospheres, seeing these as consonant with the evolution of his style in successive works and using the sensory language of colour, light, temperature, and scent to describe them. In 1887, reflecting on *Studies in the History of the Renaissance* (1873), 'the most beautiful book of prose in our literature', Arthur Symons declared that 'An almost oppressive quiet – a quietness which seems to breathe of an atmosphere heavy with tropical flowers – broods over these pages; a subdued light shadows them.'[2] In contrast he thought that Pater's next book, his novel *Marius the Epicurean* (1885), exhibited a 'a somewhat chill asceticism', while the fictional studies that make up the *Imaginary Portraits* of 1887, though characterised by the same 'self-restraint', called to mind Pater's atmospheric 'painter', each being like 'a picture painted with a brush': 'The style of Denys l'Auxerrois has a subdued heat and veiled richness of colour, which contrasts very strikingly with the silvery-grey coolness of A Prince of Court Painters, the chill, more leaden grey of Sebastian van Storck, though it has a certain affinity, perhaps, with the more variously-tinted canvas of Duke Carl of Rosenmold' (*WPCH*, 180).

No less attuned to atmosphere, George Moore, who had read *Marius* in the year of its publication, found it far from chilly: 'Well I remember when I read the opening lines, and how they came upon me sweetly as the flowing breath of a bright spring.' To him the novel was a revelation:

> I had not thought of the simple and unaffected joy of the heart of natural things; the colour of the open air, the many forms of the country, the birds flying ... A new dawn was in my brain, fresh and fair, full of wide temples and studious hours, and the lurking fragrance of incense; that such a vision of life was possible I had no suspicion.

For Moore such effects are rooted in the novel's atmospheric language, its musicality and subtle suggestion:

> *Marius the Epicurean* was more to me than a mere emotional influence, precious and rare though that may be, for this book was the first in English prose I had come across that procured for me any genuine pleasure in the language itself, in the combination of words for silver or gold chime, and unconventional cadence, and for all those lurking half-meanings, and that evanescent suggestion, like the odour of dead roses, that words retain to the last of other times and elder usage.[3]

In 1887 Vernon Lee also recalled her first reading of *Marius* 'in the earliest days of our Florentine spring', remembering how with the 'impressions from without mingled the impressions of the book: sunny, serene, bracing, like those first spring days'.[4] Nearly fifty years later she breaks off from a rather pedantic and laborious analysis of a famous passage in the novel (Marius's journey to the Temple of Aesculapius) to acknowledge 'Pater's extraordinary mastery in the reconstruction of mood'.[5] Pater's atmospheres are also clearly in her mind when, concluding her *Renaissance Fancies and Studies* (1895) with a 'Valedictory' dedicated to him, she makes plain her preference for *Marius* and *Plato and Platonism* (1893) over *Studies in the History of the Renaissance*, while noting how the early essays show 'indications' or 'characteristic germs', 'even as we find in the earliest works of a painter', that presage the later work. These 'germs', she asserts, are 'the recurrence of impressions and images connected with physical sanity and daintiness; of aspiration after orderliness, congruity'.[6] Whether or not we agree with Lee's view of the inevitable moral trajectory of Pater's work which sees him becoming 'like Plato, a teacher of discipline and self-harmony', her sense of him as signalled and informed by the characteristic atmospheres of his own work is striking. For her, he is 'the man who harped upon clearness and livingness of water, upon the delicate bracingness of air, who experienced so passionate a preference for the whole gamut, the whole palette, of spring, of temperate climates and of youth and childhood; a person who felt existence in the terms of its delicate vigour and its restorative austerity'.[7]

Atmosphere is intrinsic to Pater's style. For him the writer is a 'literary artist' who, like Gustave Flaubert (the inspiration for 'Style'), is 'Alive to the value of an atmosphere in which every term finds its utmost degree of expression' and has 'all the jealousy of a lover of words' (*A*, 13). In her 1933 essay Lee remarked on 'Pater's singularly *essential* or, if you prefer, *saturated quality*', something also noticed by John Addington Symonds.[8] Although in private Symonds was less than complimentary about Pater's style, in his 1873 review of *Studies*, he acknowledged that 'There is scarcely a superfluous word or a hasty phrase in the whole volume. Each paragraph, each sentence is saturated with thought', citing examples of sentences 'containing in brief something of the peculiar flavour which gives value to the book' and observing 'an intensity peculiar to Mr Pater's style'.[9] Arthur Symons's famous essay 'The Decadent Movement in Literature' (1893), although devoted to French writers, in its original form, contained an appreciation of Pater's prose – 'the most beautiful English prose which is now being written' – and he declared 'how far away from the classic ideals of style is this style in which words have their color, their music, their perfume, in which there is "some strangeness in the proportion" of every beauty!'[10]

As I've shown elsewhere, in conceiving his characteristic critical treatment of a subject, Pater implicitly likens his process to that of an alchemist.[11] In this he follows predecessors like Shelley and Coleridge and his near contemporary Swinburne, who draw on the language and imagery of alchemy – its notion of precious, potent, and enduring essences produced through processes of combination, fusion, distillation, refinement, and extraction – to figure literary creativity and the resulting immortal artwork. The 'function of the æsthetic critic', as described in the Preface to *Studies in the History of the Renaissance*, 'is to distinguish, to analyse, and separate from its adjuncts, the virtue by which a picture, a landscape, a fair personality in life or in a book, produces this special impression of beauty or pleasure, to indicate what the source of that impression is, and under what conditions it is experienced. His end is reached when he has disengaged that virtue, and noted it, as a chemist notes some natural element, for himself and others'.[12] Here the word 'virtue' is an old alchemical term, meaning 'essence' just as by 'chemist' Pater properly means 'alchemist'. In analysing an artist like Leonardo or Michelangelo, Pater will often see the characteristic essence of such a figure as a kind of 'alchemical marriage', an 'interfusion' or union of opposites such as 'curious beauty' or 'sweetness and strength' (*SR*, 130, 125).

Unsurprisingly then, the prose stylist as Pater conceives him is also alchemically alert to the 'virtues' of individual words, choosing them not just to convey his subject but perhaps more importantly to reflect his own unique temperament: 'His punctilious observance of the proprieties of his medium will diffuse through all he writes a general air of sensibility, of refined usage' (*A*, 13). He is anxious to 'beget a vocabulary faithful to the colouring of his own spirit, and in the strictest sense original' (*A*, 15). Pater's own characteristic vocabulary is very much a key element of his 'saturated style', with the same words gathering additional charge as they recur throughout his work. Selected from what he tellingly calls 'the delicate and evanescent region of human language' (*A*, 36), here are just some of his favourites: 'fresh', 'delicate', 'sweet', 'exquisite', 'comely', 'dainty', 'refined', 'beauty', 'grace', 'fair', 'charm', 'subtle', 'fine', 'exotic', 'strange', 'curious', 'sentiment', 'desire', 'passion', 'love', 'spirit', 'soul', 'personality', ' face', 'body', 'senses', 'sensation', 'matter', 'fascination', 'mystic', 'vision', 'sight', 'faint', 'vague', 'fade', 'passing', 'unique', 'individual', 'peculiar', 'impression', 'moment', 'essence', 'expression', 'influence', 'power', 'force', 'atmosphere', 'mood', 'dream', 'reverie', 'fancy', 'imagination', 'blend', 'combination', 'art', 'death', 'life', 'pain', 'pleasure'.

These words and their variants, along with terms that conjure the senses and sensory effects such as 'light', 'bright', 'shadow', 'rich', 'colour', 'taste', 'sound', 'music', 'touch', and others suggestive of scent and odour, are the language of Pater's own unique aesthetic sensibility, conveying his attempt to arrest and savour the fleeting shades and nuances of things, to express a series of rarefied, cultivated, and finely discriminated perceptions. Like his influential peer Swinburne, who also has a distinctive style and lexicon, he chooses to write about only subjects that attract him and meet with his approval, so that the reader attuned to Pater's particular vocabulary, although encountering fresh writings by him on new topics, will usually have a strong intuition of why that topic has been selected and how it might harmonise with Paterian ways of seeing and appreciation. And typically, what we encounter in a discursive essay by Pater is never an attempt at an objective description but an impressionistic appreciation: 'in æsthetic criticism the first step towards seeing one's object as it really is, is to know one's impression as it really is, to discriminate it, to realise it distinctly': 'What is this song or picture, this engaging personality presented in life or in a book, *to me*? (*SR*, 73).

In 'Style' Pater is at pains to show that even where prose might seem to subordinate itself to the simple transcription of facts, as in historical accounts, it is intimately shaped by the writer's subjectivity: 'Your historian, for instance, with absolutely truthful intention, amid the multitude of facts presented to him must needs select, and in selecting assert something of his own humour, something that comes not of the world without but of a vision within' (*A*, 9). And for Pater, the more a writer gives us 'The transcript of his sense of fact rather than the fact', the more his work approaches art. Thus 'Literary art ... is the representation of such fact as connected with soul, of a specific personality, in its preferences, its volition and power' (*A*, 10). Those personal preferences inevitably also determine subject matter.

In *The Picture of Dorian Gray* (1890, 1891), Oscar Wilde, Pater's friend and disciple, has the painter Basil Hallward declare that 'every portrait that is painted with feeling is a portrait of the artist, not of the sitter.'[13] It is common for critics to choose as subjects artists and writers with whom they identify or who represent either some aspect of themselves or a quality or qualities that they admire or aspire to. Not only do Pater's fictional protagonists embody traits and tendencies which he found sympathetic but we sense that the artistic and literary figures he critiques are also in his eyes kindred spirits. Arthur Symons perceptively noticed that 'As a critic ... he has selected for analysis only those types of artistic character in which "delicacy", an exquisite fineness, is the prevailing feature; or if, as with Michel Angelo he has been drawn towards some more rugged personality, ... it has been ... because he has divined the sweetness lying at the heart of the strength – *ex forti dulcedo*' (*WPCH*, 176). Pater's dedication to a personal, sympathetic, and expressive vocabulary, style, and subject matter, prompted by Swinburne but refined to another level, will prove foundational for literary Aestheticism and Aesthetic inheritors such as Wilde, Vernon Lee, and Arthur Symons.

Throughout the essay on 'Style' there is a continued emphasis on the 'vision within', a phrase Pater uses five times, as well as the word 'soul' (used seventeen times), terms that emphasise the importance of style as an authentic form of self-expression: 'Truth! there can be no merit, no craft at all, without that. And further, all beauty is in the long run only *fineness* of truth, or what we call expression, the finer accommodation of speech to that vision within' (*A*, 10); 'It will be good literary art not because it is brilliant or sober, or rich, or impulsive, or severe, but just in proportion as its representation of that sense, that soul-fact, is true' (*A*, 11). Later in the essay Pater uses the terms 'mind' and 'soul' to represent two different characterising forces in style: 'By mind, the literary artist reaches us, through static and objective indications of design in his work, legible to all. By soul, he reaches us, somewhat capriciously perhaps, one and not another, through vagrant sympathy and a kind of immediate contact' (*A*, 25). 'Mind', easier to grasp, reveals itself through the 'reasonable structure' of the work (*A*, 38), whereas 'soul', harder to define, is much more intimate and emotional, expressing the essence of the writer: 'As a quality of style, at all events, soul is a fact, in certain writers – the way they have of absorbing language, of attracting it into the peculiar spirit they are of, with a subtlety which makes the actual result seem like some inexplicable inspiration' (*A*, 25). 'Soul' is indicative of 'unity of atmosphere', while 'mind' is indicative of 'design', 'soul securing colour (or perfume, might we say?) as mind secures form, the latter being essentially finite, the former vague or infinite, as the influence of a living person is practically infinite' (*A*, 26–7). 'Soul', later rearticulated in atmospheric terms as 'that colour and mystic perfume' (*A*, 38), suffuses style with an expressive sense of the writer's individual aura as a writer, intimating the much larger nexus of subjective concerns, preoccupations, and ideas that lie behind the more limited specific utterance: 'it is still a characteristic of soul, in this sense of the word, that it does but suggest what can never be uttered, not as being different from, or more obscure than, what actually gets said, but as containing that plenary substance of which there is only one phase or facet in what is there expressed' (A, 27). To return to the statement that opened this essay, it is surely this stylistic soul-aura that the 'literary artist' channels when he aims 'at the production by honourable artifice of a peculiar atmosphere' (A, 18).

When Symonds wrote of Pater's *Studies in the History of the Renaissance* that it shows 'the elaboration of a style perfectly suited to his matter and the temper of his mind', 'temper' suggests that he saw the work as channelling Pater's own personality or 'soul' (WPCH, 58). That 'soul' looms large in Pater's own style seems evident given that his writing is consciously atmospheric in its language, rhythms, and organisation, and that it is preoccupied with evoking the author's subjective impression of artistic subjects or personalities and their own practices, often in specifically atmospheric terms. Leonardo, for example, specialises in 'the construction about things of a peculiar atmosphere and mixed lights', and 'Through his strange veil of sight things reach him so, ... as in faint light of eclipse' (SR, 133). Michelangelo's sonnets dictate the conditions of their own reading; indeed their 'spirit ... is lost if we once take them out of that dreamy atmosphere in which men have things as they will, because the hold of all outward things upon them is faint and uncertain' (SR, 119). In 'The School of Giorgione' (1877) included in the third edition of *The Renaissance* (1888), Pater registers the more palpable atmosphere of the material work, a careful composition of light and colour inspired by observation of real effects: 'that weaving of light, as of just perceptible gold threads through the dress, the flesh, the atmosphere, in Titian's *Lace-girl*, that staining of the whole fabric of the thing with a new, delightful physical quality' (SR, 144). Later he observes that 'in Italy all natural things are as it were woven through and through with gold thread' and that 'it is with gold dust, or gold thread, that these Venetian painters seem to work, spinning its fine filaments, through the solemn human flesh, away into the white plastered walls of the thatched huts' (SR, 154). Meditating also on the typical landscape of Giorgione's School as seen in the *Fête Champêtre*, 'a landscape full of clearness, of the effects of water, of fresh rain newly passed through the air, and collected into the grassy channels', he remarks: 'The air, moreover, in the school of Giorgione, seems as vivid as the people who breathe it' (SR, 154).

Pater's seminal semi-autobiographical narrative 'The Child in the House' (1878), which he described as 'the germinating, original, source, specimen, of all my *imaginative* work', traces how the 'soul' is partially made up of one's earliest material influences. Having by chance dreamt of his childhood home, Florian, the protagonist, finds that this accident of his dream was just the thing needed for the beginning of a certain design he then had in view, the noting, namely, of some things in the story of his spirit – in that process of brain-building by which we are, each one of us, what we are. With the image of the place so clear and favourable upon him, he fell to thinking of himself therein, and how his thoughts had grown upon him. In that half-spiritualised house he could watch the better, over again, the gradual expansion of the soul which had come to be there – of which indeed, through the law which makes the material objects about them so large an element in children's lives, it had actually become a part; inward and outward being woven through and through each other into one inextricable texture – half, tint and trace and accident of homely colour and form, from the wood and the bricks; half, mere soul-stuff, floated thither from who knows how far.[14]

For Pater, one's soul is thus intimately formed through an influential relationship with place, and thus we might suppose the atmosphere of that place to have a determinable effect or part to play in one's future style, 'inward and outward being woven through and through each other into one inextricable texture'. In his later essay, 'Dante Gabriel Rossetti' (1883), when Pater touches on the poet's long sonnet sequence *The House of Life*, we see the notion of the atmospheric dwelling place, and its formative links with body, soul, and the writer's literary oeuvre come together:

The dwelling-place in which one finds oneself by chance or destiny, yet can partly fashion for oneself . . . in which every object has its associations . . . ; the house one must quit, yet taking perhaps, how much of its quietly active light and colour along with us! – grown now to be a kind of raiment to one's body, as the body, according to Swedenborg, is but the raiment of the soul – under that image, the whole of Rossetti's work might count as a *House of Life* of which he is but the 'Interpreter.'   (A, 214)

Certainly, Pater's fictional protagonists have complex intimate relationships with place and atmosphere that are integral to their stories of development. Sebastian van Storck's nihilistic philosophy which prescribes detachment and self-erasure echoes his fascination with the wide empty vistas of Dutch landscapes that might be so easily overtaken by the encroaching tidal waters which threaten the obliteration of man's mark. The excavated legend of Denys l'Auxerrois, a possible god in exile in medieval France who shifts through three marked phases of temperament, seems an attempt to account for the present-day mixed 'characteristic atmosphere' of Auxerre, 'attractive in part for its melancholy' (IP, 170). The beautiful 'pensive' and 'cloistral' atmosphere of 'White-Nights', Marius's boyhood home, provides him with an ideal 'which through all the rest of his life he seemed . . . to be ever seeking to regain.'[15] As a boy he also learns a lesson which he later finds mirrored in a theory in Plato's *Phaedrus* 'which supposes men's spirits to be susceptible to certain influences, diffused, like streams or currents, by fair things or persons visibly present – green fields and children's faces, for instance – into the air around them; and which, with certain natures, are like potent material essences, conforming the seer to themselves as by some cunning physical necessity' (*ME*, 25).

As readers of Pater's fictional narratives and essays, we share in these compelling sympathetic and influential atmospheres which are also indicators of 'soul', enriching our understanding of specific characters and personalities as well as conveying a deeper sense of Pater's own character as a writer. In another of his stories, the unfinished imaginary portrait 'An English Poet', the impressionable young poet-protagonist, disappointed in his immediate 'meagre' surroundings, finds that

> The good book would be like an actual place visited, and to which one might return again and again at discretion for the infallible exercise therein of a special recognised influence, a certain controlling atmosphere, always to be experienced there, when one had a will to turn the key, acting almost independently of effort on one's own part, and remaining as an objective material fact while the pilgrim shifts to and fro. The shore with its tang of salt air, the house where you are to hear such or such songs, see such pictures, meet such people, or that great temple to which the sick came from afar to sleep, sure that a sacred dream would come to reveal how the sickness might be healed and with no fee due to the priests from the poor boy for letting him lie there; the genuine literary creations of past time have been not less palpable in influence; and a true education mainly consists in the well-pondered experience of what we shall find on demand in these places. (*IP*, 107)

Books themselves become the doorways to 'actual place[s]', these being both depictions of specific locations and intuitive spaces in which one experiences 'a special recognised influence, a certain controlling atmosphere', undoubtedly the stylistic soul-aura of the writer. Unsurprisingly as the young poet becomes a voracious reader of older English literature, what stands out most is his 'savour before all things of the style – how things were said – of manner – those elements of taste or of literary production which, because they are so delicately and individually apprehended and are yet so real, resemble physical sensations and may rightly be said to be the matter of a literary sense' (*IP*, 109). His aesthetic temperament means that he is perpetually seeking stylistic atmosphere, that essence or soul perfume of the individual author:

> the boy required from words, and not in vain, in books, the picture, the tuberose, the marble face, the fading light on ancient cities, all that was not

actually there for ear and eye, above all the genius of refinement; and this not as the new subject of writing, its more obvious and immediate presentations, but by a subtler operation from the style, the ether-like manner of the thing. So written language came to be form and colour as well as sound to him, exotic perfume almost. Having nothing else to live on, he extracted all they could yield from words, and his sense of them came to be curiously cultivated at all points. (*IP*, 110)

This clearly echoes Pater's own appreciation of style and his 'curiously cultivated' atmospheric vocabulary 'faithful to the colouring of his own spirit' and 'his peculiar sense of the world' (*A*, 15). But stylistic atmosphere is also generated by means other than vocabulary, and while it would take a much longer essay than this to detail all of these, one notable characteristic is what we might call reflective suspension, whereby having aroused or directed curiosity, Pater keeps the meaning of a complex sentence suspended or in play until the very end, at which point the reader has often to retrace the trajectory in order to grasp his meaning fully.

Pater has a fondness for starting sentences with the word 'to', used either as a preposition or as the infinitive of a verb, and in both cases starting off a sequential suspensive movement or train of reflection that is frequently not resolved until after the sentence closes when the reader must review and reconfigure all the constituent elements. Such sentences could often be rewritten in far more conventional ways, but these are not Pater's ways. Take, for example, the following from the Conclusion to *Studies in the History of the Renaissance*: 'To such a tremulous wisp constantly re-forming itself on the stream, to a single sharp impression, with a sense in it, a relic more or less fleeting, of such moments gone by, what is real in our life fines itself down' (*SR*, 198). Pater might easily have written 'What is real in our life fines itself down to [such] a tremulous wisp constantly re-forming itself on the stream, to a single sharp impression, with a sense in it, a relic more or less fleeting, of such moments gone by', or even 'What is real in our life fines itself down to a single sharp impression, with a sense in it, a relic more or less fleeting, of such moments gone by – a tremulous wisp constantly re-forming itself on the stream', both of which would have been considerably easier to follow. However, Pater's far more elusive and atmospheric sequence suspends meaning by first conjuring *in medias res* the tantalising if somewhat elusive image of the 'tremulous wisp' – possibly a fine fragment of hay or straw, possibly a small cloud of misty vapour – and making us fix on it as if we ourselves had suddenly glimpsed it from the bank or a bridge over the stream, before subsequently directing our attention to the ensuing process of perception. This ensures that, in line with the sentiment expressed, the image of the wisp imprints itself on our consciousness as the fragile but enduring visual mnemonic or relic of the moment, while the end of the sentence which ultimately delivers the postponed verb ('fines' meaning 'refines') falls with increased and sober emphasis.

'To really strenuous minds there is a pleasurable stimulus in the challenge for a continuous effort on their part, to be rewarded by securer and more intimate grasp of the author's sense' (A, 17): Pater thus singles out his true readers and keeps them exercised with a sort of 'intellectual gymnastic' (IP, 145), always avoiding the obvious while reaching for his own idiosyncratic perspectives. The Preface to Studies in the History of the Renaissance features one of his leading infinitives in its first paragraph: 'To define beauty, not in the most abstract, but in the most concrete terms possible, to find, not its universal formula, but the formula which expresses most adequately this or that special manifestation of it, is the aim of the true student of aesthetics' (SR, 73). A more conventional version of this sentence would be 'The aim of the true student of aesthetics is to define beauty, not in the most abstract, but in the most concrete terms possible, to find, not a universal formula for it, but the formula which expresses most adequately this or that special manifestation of it.' Obviously in a prefatory essay dealing with the topic of aesthetics, the definition of beauty will be important, although Pater's stance is to resist the straitjacket of pre-conceived abstract theory in favour of individual localised subjective perceptions. His sentence, which foregrounds the nuanced process of determining the nature of beauty from a subjective viewpoint, fittingly moves from abstract to concrete, ending appropriately with the 'student of aesthetics', and with an emphatic hint of redefinition in the words 'aim' and 'true'. This is an important manoeuvre as Pater is shifting the terms of a critical debate. In the next paragraph he will execute a masterly swerve of Matthew Arnold's famous statement on critical objectivity 'To see the object as itself it really is' to make it mean something like its exact opposite: 'and in æsthetic criticism, the first step towards seeing one's object as it really is, is to know one's own impression as it really is' (SR, 73).

Suspending the resolution of even a fairly simple statement like the famous watchword from the Conclusion gives a subtly altered perspective. Rather than asserting that 'Success in life is to burn always with this hard, gemlike flame, to maintain this ecstasy', Pater's formula – 'To burn always with this hard, gemlike flame, to maintain this ecstasy, is success in life' (SR, 199) – emphasises that this rarefied way of living is – against the grain of received opinion – what for him constitutes 'success' or the life well lived. The carpe diem atmospherics of the Conclusion – shadows momentarily illumined by flares of light – are also at play in the following sentence which here starts with a negative infinitive: 'Not to discriminate every moment some passionate attitude in those about us, and in the very brilliancy of their gifts some tragic dividing of forces on their ways, is, on this short day of frost and sun, to sleep before evening' (*SR*, 199). Rather than setting the scene by writing 'On this short day of frost and sun, not to discriminate every moment some passionate attitude in those about us, and in the brilliancy of their gifts some tragic dividing of forces on their ways, is to sleep before evening', Pater once more disorientates readers by throwing them urgently into the spate of action they might otherwise well miss, giving them only a brief glimpse of sunshine before springing the hard-hitting sombre reminder that death like wintry darkness closes in all too soon.

Pater clearly relishes arranging his sentences so that they help enact his meaning. This is particularly easy to see in instances where the sinuous movement of the sentence echoes physical movement, as in the journey taken upstairs to reach Sebastian van Storck's private contemplative space:

> From the midst of the busy and busy-looking house, crowded with the furniture and the pretty little toys of many generations, a long passage led the rare visitor up a winding staircase; and (again at the end of a long passage) he found himself as if shut off from the whole talkative Dutch world, and in the embrace of that wonderful quiet which is also possible in Holland at its height all around him.
> (*IP*, 150)

Here Pater's enjoyment of this atmospheric 'long passage' from bustling domesticity to meditative calm is evident, but we find more complex forms of self-reflexivity elsewhere where the movement of style is the object of contemplation. Writing about the appreciation of 'Self-restraint' or '*ascêsis*' in 'Style', he observes that 'for the reader supposed there will be an æsthetic satisfaction in that frugal closeness of style which makes the most of a word, in the exaction from every sentence of a precise relief, in the just spacing out of word to thought, in the logically filled space connected always with the delightful sense of difficulty overcome' (*A*, 17). The elegantly organised clauses of this sentence which distinguish and reflect its refinements of meaning enact the precision it describes, summarised in the singular but entirely apposite phrase 'frugal closeness'.

Another example occurs when Pater describes how the literary artist varies the type and length of his sentences, combining simple short sentences with longer more complex ones: 'The blithe, crisp sentence, decisive as a child's expression of its needs, may alternate with the long-contending, victoriously intricate sentence; the sentence, born with the integrity of a single word, relieving the sort of sentence in which, if you look closely, you can see much contrivance, much adjustment, to bring a highly qualified matter into compass at one view' (*A*, 23). Note the satisfying monosyllables ('blithe', 'crisp') used to denote the simple sentence 'born with integrity of a single word' contrasted with the twining polysyllables of the 'long-contending, victoriously intricate sentence', the sentence whose cumulative, carefully nuanced clauses are calculated to lead the reader on a journey towards a dramatic final revelation of meaning. Although we commonly associate Pater with long sentences, he is, as he suggests here, perfectly adept at varying the tension of a passage by using shorter ones. In 'Style', he asserts the literary artist's duty of rigorously removing all superfluous verbiage, following this up with the pithy declaration: 'Surplusage! he will dread that, as the runner on his muscles' (A, 19), a deliberate contraction or economy of phrasing for 'as the runner dreads excess fat on his muscles'.

Inhabiting Pater's sentences, learning to savour their reflective suspensions in order to apprehend new ways of seeing things, is integral to appreciating his style. Such sentences, along with a highly individualised vocabulary, 'faithful to the colouring of his own spirit', and a mobile repertoire of evocative images and associations that reiterate the nature and expression of artistic personality, help constitute Pater's atmospherics of style and his own pervasive stylistic soul-aura.

Notes

1. Walter Pater, 'Style', Appreciations with an Essay on Style (London: Macmillan, 1910), 15. Subsequent references to Appreciations (A) given in the text.
2. Arthur Symons, Time 6 (August 1887), in Walter Pater: The Critical Heritage, ed. R. M. Seiler (London, Boston, and New York: Routledge and Kegan Paul, 1980), 175–82; 177. Subsequent references to this useful compilation given within the text as WPCH.
3. George Moore, Chapter 10, Confessions of a Young Man (1888), in WPCH, 152, 153.
4. Vernon Lee, Preface, Juvenilia, 2 vols (London: T. Fisher Unwin, 1887), 1. 7, 8.
5. Vernon Lee, 'A Page of Walter Pater', Life and Letters 9, no. 50 (1933), 287–310 (308).
6. Vernon Lee, Renaissance Fancies and Studies (London: John Lane. The Bodley Head, 1895), 257.
7. Lee, Renaissance Fancies and Studies, 258, 257.
8. Lee, 'A Page of Walter Pater', 303.
9. John Addington Symonds, Academy 4 (15 March 1873), in WPCH, pp. 58, 60.
10. Arthur Symons, 'The Decadent Movement in Literature', Harper's New Monthly Magazine 87 (November 1893), in WPCH, 269.
11. See Catherine Maxwell, Second Sight: The Visionary Imagination in Late Victorian Literature (Manchester: Manchester University Press, 2008), 82–8.
12. Walter Pater, The Renaissance: Studies in Art and Poetry, ed. Hilary Fraser (Oxford: Oxford University Press, 2025), 74. Subsequent references given as SR in the text.

13. Oscar Wilde, *The Picture of Dorian Gray*, ed. Michael Patrick Gillespie, 2nd ed. (New York and London: W. W. Norton, 2007), 9.

14. Walter Pater, 'The Child in the House', *Imaginary Portraits*, ed. Lene Østermark-Johansen (London: MHRA, 2014), 83–84. Subsequent references to *IP* in the text.

15. Walter Pater, *Marius the Epicurean*, ed. Gerald Monsman (Kansas City: Valancourt Classics, 2008), 18, 19. Subsequent references to *ME* in the text.

4

KATE FLINT

Pater, Looking

In 1880, the Scottish poet and literary biographer William Sharp met Walter Pater for the first time. The encounter grew into a friendship, and shortly after Pater's death in July 1894, Sharp published his personal reminiscences of him in the *Atlantic*. He recalls attending a salon at the house of George T. Robinson, the designer and critic, who, together with his literary daughters, held 'delightfully promiscuous gatherings' where painters, sculptors, and musicians from a whole range of backgrounds mixed together for lively conversation. Standing next to the piano, stroking a long-haired cat, was a quiet, pale, moustachioed man, 'his eyes were fixed steadfastly on the fire. The glow fell right across them, and I could see how deep-set they were, and of what a peculiar gray; a variable hue, but wherein the inner light was always vivid, and sometimes strangely keen and penetrating'.[1]

I want, in this chapter, to think about *what* those eyes saw – or rather, what aspects of the natural world, and what aspects of art, sparked Pater's attention. But more than this, I will consider *how* Pater saw – that is, how he practiced, and thought about, the very act of looking. For him, this was both an acutely personal act, and something demanding recognition that the object looked at has its own specificity – material, historical, and contextual. I ask what qualities he retained as visual touchstones across the broad historical timespan from the Greeks to the present day, and address the variety of different modes in which he captured objects of sight – essays, reviews, fiction, and imaginary 'portraits'. All are unified by Pater's habits of looking and by the process of translation into verbal language. This chapter explores the variety of places, buildings, art works, and objects that Pater looked at, and his habits of selection as he translated what he saw into language. It looks at the attention that he paid to form and to colour. Finally, it considers how his aesthetic thought was closely connected to contemporary science, especially that concerned with physiology and perception.

Pater responded to the visible and material aspects of the world – buildings, natural surroundings, paintings, and sculptures – with a sustained intensity. But all this solidity readily melted – not exactly into air but into prose that responded to what he himself called our 'inward world of thought and feeling'.[2] Above all, looking was, for Pater, inseparable from an inwardly-held impulse that sought and relished beauty – a category that was far from simple since, for him, beauty was not a matter of aesthetic convention, but was what an individual observer with a strong capacity for sensory perception found beautiful. In turn, he transmuted his impressions into prose that strove, elegantly, to capture the essence of what he saw: something mediated by individual personality; by his careful choice of public-facing language (he notoriously left scant evidence of his immediate reactions to what he saw in letters, journals or notebooks); by his careful masking of preferences that might be too obviously homosexual; by his knowledge of, and interest in, contemporary theories about the physiological use of the eye, and the connection between eye and brain; and by his broad knowledge and understanding of philosophical aesthetics. But it's not my intention here to explore the more conceptual implications of Pater's aesthetics. Rather, I explore the very first stage of the process: What did Pater see, and what can we know of what looking, and seeing, meant to him?

What Pater saw

Pater's immediate surroundings in Brasenose College, Oxford, had – Sharp tells us – a 'delicate austerity' to them, a 'quiet simplicity' that was the product of 'scrupulous selection'. His study was an uncluttered room: as he wrote, his eye was not distracted. As well as carefully organised books – Greek and Latin classics, German and French aesthetics, French and English imaginative literature –

> the first thing to catch the eye was a large and fine *alto-rilievo*, a Madonna by Luca della Robbia, the exquisite delicacy and soft cream-white tone of which not only harmonized with, but seemed to focus the other things in the room, – the few etchings against the dull yellow wall-paper, one or two old Italian bronze ornaments that caught the sheen of sunlight or lamplight, a low wide piece of Wedgewood [sic] full of white flowers, a slim gold-brown vase on the broad sill, containing wallflowers, or flowering lavender, or chrysanthemums, or winter aconites, as the season went.   (Sharp 806)

Although the wall colour changes over the years – some accounts describe his rooms as blue, or white, or primrose, or greenish-white – Pater's preferences for carefully chosen art works and flowers are apparent from all the accounts of those who visited him. The same decorative principles held true at the house he shared with his sisters in Bradmore Road, Oxford: William Morris wallpaper; 'a sparing allowance of blue plates and pots'; engravings after Botticelli, and a crewel-work embroidery that his sister Hester executed of *The Birth of Venus*.[3]

The habit of visual selection, focusing on singular objects of vision, is a hallmark of Pater's looking. It allows for a meditative engagement with art and with natural surroundings. It was not just art and architecture that seized Pater's attention: far from it. Sharp describes going for walks in Christ Church meadows and by the banks of the Cherwell: 'He was singularly observant of certain natural objects, aspects, and conditions, more especially of the movement of light in grass and among leaves, of all fragrances, of flowing water . . . ' (Sharp 807). As this indicates, Pater did not just take note of visible detail: his attention was synesthetic, alert to the sounds and textures and smells accompanying the visual. Scents, indeed, held a particular power over his memory. A little later, in 1884, walking at sunset in the meadows by the Cherwell, Pater told Sharp that 'certain flowers affected his imagination so keenly that he could not smell them with pleasure; and that while the white jonquil, the gardenia, and the syringa actually gave him pain, the meadow-sweet generally gave him a sudden fugitive sense of distant pastures, and twilit eves, and remote scattered hamlets' (Sharp 809–10). Although Pater never advocated, as Ruskin did, for the meticulously close observation of natural phenomena, he was attentive to the descriptive words that both conjured up the precise appearance of a plant, and, through apt metaphor, used it to intensify the tone of a scene. Thus, in the increasingly ominous narrative of 'Emerald Uthwart', we read how Uthwart, in Oxford, spent 'May evenings among the fritillaries . . . in colour like rusted blood, as if they grew from some forgotten battle-field, the bodies, the rotten army'.[4]

Despite the contemplative visual stability afforded by his living and writing spaces, Pater's viewing practices were driven by a continually questing mind. In his first published work, he maintains that

> What constitutes an artistic gift is first of all a natural susceptibility to moments of strange excitement, in which the colours freshen upon our threadbare world, and the routine of things about us is broken by a novel and happier synthesis.[5]

He emphasised the importance of curiosity, praising Romanticism for its 'restless curiosity' – something that the writers of the period added to their 'desire of beauty'.[6] Pater believed in the principle of creative renewal through new contacts and experiences – whether for critic or artist. Describing the artistic development of Luca Della Robbia, he tells how the sculptor worked first in plain white earthenware, and then responded to the 'strange, bright colours' of oriental pottery and the colours of Roman pottery dug up in his neighbourhood.[7] 'Strange', we might note, is an adjective that Pater repeats again and again throughout his work: it signifies a striking, yet indefinable quality that disrupts one's habitual ways of seeing; on occasion, as was also the case with Oscar Wilde's use of the word, it has homoerotic undertones.

Pater's own artistic consumption was unquestionably curious and very varied. Florian, in 'The Child in the House' – the closest that Pater came to writing an autobiographical piece, although all his protagonists are invariably suffused with his own preoccupations and capacities – manifested 'early the activity in him of a more than customary sensuousness, "the lust of the eye", as the Preacher says.[8] This 'lust of the eye' is no bad thing: it represents an eager hunger for visual experience. Pater's artistic eye was trained on the architecture and galleries that he saw on his 1864 trip to Paris, where he almost certainly encountered the *Mona Lisa* and other works attributed to Leonardo; his 1865 trip to Italy with his good friend Charles Shadwell, when they visited Florence, Pisa, and Ravenna; on the Gothic cathedrals and churches of Northern France seen on summer holidays with his sisters; and by the art-crammed month that he spent in Rome in late 1882, when writing *Marius the Epicurean*. He was very familiar with works in the National Gallery, Oxford's Ashmolean Museum, and the British Museum, where his friend Charles Newton was Keeper of Greek and Roman Antiquities. This gave him first-hand knowledge of the many new developments in archaeology in the later decades of the nineteenth century.

Pater was particularly drawn, too, to the Parthenon sculptures, which the Museum received in 1816: 'If one had to choose a single product of Hellenic art, to save in the wreck of all the rest, one would choose from the "beautiful multitude" of the Panathenaic frieze', he wrote: 'that line of youths on horses, with their level glances, their proud patient lips, their chastened reins, their whole bodies in exquisite service' ('Winckelmann' 189). He calls the reader's attention to one of the 'very pleasantest human likenesses', a statue of Trypho, son of Eutychus, who died young; he closely observed the tall statue of Demeter – and compared her to 'the homely figure of the roughly clad French peasant woman' who hurries through a twilit landscape in one of Camille Corot's pictures.[9] This comparison to Corot exemplifies Pater's familiarity with a wide range of art. In turn, this tells us something about his tacit assumption that his readers carry the same mental art gallery around with them.

Corot, with his subdued, melancholy, misty grey-green landscapes, was a favourite point of reference for Pater (and the subject of an unfinished essay).[10] Pater had a strong interest in modern art. He visited the studios of Dante Gabriel Rossetti and William Bell Scott; he was friends with Simeon

Solomon and owned a drawing by Solomon, the awkward threesome of *The Bride, the Bridegroom, and the Friend of the Bridegroom*. Solomon executed a portrait sketch of Pater; the writer referred to Solomon's painting *Bacchus* in 'A Study of Dionysus', which he had seen at the Royal Academy in 1867, and praised his ability to convey the idea of 'a melancholy and sorrowing' Dionysus even more strongly than the Mocetto engraving, after Bellini, in the British Museum.[11] Pater was a regular attendee at Royal Academy summer exhibitions, and at more forward-looking venues for displaying art, including the Grosvenor Gallery and the Dudley Gallery. Reviewing George Moore's *Modern Painters* in 1893, he seems entirely comfortable discussing Millet and Sisley, and commends Moore's recognition of the particular qualities of Whistler and Sargent. Elsewhere, he alludes to the work of the so-called Idyllists Frederick Walker and George Mason; he draws J. M. W. Turner, Edward Burne-Jones (especially his painting *The Day*), and Alphonse Legros's etchings into his essays. His 1885 review of Ernest Chesneau's *The English School of Painting* shows him writing not just about contemporary painting but with authority about William Hogarth.

In other words, Pater looked at an eclectic variety of art. He regarded artefacts of the past not as static objects of appreciation but as contributing to a continuing tradition of creativity, and informing our contemporary responses. Taking up a notably Ruskinian topic, Gothic architecture, he calls our attention to 'certain modern churches in London', to which posterity may well look back with puzzlement.[12] Rather than being the product of an age when Gothic art was somehow a spontaneous manifestation of creativity – as a simplified reading of Ruskin would have it – the architects and artisans here 'through long, large, devoted study of the handiwork of the past, have done the thing better, with a more fully enlightened consciousness, with full intelligence of what those early workmen only guessed at'.[13] Pater's thinking eye was turned not just to museums, galleries, and cathedral interiors but to the public works in the changing, modern city around him.

Form and colour

When William Sharp asked Pater what he personally considered 'the most memorable passage in George Eliot', he surprised him by saying, '"it was the remark put into Piero di Cosimo's mouth, in *Romola*"' – Eliot's novel of Renaissance Florence – '"The only passionate life is in form and color"' (Sharp, 810).

The 'mere matter' of a picture, Pater claims in his essay on Giorgione, is 'nothing without the form'.[14] In terms prefiguring Clive Bell's comments about 'significant form' in *Art* (1914), Pater claims that the 'handling' of form 'should become an end in itself'.[15] His attention to form is most apparent in his earlier writings on sculpture, both Renaissance and classical. A statue, he said, was something that could be taken in isolation, bound by its own materiality, an example of an art that 'threw itself upon pure form' ('Winckelmann', 186). Unlike many paintings, 'it has no backgrounds, no sky or atmosphere, to suggest and interpret a train of feeling; a little of suggested motion, and much of pure light on its gleaming surfaces, with pure form' ('Winckelmann', 186). We are obliged to begin and end 'with the finite image' ('Winckelmann', 183). Yet in writing of Michelangelo he explains that looking at art is by no means a passive process: these particular sculptures offer a strong instance of how our own looking must break through that finitude. In Michelangelo's work he isolates a particular quality – 'studied incompleteness'.[16] For him this is a form of idealisation 'which in Greek sculpture depends on a delicate system of abstraction, and in early Italian sculpture on lowness of relief', and, he says, 'trusts to the spectator to complete the half-emergent form'.[17]

Pater's own descriptions often had something of 'studied incompleteness' about them, making it difficult for his reader to pull things together in a visual whole, unless they draw on prior knowledge. Furthermore, he had a restless eye, whether looking at an individual painting, or a range of buildings – we see this clearly in 'Art Notes in Northern Italy' (1890), where this eye darts from paintings inside a church, to pumpkins and mulberry trees, to more paintings, to the beauty of sub-Alpine towns in the 'purple mystery of evening', to rich and coloured church woodwork.[18] His essays and fictions are more remarkable for style than for their own form, even as they convey a broad responsiveness to form and colour that underpins Pater's acts of visual attentiveness. He repudiates the dominant narrative and moralising strands in criticism of contemporary art, claiming, in 'The School of Giorgione', that

> [i]n its primary aspect, a great picture has no more definite message for us than an accidental play of sunlight and shadow for a few moments on the wall or floor, is itself, in truth, a space of such fallen light, caught as the colours are caught in an Eastern carpet, but refined upon, and dealt with more subtly and exquisitely than by nature itself.[19]

Describing Troyes cathedral in 'Denys L'Auxerrois', this preference for qualities of light and colour above the matter of representation is clear when he is struck by 'one of the richest of its windows, [in which] certain lines of pearly white run hither and thither, with delightful distant effect, upon ruby and dark blue' – a concern with design supersedes the subject matter: Biblical travellers.[20] Similarly, fleeting, accidental moments of beauty are more powerful and suggestive than, say, the over-opulent, richly panelled and perfumed villa that Apuleius visits in *Marius the Epicurean.*

The images lodged within Pater's memory formed an associative connective tissue. His writing is, in this respect, highly palimpsestic, building on layers of visual allusion. He purposed this storehouse of images to evoke moods and impressions, rather than to delineate and describe. In doing so, he frequently confounded historical logic – for example when, in *Marius*, the narrator notes the farms reverting to wildness; villas 'partly fallen into ruin. The picturesque, romantic Italy of a later time – the Italy of Claude and Salvator Rosa – was already forming, for the delight of the modern romantic traveler'.[21] By Chapter XXIV, Rosa seems to have melded with John Martin – or perhaps Turner – as, approaching Rome among the ruined tombs, a 'blood-red sunset was dying angrily' (*Marius* II 169).

But Pater's favourite visual effects, the ones that draw his eye and imagination back again and again, were habitually far more subtle than this apocalyptic moment. As with Corot's misty greys, he gravitated towards subdued, often shadowy tones: the 'uncertain twilight' that represents our speculation about Abelard's hypothetical later life; a preference, in 'A Prince of Court Painters', for a Madonna by Pieter Paul over Rubens's work – '[h]er robe of shadowy blue suits my eyes better far than the hot flesh-tints of the Medicean ladies of the great Peter Paul'.[22] This visual propensity both betokened an emotional pull towards the melancholic – just as he noted Botticelli's 'predilection for minor tones' and the sadness this lends his work – and could be turned to comment on phenomena that reach far beyond a work's original ends.[23] Writing of Leonardo's damp and deteriorating *Last Supper*, he considers the painting of Christ's head, which certainly owes 'part of its effect to a mellowing decay'.[24] But it also sums up, for Pater, the whole assembly of disciples and the Christianity that they signify:

> this central head does but consummate the sentiment of the whole company –
> ghosts through which you see the wall, faint as the shadows of the leaves upon
> the wall on autumn afternoons; this figure is but the faintest, most spectral of
> them all. It is the image of what the history it symbolises has been more and
> more ever since, paler and paler as it recedes from us.[25]

John Morley, reviewing *The Renaissance* in the *Fortnightly Review*, was right in remarking on 'the attraction to him of hints of beauty and faintly marked traces of exquisite particularity, rather than the noon-day splendour of master works'.[26]

Certain colours, as well as tonal effects, recur repeatedly. Lene Østermark-Johansen calls our attention to 'the long golden thread that runs through Pater's writings', from the 'gold dust, or gold thread' with which Venetian painters seem to work, to his description of the Italian countryside as 'woven through and through with gold thread', to the ray of sunlight that, in *Marius*, transforms 'the rough grain among the cool brown shadows into heaps of gold' (*Marius* I, 59).[27] Sharp claimed that the ray of sunlight extending from a shadowed corner in Pater's study caused him to exclaim that gold is 'the primary colour of delight' and, even if apocryphal, this foregrounds gold's ability to connect the natural world with careful craftsmanship (Sharp, 806). The other dominant colour in Pater's work is white. Thomas Wright's 1907 biography of Pater is wildly inaccurate in many respects, but he is completely correct in calling attention to Pater's fondness for white, something implanted in him by the rooms he knew as a boy: 'As he grew older this passion for whiteness and cleanness increased. He stands for white marble. He is the Alma-Tadema of English Literature.'[28]

Strikingly, in his later writings, Pater's visual interest seems to shift. Instead of shadows and obscurity, there is a new emphasis on brightness, light and clarity. But by the time of 'The Beginnings of Greek Sculpture' (1880) – and this is one of the most notable realignments in Pater's aesthetic approaches – he had become frustrated with the isolation of marble sculptures from their original contexts. He was in favour of restoring the original colouring to Greek sculpture – or at least reminding us that these statues were not always monochromatic. 'The whole black and grey world of extant antique sculpture [needs] to be translated back into ivory and gold, if we would feel the excitement which the Greeks seem to have felt in the presence of these objects', he wrote: this would 'relieve the air of our galleries and museums of their too intellectual greyness. Greek sculpture could not have been a cold thing.'[29] He was not consistent in advocating antiquarian restoration. Visiting Notre Dame d'Amiens, he admires its airiness and cheerfulness, in contrast to

> the broad but subdued sunshine which falls through range upon range of windows, reflected from white wall and roof and gallery, soothing to the eye, while it allows you to see the delicate carved work in all its refinement of touch, it is only as an after-thought, an artificial after-thought, that you regret the lost stained glass, or the vanished mural colour, if such to any large extent there ever were.[30]

Such lucidity conveys 'amazing cheerfulness' by contrast to the 'mortified light' of Vézelay's abbey, that still evokes a gloomy aura of monasticism and repression.[31] He praises the transformation of the church of Saint Hubert at the hands of Gaston de Latour – 'an enemy of all Gothic darkness or heaviness'.[32] In the past, the stained glass 'admitted only an almost angry ray of purple or crimson, here or there, across the dark roomy spaces;' now, this was changed through 'cheerful daylight, refined, but hardly dimmed at all, by painted glass mimicking the clearness of the open sky'.[33]

Yet light and whiteness have their tipping point. In certain of Pater's later writings, they morph on occasion into the white heat of violence. Writing of *Measure for Measure*, and Isabella's fury at her brother Claudio's willingness to let the law-maker Angelo take her virginity in order that he might live, Pater describes, '[t]he swift, vindictive anger leaps, like a white flame, into this white spirit'.[34] In the shocking scene in 'Apollo in Picardy' (the myth of Apollo, Dionysus and Hyacinth transposed to the Middle Ages), when Brother Apollyon stands in cold white light on the moonlit turf,

> crouching, right foot foremost, and with face turned backwards to the disk in his right hand, his whole body, in that moment of rest, full of the circular motion he is about to commit to it, he seemed – beautiful pale spectre – to shine from within with a light of his own, like that of the glow-worm in the thicket, or the dead and rotten roots of the old trees.[35]

Like an inwardly illumined version of the *Discobolus* (a Roman marble copy of a lost Greek bronze sculpture by Myron, with which Pater would have been familiar from the British Museum), he releases the discus that slices, horrifically, through Hyacinth's face.

Seeing and science

The *Discobolus*, like all sculptural representations of the human body, suspends life. Pater's attention was often drawn to figures of young men whose beauty was permanently caught at a moment of physical perfection, and he suffused these with melancholy, for it is impossible to preserve such beauty in real life. Pater was acutely attuned to living in a world in flux.

The Conclusion to *The Renaissance* is best known for Pater's comments about the fluidity of our impressions of the material world – 'unstable, flickering, inconsistent' – and his description of each individual as, ultimately, isolated within their own mind.[36] We may all go to the same Royal Academy exhibition, or stand in front of the *Mona Lisa* or a small bronze statuette of Apollo of Canachus, but in the end, 'the whole scope of observation is dwarfed into the narrow chamber of the individual mind . . . Every one of those impressions is the impression of the individual in his isolation, each mind keeping as a solitary prisoner its own dream of a world' (Conclusion, 198). Read in the context of his aesthetic practice, however, this is not a manifesto in support of exquisite, sensory-stimulated subjectivity but rather the end point of ascesis: a self-disciplined form of looking and contemplation that leads to a kind of dissolving of the self. Pater remained focused on what was outside of himself, not within – however mediated this exterior world might be by personal experience. As George Levine explains, '[e]xperiencing sensation is one thing; literally knowing it, discriminating it, entails repression of self, almost a denial of the sensation being experienced. Pater is arguing for a way to be objective about subjectivity, to find a position outside experience from which to experience it and possess it.'[37]

Yet the separation between outer and inner was not, for Pater, an absolute one – as we see in the first paragraph of the Conclusion. The human body partakes of the same elements – 'phosphorus and lime and delicate fibres' – as are found in the non-human world, and it is subject to the same forces (Conclusion, 197). The eye is not just an instrument through which this visible world is transmitted to the brain but is likewise part of an ever-changing and re-amalgamating combination of elements that constitutes 'the whole physical life' (Conclusion, 197). Our physical existence 'is a perpetual motion' of these elements: 'the passage of the blood, the waste and repairing of the lenses of the eye, the modification of the tissues of the brain' by every ray of light and sound (Conclusion, 197).

Pater was very well versed in debates in contemporary science about materiality, especially the issue of whether or not what one sees in the physical world is all that there is, or whether there is something bigger and ineffable lying behind it, of which the visible world is just a manifestation. This is the question that Marius works through in Chapter XIX of *Marius the Epicurean*, 'The Will as Vision' – a chapter in which, effectively, Marius serves as Pater's representative, debating these issues with himself. 'Might not this entire material world, the very scene around him, the immemorial rocks, the firm marble, the olive gardens, the falling water, be themselves but reflections in, or a creation of, that one indefectible mind', he asks, concluding that this is the most plausible of all hypotheses (*Marius* II, 174). The thought was attractive to him because it allowed one to go beyond the material aspects of both observer and observed: 'It was easier to conceive of the material fabric of things as but an element in the world of thought, as a thought in a mind, than of mind as an element, or accident, or passing condition in a world of matter (*Marius* II, 175).'[38]

This idealist position was but one side of the contemporary debate, and Marius soon loses the certainty he expressed here – as, after all, is consistent with a world permanently in flux. In recent years, Gowan Dawson, George Levine, Benjamin Morgan, and others have written illuminatingly about Pater's familiarity with mid-late century discussions of physiological aesthetics, of the interwoven relationship between mind and matter. Many of these discussions appeared in the same periodicals in which Pater himself published, especially the *Fortnightly* and the *Nineteenth Century*: Pater's own audience, in other words, would very likely have been fully aware of this intellectual context. As we saw in the previous section, Pater was drawn to the shadowy, the visually impenetrable, the indistinct – that which was 'strange' rather than that which was crystalline clear. But this did not mean that he believed that there was some numinous, identifiable power behind the veil. Indeed, the remainder of *Marius*, despite the protagonist's movement towards tentative Christian belief in the final chapters, may be seen as a rebalancing of the perceiving self after that apparent instant of enlightenment in the olive grove. It reads as a demonstration of the fact that although we may interrogate ourselves about how we exercise the facility of looking; and although we may be conscious of the tension between what we see in the material world – and the material aspects of mind – and a spiritual realm that may lie beyond it, such an awareness is bound to dissipate in the ordinary, everyday practices of looking at and responding to the physical world of nature and art as it presents itself to our eyes. That which has material, corporeal existence is always, undeniably, *there*, and ultimately tends to command our attention. For Pater, the perennially present commonplace was, however, ready to be transformed by a sunbeam into something magical, or attracting one's vision with a sudden striking effect, like 'those whites and reds through the smoke on very homely buildings, and . . . the gold of the dandelions at the road-side' that strike Florian's young, untrained eye in 'The Child in the House'.[39]

Physiological aesthetics, as understood in the last few decades of the nineteenth century, explored how the brain processed what the eye saw, and did so in terms that overlapped closely with Pater's preoccupations. For example, James Sully, in 'The Undefinable in Art', similarly shows himself wondering if the scientific and the contemplative can be held in balance, as simultaneous, and complementary approaches to looking at a work of art. He also explains how, when looking at a painting, the eye works in a highly selective way, ranging over the canvas surface: 'we are at each successive moment elevating one impression or group of impressions after another into clear consciousness, while the rest fall back into the dim regions of the sub-conscious.'[40] The eye and corresponding mental processes home in on particular aspects of a painting – a description which perfectly fits Pater's visual habits of singling out details within a whole. And Sully, like many of his contemporaries, was fascinated by the processes of mental visualisation, whether constructing scenes from a mental storehouse of visual references, or drawing on specific memories – for Pater, most frequently taken from the rooms, gardens and buildings of his childhood. Sully, like him, was particularly fascinated by how early impressions became part of the texture of the mind.

Seeing 'in the mind's eye' was a powerful tool for Pater, writing, in *The Renaissance*, of Platonists' habit of 'the act of *shutting the eyes*, that one may see the more, inwardly'.[41] This was not just so that one could understand the essence of what one had been looking at. It was, perhaps particularly, so that one can draw on embedded trains of associations and visualise some remembered scene, or some other work of art, or even call into visual being a lost object from textual hints and archaeological knowledge, like the Chest of Cypselus described by Pausanias.[42] This Platonic philosophy was connected, too, to Pater's understanding of the world through the terminology of modern science, with its attention to the constant flux of matter, and to the doubling of forces in our bodies and the wider world. This was an understanding, as he was to explain in 'Myth of Demeter I',

> more of instinct than of the understanding, the mental starting-point of which is not an observed sequence of outward phenomena, but some such feeling as most of us have on the first warmer days in spring, when we seem to feel the genial processes of nature actually at work; as if just below the mould, and in the hard wood of the trees, there were really circulating some spirit of life, akin to that which makes its energies felt within ourselves.[43]

Conclusion

What happens within the individual as these energies start to ebb and disperse? In 'Poems by William Morris', Pater directs us to examine our thoughts as we contemplate our own death. The picture that forms in the mind's eye is momentarily specific – a drowning form, or maybe the body of one recently dead: 'the image of one washed out beyond the bar in a sea at ebb, losing even his personality, as the elements of which he is composed pass into new combinations'.[44] This practice of dissociation, looking at oneself as though from the outside, a dispassionate if curious observer, recurs in 'The Child in the House'. As Florian felt the

> pressure upon him of the sensible world, then, as often afterwards, there would come another sort of curious questioning how the last impressions of eye and ear might happen to him, how they would find him – the scent of the last flower, the soft yellowness of the last morning, the last recognition of some object of affection, hand or voice; it could not be but that the latest look of the eyes, before their final closing, would be strangely vivid; one would go with the hot tears, the cry, the touch of the wistful bystander, impressed how deeply on one! or would it be, perhaps, a mere frail retiring of all things, great or little, away from one, into a level distance?[45]

In this almost unbearable passage, Pater speculates about how we may take impressions on board at the hour of our death, when there is no chance of them being translated into language; no opportunity to give them form and structure; no possibility of them being stored in the memory.

Whatever cultural associations and verbal formulations may take place in the crucible of the mind, awareness of what we are looking at any given moment is, ultimately, all we have. Pater's demand, in other words, is for paying attention, both to the qualities of what we are looking at and of our own immediate response. For at the end, we will be compelled to live in the moment, and to recognise in our impressions, *at* that moment, the pleasure that they can give.[46]

Notes

1. William Sharp, 'Some Personal Reminiscences of Walter Pater', *Atlantic Monthly* 74 (December 1894): 801–814, 801. Hereafter references to Sharp are included in the text.
2. Walter H. Pater, 'Winckelmann', *The Renaissance: Studies in Art and Poetry*, ed. Hilary Fraser (Oxford: Oxford University Press, 2025), 197. Hereafter 'Winckelmann' is cited in the text.
3. Mrs Humphry [Mary] Ward, *A Writer's Recollections* (London: Collins, 1919), 123.
4. Pater, 'Emerald Uthwart' (1892). *Miscellaneous Studies: A Series of Essays* (New York and London: Macmillan, 1895), 198.
5. Unsigned review [Pater], 'Coleridge', *Westminster Review* 85 (January 1866): 106–132, 123. This passage was omitted when the essay was reprinted in *Appreciations*.
6. Pater, 'Romanticism', *Macmillan's Magazine* 35 (November 1876): 64–70, 65.
7. Pater, 'Luca della Robbia', *Renaissance*, 110.
8. Pater, 'Child in the House', *Miscellaneous Studies*, 155.
9. Pater, 'The Age of Athletic Prizemen' (1894), *Greek Studies. A Series of Essays* (New York and London: Macmillan, 1897), 289; 'The Myth of Demeter and Persephone' (1875), *Greek Studies*, 150.
10. Pater, 'Corot', unpublished manuscript notes. Houghton Library, Harvard University. bMS Eng 1150(25).
11. Pater, 'A Study of Dionysus', *Greek Studies*, 37.
12. Pater, 'Mr Gosse's Poems', *Guardian* (29 October 1890.) Reprinted *Essays from 'The Guardian'* (London: Macmillan, 1901): 105–118, 107.
13. Pater, 'Mr Gosse's Poems', 107–108.
14. Pater, 'Giorgione', *Renaissance*, 145.
15. Pater, 'Giorgione', *Renaissance*, 145.
16. Pater, 'Luca della Robbia', *Renaissance*, 110.
17. Pater, 'Michelangelo', *Renaissance*, 114.
18. Pater, 'Art Notes in Northern Italy', *Miscellaneous*, 78.
19. Pater, 'Giorgione', *Renaissance*, 144.

20. Pater, 'Denys L'Auxerrois' (1886), *Imaginary Portraits* (London: Macmillan, 1887), 53.
21. Pater, *Marius the Epicurean*. 2 vols. (London: Macmillan, 1885), I. 164. Hereafter cited in the text.
22. Pater, 'Two Early French Stories', *Renaissance*, 80. The first edition of *The Renaissance* contains an earlier version, 'Aucassin and Nicolette', which does not include this phrase; 'A Prince of Court Painters', *Imaginary Portraits*, 12.
23. Pater, 'Sandro Botticelli', *Renaissance*, 105.
24. Pater, 'Leonardo da Vinci', *Renaissance*, 138.
25. Pater, 'Leonardo da Vinci', *Renaissance*, 138.
26. The Editor [John Morley], 'Mr Pater's Essays', *Fortnightly Review* 14 (April 1873): 469–477, 473.
27. Lene Østermark-Johansen, "The primary colour of delight': Walter Pater and Gold', *Polysèmes* 15 (2016): 1–14. https://journals.openedition.org/polysemes/889?lang=en. Accessed 6 May 2023; Pater, 'Giorgione', *Fortnightly*, 537.
28. Thomas Wright, *The Life of Walter Pater*. 2 vols. (London: Everett, 1907), I. 23.
29. Pater, 'Beginnings of Greek Sculpture I', *Greek Studies*, 199.
30. Pater, 'Notre-Dame d'Amiens', *Miscellaneous Studies*, 96–97.
31. Pater, 'Vézelay', *Miscellaneous Studies*, 112.
32. Pater, *Gaston de Latour. An Unfinished Romance (1888)* (London: Macmillan, 1896), 7.
33. Pater, *Gaston*, 6 and 7.
34. Pater, *'Measure for Measure' (1874)*, *Appreciations. With an Essay on Style (1888)* (London and New York: Macmillan, 1889), 184.
35. Pater, 'Apollo in Picardy', *Miscellaneous Studies*, 143.
36. Pater, Conclusion, *Renaissance*, 198. Hereafter cited in the text.
37. George Levine, *Dying to Know: Scientific Epistemology and Narrative in Victorian England* (Chicago: University of Chicago Press, 2002), 249.
38. Levine, *Dying to Know*, 175.
39. Pater, 'Child in the House', *Miscellaneous Studies*, 150.
40. [James Sully], 'The Undefinable in Art', *Cornhill Magazine* 38 (1878): 559–72, 561.
41. Pater, 'Pico della Mirandola', *Renaissance*, 94.
42. Pater, 'The Beginnings of Greek Sculpture', *Classical Studies*, ed. Matthew Potolsky (Oxford: Oxford University Press, 2020), 131, 133.
43. Pater, 'Myth of Demeter I', *Greek Studies*, 96.
44. Pater, 'Poems by William Morris', *Westminster Review* 34 (October 1868): 300–312, 311.
45. Pater, 'Child in the House', *Miscellaneous Studies*, 162–3.
46. Pater's own death, however, occurred from a massive heart attack as he recovered from a serious bout of pleurisy. According to Gosse, he died as he started to come downstairs at 64 St Giles, in Oxford: in his last conscious moment, he may well have registered not flowers, nor the light of dawn, but the presence of his sister Clara, in whose arms he died.

5

JONAH SIEGEL

Pater's *Renaissance*

Boldly original though they are, the essays that comprise *The Renaissance* are run through with the words of others. Acknowledged and unacknowledged quotations and adaptations of earlier thinkers abound in a work designed to feature an originality that shows no interest in escaping citation and reference. This play between originality and reference is just one of the many challenges that confront the modern reader of the volume that more than any other established Pater's reputation. The topics addressed in the work can also seem dizzyingly varied; its title appears clear enough, promising as it does studies of the art and poetry of one particular period, and yet Pater does not limit himself to the creative arts, but cites philosophers and scientists in essays that in any case roam with unusual freedom from antiquity to modernity, and that even make claims about periods typically held to be entirely and of necessity distinct from the Renaissance – notably the middle ages, the Enlightenment, and the Romantic era. The conceptual claims one might make about the text are also liable to complications in practice. For example, although the book marks a milestone in the history of the emergence of formalism as a dominant value in the arts, its biographical preoccupations are of the sort that in a later era work against any kind of pure formalism. Then again, as my brief and incomplete list of apparent contradictions may suggest, *The Renaissance* is not interested in purity, a value that is present insofar as it is understood to be a historically bound phenomenon with powerful cultural effects but which is decidedly limited in lived experience.

Five of the eleven pieces that comprise *The Renaissance* were first published as free-standing articles in the periodical press. The earliest, 'Winckelmann', an essay in which the sensitive reader will find a deeply confessional quality combined with a remarkably sophisticated practical application of Georg Wilhelm Friedrich Hegel's philosophy, was originally published in 1867. The last, the astonishing reflection on form and medium that is 'The School of Giorgione', first came out a full decade later, and was only added to the third edition of *The Renaissance* in 1888. The notorious

Conclusion started life as part of a review of William Morris's poetry in 1868 and was famously suppressed by the author in the 1877 edition, only to return in a slightly revised form in the third edition. Another challenge for the reader, then, is to formulate a sense of the whole that does justice to the integrity of the book without doing violence to the particularity of each essay – or to the way each essay is itself compendious.

Pater's achievement in *The Renaissance* emerges with real force when what can feel at first like a wilful embrace of paradox for its own sake is recognised as a commitment to the inescapability of mixed conditions in culture, as in every other facet of our existence. Although the topic blazoned in its title is based on a powerful historical claim – that there was an important moment when a lost culture was recovered or *reborn* – the text refuses to stabilise itself at one temporal location, but instead triangulates its claims in relation to three points: the moment of cultural production of prized works of art, that of encounter with an admired object at a later occasion of citation or reuse, and then the yet-later moment of reception or reflection (Pater's own time, the reader's) when the meaning of both the original object *and* its recovery may be found to signify anew.

But this is to make Pater sound more bloodless than he ever should feel in the reading. At every point *The Renaissance* refuses to separate culture from other elements of human experience such as longing, passion, and loss. The challenges Pater sets himself may be variously described, but they all have at their heart the difficulties attendant on recognising the emotional power of mixed conditions: how to make one clear thing out of a collection of things, how something new may emerge from the accumulation of old material, how to express oneself by reflecting on what one loves in others. While any responsible reading of *The Renaissance* will recognise the distinct nature of these projects, it would be a loss to miss the fact that they amount to one thing: a radical and emotionally urgent recalibration of what it means to be a critic that affects both the substance and the form of the book.

It is not simply that the chapters of *The Renaissance* are wide-ranging, addressing topics from the meanings of classical sculpture to the nature of the modern world given the insights of science, from the passions manifested in medieval romances to those hidden in plain sight in the paintings of Botticelli and Leonardo or the poetry of Michelangelo. The scope of Pater's references, which move from Heraclitus to Pascal, from Hegel to Charles Darwin, pausing from time to time on Charles Baudelaire and Victor Hugo and other nineteenth-century luminaries, adds to the feeling of an erudition that can seem too idiosyncratic to form the basis for a claim of authority. Pater's display of learning is designed less to compel assent through his performance of cultural mastery than to move his reader to feel the pleasure of knowing things and of admiring formulations that capture with unusual elegance the nature of issues the longevity of which testifies to their impossibility of resolution. Sometimes it is clear that Pater has set himself the challenge of making a perfect setting for a particularly apposite quotation. At other times his references are designed to jar the reader by an unexpected juxtaposition. This play between citation and argument hearkens back to the earliest days of the essay form, its emergence out of the commonplace book, the compendium of telling or evocative quotations that was so important in the Early Modern period. As in Michel de Montaigne, that ultimate source for all essayists, the energies of the creative writer are not to be distinguished from the attempt to place found material in a new context. In that sense, the essayistic impulse and the critical one are closely allied. The challenges of analysis are also intimately bound up with the anticipation of something like a relationship. How to make you see what I do in this fragment of text, this novel idea? How to make you feel its significance anew by leaving a record of my own response? But also, how much can I make you feel me in my prose? Can writing about culture and ideas be a kind of confession? Are reflections on art or education places where personal intimacies take place?

The Renaissance also has immediate sources in its own period. It is a relatively late and deeply self-conscious manifestation of the great efflorescence of prose writing in the nineteenth century that had so many causes and so many still ongoing after-effects. The era had seen an epochal expansion in literacy and in technological developments that made the creation and widespread distribution of the written word possible at an extraordinary scale. The emergence of a newly powerful middle class and the pressures of the developing mass politics that would reshape the world for the foreseeable future created a sense of urgency when it came to the diffusion of knowledge. Readers hungry for ideas and information about a changing world sustained the proliferation of periodicals containing not only fiction, poems, and news but also essays and reviews summarising and characterising recent work in a wide range of fields. The forms these texts would take at their most ambitious were inevitably shaped by earlier models such as the sermon and the popular lecture, as well as by the essay form itself, which had had many important British practitioners. Like many of his contemporaries, when Pater wrote, he was placing himself in the ever-expanding world of the periodical press, but he also had the longer tradition in mind. That he was keenly aware of the traditions in which he worked is indicated by his alert responsiveness to the writings of his more recent antecedents, including Matthew Arnold, Thomas Carlyle, Ralph Waldo Emerson, John Henry Newman, and John Ruskin. His work responds directly to the claims of these authors and others in the English-speaking world and on the continent, writers whom he sometimes cites directly, and sometimes merely evokes by touching on their characteristic concerns or formulations.

The proliferation of newly specialised fields of humanistic inquiry is a characteristic of the nineteenth century that Pater's work registers and also may be said to resist. As insights from art history, archaeology, anthropology, the natural sciences, and, of course, the history of antiquity all shape Pater's responses to his literary and intellectual predecessors, we find in his work a set of object lessons on the merits of aiming always towards a 'complete type of general culture'.[1] Emerging academic fields aside, Pater was also deeply responsive to the Europe-wide intellectual ferment that followed the French Revolution, notably the idealist philosophical tradition that culminated in the work of Hegel and romantic and post-romantic literary innovations coming from the continent, including such distinct French men of letters as Victor Hugo and Charles Baudelaire as well as Hippolyte Taine, and Jules Michelet. Nowhere is Pater more clearly participating in the great tradition of the essay going back to Montaigne than when he wields a deeply self-reflexive prose combining quotation, citation, and allusion in order to develop his arguments in relation to the wide range of authors and fields that shapes modern thought. So it is that Pater's Darwin is inflected by his Hegel – and they both shape his account of classical antiquity and of contemporary literature. His evocative responses to the biographical elements in Vasari's foundational art history are reshaped by the cutting-edge archival research in works such as Joseph Archer Crowe and Giovanni Battista Cavalcaselle's *New History of Painting in Italy* (1864–66), even as his sense of the stakes of art-historical claims emerges in response to the general cultural claims he finds in Ruskin's moralised accounts of history.

The sections of this chapter are designed to provide an overview of elements that link the essays, and that make *The Renaissance* more than a collection of disparate writings on culture. I focus first on the limits of conventional concepts of periodisation in Pater, and the power of those categories when their limits are recognised. I then address the nature of the aesthetic critic Pater describes and whose work the essays illustrate, focusing on the range of interests that are included in what such a critic might contemplate, and on the primacy of the impression as an object of reflection. The final two sections address the multivalent power of desire and the place of representative figures in Pater's writing. Pater is as interested in the erotic passions that lead individuals towards each other as in the drives that motivate them towards learning, but most interested of all in the occasion when those motivations coincide. My division of these topics notwithstanding, the reader will find that in Pater they are always inextricably and fundamentally connected, his teaching always including the lesson that the main virtue of identifying a limit is in immediately recognising the things always breaking through its edges.

Periodisation in *The Renaissance*

The term 'Renaissance' was of recent vintage when Pater adopted it as the title for his volume.[2] It had emerged in French circles in the 1820s, and entered English in the 1830s, but the art-historical implications of the period had been established for nineteenth-century England by its particularly tendentious evocation in Ruskin's work, especially *The Stones of Venice* (1851–53), where the critic was concerned to draw important distinctions between the socially enmeshed imperfect work of the medieval craftsman and the individualistic, specialised – not to say egotistical and showy – art of the period following the end of the Middle Ages. The distinction Ruskin developed was part of a Europe-wide re-valorisation of medieval work that would be manifested in the British context in the second part of the century by the rise of the Pre-Raphaelite Brotherhood and before that by various forms of Gothic revival in architecture, but it was based on claims of stark period differences that Pater was never interested in endorsing. Indeed, Pater is principally concerned with characterising periods in order to demonstrate the relations among them – not to make claims about absolute breaks. 'Theories which bring into connexion with each other modes of thought and feeling, periods of taste, forms of art and poetry, which the narrowness of men's minds constantly tends to oppose to each other', he proposes in 'Two French Stories', 'have a great stimulus for the intellect, and are almost always worth understanding'. If putting apparently distinct periods into relation is a worthwhile practice, that is in part because the claims of absolute distinction are so often inaccurate. Hence, Pater's description, with Ruskin certainly in mind, of 'that rupture between the middle age and the Renaissance which has so often been exaggerated' (78).

The tendency to divide the past into periods is an old one, but it had been given new technical impetus by the reflections of philosophers of the eighteenth century and a new scope in the practical sphere by the experience of irreparable social ruptures that followed the years of political revolution at the end of the century and accompanied the Industrial Revolution. As philosophy itself came to be oriented towards history, it found in art an important index of change, notably in the work of Friedrich Schiller in *The Aesthetic Education of Man* (1794) and *On Naïve and Sentimental Poetry* (1795) and then in the systematisations of Hegel in the *Phenomenology* (1807) and in the *Aesthetics* (1835). It was not in cultural productions alone that the pervasive sense of inevitable change and development was

69

manifested, however. Geology, and eventually biology, would give newly compelling force to the idea that the conditions of life needed to be understood as fundamentally distinct at different points in time. Ultimately the concept of the descent of man from more primitive organisms and the endless horizons of development opened up by Darwin made the theme of fundamental change not just unavoidably personal but simultaneously a quality each human being shared with every element in organic life. Recent work on materialism and in environmental humanities has moved in the direction of Pater's full-bodied recognition of the place of the human in nature, but his texts are characterised less by the drama of such recognitions (that we are animals, that we exist in a natural world of which we form a part, and so on) than by the desire to dwell on the implications of the intermediary stages between conditions of being and the concepts the critic might bring to bear in understanding those conditions. The later nineteenth century was fascinated with half tones, with unresolved states, with dawns, and the coming of twilight. Pater charges this sensibility with an energy that amounts to something far more than vagueness. The evocative mysteries of the paintings of Botticelli received renewed attention in the nineteenth century, and both Ruskin and Pater have been identified as pioneers in establishing the modern fame of this artist.[3] For Pater, Botticelli anticipates the intellectual preoccupations of later eras, so he is one of several transitional or intermediary figures that interest him because of the way his paintings appear to push beyond the limits of simple faith using conventional religious subjects to project ideas and feelings that are the opposite of pious, that anticipate modern uncertainties. Botticelli's work, in Pater's telling, is characterised by the ability to make sacred subjects speak even of topics quite distant from those one might expect from an altarpiece: 'the genius of which Botticelli is the type usurps the data before it as the exponent of ideas, moods, visions of its own' (103). The remoulding of conventional material into something new is the chief project of the kind of culture that fascinates Pater, and he will tend to pause over instances where that remaking is marked – as in the case of Botticelli transforming Mary, the mother of God, into an anxious thought-beset modern. The role of the Virgin in interceding for a fallen humanity is an orthodox idea, but the ways in which that function is manifested by Pater's Botticelli is extraordinary: 'He paints Madonnas, but they shrink from the pressure of the divine child, and plead in unmistakable undertones for a warmer, lower humanity' (106).

Michelangelo's longevity makes him towards the end of his life a figure outside of time, his physical existence continuing into cultural moments in which he cannot fully participate, but the temporal dislocation of

Michelangelo is more than a biographical accident in Pater's account of the artist. It is central to the story he tells about the sculptor.[4] Pater adapts Michelangelo's notorious irascible independence into another way of representing the feeling of living in a time not fully one's own. On the other hand, the sweetness Pater emphasises in his work hearkens back to the reserve the artist learned from his study of Tuscan sculptors of the very early Renaissance. One practical effect of these dislocations is that Pater manages to separate Michelangelo from the Mannerism with which he has been associated in traditional accounts of the arc of the Renaissance, and which has conventionally been seen as a falling off from the great successes of the period. As Pater loosens the artist's location in time, Michelangelo's achievement is no longer marred by the heritage of lesser artists following his model but unable to match his accomplishments. Indeed, Pater looks to the nineteenth century to identify figures approaching the blend of strength and sweetness he finds in Michelangelo, citing a surprising pair at various points in the essay: William Blake and Victor Hugo. The anachronistic quality of an artist who hearkens back to a period in sculpture from centuries before his birth and anticipates distinct strands of Romantic creativity in the visual arts and literature not only evidences the complex nature of the concept of periodisation with which Pater works but also illustrates the centrality of the place of the modern subject in his approach to aesthetics. There is no straightforward historical argument that will link a Tuscan sculptor who flourished in the fifteenth and sixteenth centuries with a British engraver and French novelist from the nineteenth. They meet only at the point created by the sensibility of the modern critic.

The Aesthetic Critic and What Is Real in Our Life

The Preface to *The Renaissance* establishes three things: the concept of culture with which Pater is working, the claims of the concrete he intends to advance in the face of a tendency towards abstraction in thinking about beauty, and the centrality of the subject in all aesthetic matters. All of these elements come together in the figure of the critic, the key protagonist in *The Renaissance* – along with Pater's urbane style of informed, judicious reflection, which itself is a practical manifestation of the presence of the critic. It is his carefully developed tone that makes some of Pater's more surprising transitions or changes in register effective, and indeed allows some of them to pass without notice, as can happen even with that notorious moment when Pater appears to wholeheartedly agree with Arnold's bracingly straightforward claim that 'to see the object as in itself it really is' is the object of all criticism, only to turn the meaning of that claim on its head: '"To see the object as in itself it really is," has been justly said to be the aim of all true criticism whatever; and in aesthetic criticism the first step towards seeing one's object as it really is, is to know one's own impression as it really is, to discriminate it, to realise it distinctly' (73). Pater's elaboration of his initial consent to a proposition that purports to ground all criticism in the objective world (on the object as it is, free of all elements that might be imported by the subject) blithely moves towards a full reversal of what it purports to agree with by the simple expedient of identifying the only objects available to the mind as the mind's own impressions. The impression itself is the thing that requires to be seen as in itself it really is, and the key point about any impression, of course, is that it is an instance of subjective experience. Although the question that Pater identifies as fundamental for the aesthetic critic, what is this thing 'to *me*?' appears to have two elements in view, the perceiving self and the object of perception, they ultimately come down to one: this thing *to me* (103).

The process by which Pater leads the reader to a reversal of Arnold's aspiration towards objective perception is of fundamental importance to the book. The assured reuse of prior ideas is not simply an exercise in misdirection; it is predicated on a claim about the circumstances in which the critic works. The individual point of view is not the clear ground on which to stand and assess the object world. Experiences the world makes available, whether material or intellectual, are disparate and challenging; it is the consciousness of the critic that recognises the essential parts – of Wordsworth, say, or Leonardo – and lets the rest go, who identifies how the disparate elements that emerge at a particular time amount to a culture. But, the only way recognition can take place and identification will be possible is by fully engaging with a question that is nowhere as easy as it sounds: *what is this thing to me?* To embrace the question that Pater poses for the aesthetic critic is to make every work of criticism a confession. It is impossible to tell you what something is to me without revealing my own nature. The personal limits and extension that determine what one sees are shaped by what one's individual nature allows one to recognise in the world. Pater's critic consistently confesses his vulnerabilities – what he fears as much as what he desires. While Pater's concept of the aesthetic critic places the individual response – understood as in itself the primary object of analysis – at the centre of any account of the encounter with the aesthetic object, the poignancy of the self-revelation entailed in the work of the critic becomes all the sharper given full range of things that may call out to one from the world. Indeed, Pater's lists of the categories that will interest the aesthetic critic include items that will never appear in any curriculum of formal study:

> The objects with which aesthetic criticism deals – music, poetry, artistic and *accomplished forms of human life.*
>
> What is this song or picture, *this engaging personality presented in life* or in a book, to *me*?
>
> [A]ll the objects with which he has to do, all works of art, and *the fairer forms of nature and human life* ...   (73–74; my italics)

Life appears repeatedly ranked alongside aesthetic objects drawn from the plastic, literary, or musical arts that one might have expected: life – fairer, engaging, accomplished human life. These moments in the Preface forecast what will be a constant preoccupation in *The Renaissance*, but it is worth spending a moment on what it means for life to be placed in the same register as other aesthetic objects. There are some obvious answers, familiar to the reader of later aesthetes: the idea that life may be led artistically, that its relationship to artifice is closer than generally thought. But the subject Pater is particularly interested in is the one written into his title, *The Renaissance*. The *return* to life is a topic which in a Gothic register might suggest something morbid, but when it enters reflections on our actual existence may simply suggest something far more powerful, though more mundane: that it is possible to not fully live, and therefore that we may have the option to start to live anew. Rebirth, renaissance and vivification are closely related terms, and in Pater they always involve a claim for a new life, not simply the rebirth of the culture of one era in another but the beginning of a process of constant rebirth including the desires of the body and the fascinations of the mind (elements this text full of scholar-lovers is never interested in separating).

The desire for a rebirth into the body will always become especially charged when the manifestation of longing has been balked by the denial of the claims of physical desire. In that sense individual renaissances will be the aspiration of every subject during a time of ascetic constraint, whether it is the constraints of medieval Christianity or of Victorian morality that are at work. It is also available for us to understand even profoundly repressive cultural movements as emblematic of a more overwhelming loss, that of death itself or of the wasted opportunities that amount to a living death – to not living at all in the sense Pater means the term in this text: 'on this short day of frost and sun', as Pater will write in the Conclusion, 'to sleep before evening' (199). On the other side of such a premature sleep is a passionate personal engagement with life.

The first lines of Pater's most famous text, the Conclusion of *The Renaissance*, are among those that readers often rush through, and they can be forgiven for doing so, given the passage's muted generalisations: 'To regard all things and principles of things as inconstant modes or fashions has become more and more the tendency of modern thought' (197). It is worth pausing on this opening sentence, however, that is so characteristic of its author in its combination of a proposition of extraordinary reach with a prose that disarms resistance by camouflaging its tendentious nature – in this case by appearing to be little more than a citation of received opinion. Typical of Pater's style also is the way the passage suggestively opens up a topic or line of thought that it never quite closes at its end. The reader anticipates a turn that never comes and the absence of which is then not quite remembered as the text moves on. In short, the text suggests a number of clear directions the argument is likely to pursue, all of which it proceeds to ignore.

Readers today (as in the nineteenth century) are used to claims about fashions and tendencies and modern thought, so the eye barely registers the two key words that give this apparently bland opening its force: 'all' and 'principles'. Were we to pause on the boundless nature of the formulation, which would require us to credit the precision of the author, the weight of its implications would be unmistakable: the inconstancy goes all the way down to principles – and it is absolute (including, as it does, *all* things). Pater provides no opportunity for pause, however. The opening claim calls out for a balancing antithesis that never comes, an absence that augments the force of original proposition, that reinforces the claim of inconstancy rather than mitigating it in any way. Propositions about 'modern thought' or about how people 'regard' things tend to be followed by mollifying, nuancing claims – about the way that facts show us the limits of thoughts, perhaps, or about how seeming is ironised by being, or about how our unmistakably real experiences of the permanence of things make the claims of inconstancy and fashion trivial and possibly pernicious. Such corrective moments would seem to be called for especially when it is *all* things and principles of things that are at issue. However, the reader will wait in vain for any correction or limit to the bold opening. Instead, where revision or nuancing of the scandalous proposition should be, one finds simple and concrete development. In a quiet reversal of expectation, the inconstancy modern thought tends to find in all things is retrospectively revealed to be *not* erroneous or overstated at all, so much as a relatively straightforward description of circumstances.

'Let us begin with that which is without – our physical life', the passage continues (197), with Pater turning away from general terms to something that seems entirely distinct from inconstancy or the mental states we might associate with how we regard things, and especially the principles of things. Or, does this second sentence retrospectively make the original claim some- thing close to an axiom calling for illustration? – Otherwise, what are we

74

beginning? Without elaboration, Pater moves from what appears on first reading to be a discussion of perception or conceptualisation – one that seems to call on the reader to begin to distinguish between how things are regarded and how they simply *are* – to language suggesting that what one has just read is a premise that can be demonstrated through observation itself (of 'that which is without – our physical life'). But this is all dry stuff compared to what is coming: a third sentence in which a direct imperative that addresses the reader personally (making the 'let us begin' of the previous sentence retrospectively more personal and intimate than it at first appeared) concludes with a deeply physical experience: suddenly the reader is taking a plunge and having sensations that are unavoidably also those of the writer who relishes the memory of our physical life: 'Fix upon it in one of its more exquisite intervals', says a voice now clearly become seductively intimate, 'the moment, for instance, of delicious recoil from the flood of water in summer heat'. *Delicious*: unexpectedly we are in the water on a hot day accompanied by an author who is apparently not interested in arguing about how we regard things or principles of things so much as in bringing us along with him, or rather in making us recognise with a kind of Whitmanesque identification that we have been where he is all along, that we have both felt something delicious, though we have not been thinking about that experience until just now.

Pater moves in three quick sentences from the passive voice and general claims about 'things', indeed about 'principles of things' – what could be drier and more abstract! – to a direct address intended to make us remember our bodies (that which feels the 'exquisite interval', the 'delicious recoil'). The transitions effected and links suggested across these lines of prose illustrate the nature of the connections the author is interested in establishing. Pater's goal is not the kind of demystification that moves decisively from the illusion of general claims or seeming to real experience understood as an alternative solid ground – far from it. The evocation of physical sensations, which would, in some forms of the argument Pater might have been pursuing, work against the bloodless non-experience of 'principles' and 'things', does not ultimately give the reader a place for constancy and permanence in the face of distressing abstraction. To 'fix', in this argument, is not to attach, to stop from motion – it is to look attentively. And any attentive look in/at the world he describes will reveal inconstancy. When Pater turns to the mind itself ('the inward world of thought and feeling'), the speed of change, and its ultimately destructive nature, is all the clearer ('the whirlpool is still more rapid, the flame more eager and devouring'). It is here, in this inward world, that 'what is real in our lives' will be revealed. But, the promise of reality amounts to an extraordinarily insubstantial impression: 'To such a tremulous wisp constantly re-forming itself on the stream, to a single sharp impression, with a sense in it, a relic more or less fleeting, of such moments gone by, what is real in our life fines itself down' (198).

'*What is real in our life*': to think about the conditions in which this evocative formulation might make sense is to begin to realise how much its terms assume and how much they take away. We are apparently together in this moment; the lived condition at issue is *ours*, shared. But this companionship is recognised in (may well be a compensation for) the condition the phrase also suggests is the case: that there is some portion of our life that is not real. The phrase assumes that the real only makes up a part of life. This is not an unusual claim in the nineteenth century or today – the idea that much of our existence is in some measure not real, and that those moments in which reality is truly experienced are rare and to be prized. Indeed, a locution such as 'what is real in our life' – with all the poignancy it carries – might be said to describe the goal motivating much of nineteenth-century culture whether we think of Wordsworth seeking a realer language for poetry, or the great realist novelists searching for forms that would make the nature of social experience visible to their readers, or even scientists plumbing the fossil record or studying the starry firmament to establish the principles of things. Nevertheless, and with these distinct traditions clearly in mind, Pater does not identify 'what is real in our lives' with a solid level of human knowledge or individual experience, but rather with 'a tremulous wisp', an unstable vapour hovering over the water of which it is sometimes a part, but which is always something even more unsteady and evanescent than the liquid element over which it forms.

In order to be recognised for the call to alertness that it is, the famous description of the experience of art in the Conclusion as a kind of brief erotic encounter needs to be understood in the context of the seductive nature of the text as a whole. Seduction here is an invitation to a kind of self-recognition only available from a full engagement with the transient world that the rest of the text describes. As I have been suggesting, the extraordinary scope of the brief five paragraphs that make up the Conclusion of *The Renaissance* is achieved through writing strategies that amplify the force of the prose through the bold juxtaposition of elements. Which is to say that a great deal of the work of the writing takes place in the spaces that are left unelaborated, a suggestive style that creates the conditions for an argument in which intimate encounters and general claims come together into an invitation to recognition of one's own fears and desires in the words of another. We might call the style seductive, if we understand that term to describe the urgent moment when a need and an opportunity arrive at the same time.

A marked instance of the way Pater uses the gaps he leaves between the expectations his sentences create and what they proceed to offer to generate a retrospective sense of the meaning of the prose we have just read is to be found at the odd opening of the final paragraph of the Conclusion, which begins with an utterly unprepared-for evocation of a moment in Jean-Jacques Rousseau's *Confession* (a text that is only mentioned once before in the whole volume, and then simply to provide a point of comparison with the confessional qualities of Joachim du Bellay). 'One of the most beautiful passages of Rousseau', Pater abruptly declares following a paragraph the tenor of which had been the need to recognise in philosophy not the claims of its abstraction but the fact that it ought to startle us into paying attention to life, 'is that in the sixth book of the *Confessions*, where he describes the awakening in him of the literary sense' (199). The sentence is typical of Pater: it suggests by its location a connection with what has preceded it without fully spelling out what the link is; it augments its performative erudition with an authoritative use of technical detail (the fact, in this case, that the moment cited is in the *sixth* book), and it deploys an aesthetic sensibility that suggests that to the specific knowledge he wields the author also adds an ability to make nuanced judgements of taste (there are evidently other beautiful passages in the book, some less beautiful than this one; the critic knows them and can rank them). The passage is also, of course, typical of the interest in the interior lives of representative men that characterises *The Renaissance* (and we may remember that Rousseau is one of the figures Carlyle featured in the chapter on 'The Hero as Man of Letters' in his *Heroes, Hero-Worship and the Heroic in History* (1841))). In that sense, although I have described the placement of the allusion as abrupt, the text as a whole has prepared the reader for this moment, which represents a kind of internal rebirth into something it would be difficult to describe as either an emotion or a form of knowledge, but which seems to combine both into a promising new creative ambition ('the awakening in him of a literary sense').

The energy of the sentence arises between the authoritative clarity of its presentation and its basic mysteries. Why should I care about this eighteenth-century man of letters? Why is the author talking about him now? Pater quickly explains that what interests him in this part of the *Confessions* is the fact that what he is calling the literary sense arose in Rousseau as a response to a pervasive sense that he was mortally ill. If the reader misses or forgets the idiosyncratic nature of the opening of the final paragraph of the Conclusion of *The Renaissance*, it is because Pater so quickly and effectively suggests the general nature of the condition at issue. By way of explanation he quotes Hugo's melancholy declaration that 'we are all under sentence of death, but with an indefinite reprieve' (199). As he did at the opening of the Conclusion,

Pater reaches out to his readers and declares us all to be in the same condition (sharing the same sentence – literally and figuratively). What we do not know is if we will feel a newly quickened passion in the face of a death that is at once inevitable as a destiny and unpredictable in nature. Pater celebrates a passion that will be most fully rewarded by the encounter with art precisely because art elicits disinterested emotions that make no claims of permanence. What is this to me *now* turns out to be the full expression of the question for the aesthetic critic, with the 'now' understood to mean both *for the time being* and *in the context of modern thought*. The experience of beauty gives you precisely what it promises at the moment of encounter. This world that takes so much from us, the Conclusion suggests, whether we notice the loss or not, might also give things back if we begin to pay attention to all it offers at every moment.

The rebirth written into Pater's *Renaissance* is a phenomenon that is not limited to one historical period because it is always about individuals as much as it is about the general culture. However, the realisation of the promise of renaissance depends on the recognition of the fundamental condition of evanescence. The refusal to acquiesce in abstract principles that falsify the endless variety of actual experience is the moral call to life of the text, but the certainty that the experiences of the mind are as powerful as those of the body, or, rather, that they are mutually shaping make Pater's recourse to experience, to life, unusually sophisticated. When *what is this to me?* is the only question that stands a chance of revealing what is real in our lives, individuals are bound to only ever reach partial satisfactions that leave them desiring more. The things we think we know provoke desires: for more knowledge, for more beauty, for something that will fill the moments we have with significance without falsifying the condition of transience (of conditions, of selves). Inconstancy is loss only when permanence is thought to be possible. To regard all things as inconstant is to be committed to a sense that the widely recognised fact that culture is change may align it not with what is not important because it is transient but with all the most important transitions we know – notably those that entail death at one end and the possibility of new birth at the other.

Desire

Nowhere is Pater more tantalising to the modern reader than when the centrality of desire in his work comes to the fore. With a kind of polymorphous perversity, longing proliferates in his text in ways we might want to endorse when it comes to his refusal of the repressions he associates with the Church, or when he opens the door to a frank manifestation of the force of same-sex desire, as in his account of Johann Joachim Winckelmann, or Pico della Mirandola, or of Leonardo's relationship with his treasured students, or even when he proposes that the poignant romance in Chaucer's 'Knight's Tale' is a love triangle, in which each line is equally deeply etched: 'one knows not whether the love of both Palamon and Arcite for Emelya, or of those two for each other, is the chiefer subject' (80).[5] In his brief first essay on some medieval French stories, which includes his retelling of a number of passionate relationships, including those of Palamon and Arcite and Heloise and Abelard, as well as of Aucassin and Nicolette and Amis and Amile, Pater illustrates a period characterised not by its harmonious social organisation and its piety (as Ruskin might have had it, along with a number of Catholic authors in the period) but by a nascent rebelliousness against constraint that is driven by the new recognition or valorisation of desire:

> One of the strongest characteristics of that outbreak of the reason and the imagination, of that assertion of the liberty of the heart, in the middle age, which I have termed a medieval Renaissance, was its antinomianism, its spirit of rebellion and revolt against the moral and religious ideas of the time. In their search after the pleasures of the senses and the imagination, in their care for beauty, in their worship of the body, people were impelled beyond the bounds of the Christian ideal; and their love became sometimes a strange idolatry, a strange rival religion. (88)

Pater creates an extraordinary context for thinking about the human affections when he goes on to compare this passionate outbreak favourably to the violent changes that marked the coming of the Reformation and the French Revolution. The analogy suggests the epochal nature of the (re)turn to the body but also highlights the universality of the phenomenon.

Given Pater's celebration of passion, however, it is worth pointing out some of the more shocking elements in the vision of desire in *The Renaissance*, at least for the modern sensibility that tends to view satisfaction as the only acceptable response to desire, and that still often confounds erotic gratification with the consolidation of the individual personality. Not only are love and pedagogy allied in Pater in ways that might make contemporary readers uncomfortable, as in his treatment of the passion that overwhelms Abelard and Heloise or of the love determining the relationships of Leonardo and his students, but such affiliations might result in the loss of one identity within another, as is the case with artists whose creative endeavours become no more than emulations of the teacher they love and serve. Ultimately, Pater's responsiveness to the power of longing means that its presence is far more marked in his texts than that of any forms of satisfaction, a tendency that the reader might identify as the confession of individual need, but that

Pater himself indicates is more than personal. His treatment of the topic is informed as much by his inheritance of that line of the Romantic sensibility preoccupied by the pleasures of unsatisfiable desire as by his responsiveness to a modernity of which the keynote is change. Constant alert recognition of those moments in which an ever-changing world appears to promise to meet our needs may be another way to describe the experience of desire in this work, and, ultimately, the relationship between longing, success and failure developed in the essays. Leonardo's master, Verrochio, is a perfect crafts-man, but his ability to fully and satisfactorily realise what he envisions is the reason for the relatively limited interest his work holds for later periods. It is his student, Leonardo, always pursuing new interests, pushing himself to new attempts, new failures, new partial successes, who stands for the Renaissance spirit that fascinates Pater. The 'way to perfection', Pater writes quoting Baudelaire as he works to make sense of Leonardo's vast catalogue of unfinished projects, 'is through a series of disgusts' (129).

Each art, the critic posits in the essay on the School of Giorgione, pushes beyond its own limits. In that sense, the famous proposition that all art aspires to the condition of music needs to be understood as the fullest manifestation of a longing that characterises every creative endeavour. Pater was never likely to give us a theory of dissatisfaction or of longing, given his resistance to any kind of abstracting thought. Nevertheless, the proliferating instances of desire in *The Renaissance* suggest that what he is describing are so many concrete manifestations of a feeling that is impossible to separate from thought itself. It is not just that the desires of the body, the concepts of the mind, and the urgings of the heart are more closely allied in Pater than is typical; he insists on their interdependence phenomena. To say that ideas shape emotions and so the desires of the body would be one way of understanding the relationships involved, but the matter can also be run other ways. The desires of the body inevitably register on the affective and intellectual life of individuals in Pater. The attention we give the world is motivated by the desires driving us and the concepts that motivate us, desire, and idea articulating us with a world of things and principles of things that our concepts might tell us is shifting ever more as we look at it. While our forms of attention are shaped by our ideas, then, our experience of what we encounter in the world inevitably reshapes anew our feelings and desires.

Renaissance, or 'the Chief Use in Studying Old Masters'

Pater's essays range restlessly from the days of his subjects to the earlier periods they had come to admire and forward to a modernity we still share with him. Artists and intellectuals are at the heart of Pater's analysis of culture, in particular the way their lives and works might be understood as central to the attempt to place oneself into relationship with the periods they lived in, shaped, or dreamed about. But, as culture is no simple matter in Pater, involving as it does all the unevenness attendant on variations and contradictions and processes never fully realised, the critic's project does not come down to simple sociological determinations of the kind one sometimes encounters in historicist studies of culture. The figures he writes about are always to be placed in relation to some tendency or characteristic of the period in which they lived, but as that tendency will itself be in the process of metamorphosis, the relationship of a creative figure to the vicissitudes of an era will never be fully settled.

It would be a failure of response to the vivifying project of *The Renaissance* and to its commitment to delayed rebirths and rediscoveries, to longings provoked by cultural material from far away, to leave its seductions on the page in which we find them, or strand them in the period in which they arose, and indeed, they never remain there. 'That strange interfusion of sweetness and strength', Pater writes at the end of his essay on Michelangelo, 'is not to be found in those who claimed to be his followers; but it is found in many of those who worked before him, and in many others down to our own time' (125). This flamboyant anachronism Pater identifies in the artist is part of an attempt to rescue Michelangelo's legacy by saving him from being remembered as the inspiration of a Mannerist school that even today gets less admiration than it might, but which in the nineteenth century was certainly out of favour in advanced thought, understood as it was as a falling away from, or hollowing out of, the great achievements of the Renaissance. As I noted above, the artist is instead identified with the passionate force manifested in Blake's prints and Hugo's novels. While such an ahistorical leap sustained only by the power of the critical sensibility would be difficult to make today, it is hard not to think that it is a loss to the student of culture to no longer be able to propose categories, whether formal or intellectual, that compellingly link disparate periods. 'Though not of his school, and unaware', he says of these nineteenth-century figures, they are 'his true sons'. To be a true son is a family relationship he then glosses as follows: 'and help us to understand him, as he in turn interprets and justifies them. Perhaps this is the chief use in studying old masters' (125).

It would be wrong to suggest that a writer whose self-confessed followers include such thoughtful and passionate acolytes as Oscar Wilde or Lionel Johnson, or whose influence on so diverse a set of authors as Gerard Manley Hopkins, William Butler Yeats, and Henry James is so clear, could be said to lack intellectual offspring. And indeed, the centrality of Pater's *Renaissance* for important lines of Modernism in the English-speaking world and else-where has been pretty clearly established at this point.[6] As literary studies rediscovered Walter Pater after a long hiatus in which his work was in bad odour in the first half of the twentieth century, it found in his writings antecedents not just for later literary movements but for theoretical approaches to literature such as deconstruction, and certainly for the com-plex representation of same-sex desire. In that sense he interprets and justifies offspring he never knew he had. Nevertheless, if we are still learning to be Pater's heirs, that is in no small measure because of a widespread tendency to doubt something he never did, the dynamic and unresolved quality of the nineteenth century itself. The pleasures and challenges of the book that has beyond all others been responsible for Pater's reputation are clear enough, though easy to lose sight of as developments in culture have made his innovative concepts appear more conventional than they were at the time of formulation. Still, spending time with Pater's text will reveal that in their committed response to ideas that contemporary culture apparently shares with him – about the inevitability of change, say, or the power of desire, or the nature of form – Pater's formulations may offer more challenges that the conventionalising of their radical nature will sometimes allow us to see.

Notes

1. Walter Pater, *The Renaissance: Studies in Art and Poetry*, ed. Hilary Fraser (Oxford: Oxford University Press, 2025), 76. Subsequent references to *The Renaissance* are parenthetical.
2. The original title that Pater gave the book, *Studies in the History of the Renaissance*, probably called for too sophisticated a sense of what Pater means by history to ever seem accurate to the superficial reader. Starting with the second edition it was changed to *The Renaissance: Studies in Art and Poetry*.
3. For the fullest account of the reception of the artist, see Jeremy Melius, 'Art History and the Invention of Botticelli' (PhD Thesis, University of California, Berkeley, 2010).
4. Carolyn William's *Transfigured World: Walter Pater's Aesthetic Historicism* (Ithaca, NY: Cornell University Press, 1989) is still the best resource on the play between history and concept in Pater. Heather Love writes of Pater's 'temporal ambivalence' in a rich study that identifies the author himself as a figure for the kinds of displacements that fascinated him. Heather Love, *Feeling Backward: Loss and the Politics of Queer History* (Cambridge, MA: Harvard University Press, 2007), 8, 53–71. While it does not address Pater, the most sophisticated recent study of the kinds of generative temporal disjunctions in the reception of art that run through the critic's work is probably Alexander Nagel and Christopher S. Wood, *Anachronic Renaissance* (New York: Zone Books, 2010).
5. The place of same-sex desire in Pater has received sustained attention since at least Richard Dellamora's groundbreaking *Masculine Desire: The Sexual Politics of*

Victorian Aestheticism (Chapel Hill, NC: University of North Carolina Press, 1990), and has been enriched by a number of more recent studies, including Heather Love and Jacques Khalip, 'Pater's Sadness', *Raritan* 20.2 (Fall 2000): 148–149. Dustin Friedman, *Before Queer Theory: Victorian Aestheticism and the Self* (Baltimore, MD: Johns Hopkins University Press, 2019), is a particularly ambitious attempt to link the topic to Pater's aesthetic thought. On Leonardo and his students, see Jonah Siegel, 'Schooling Leonardo: Collaboration, Desire, and the Challenge of Attribution in Pater', in *Walter Pater: Transparencies of Desire*, ed. Laurel Brake, Lesley Higgins, and Carolyn Williams (Greensboro, NC: ELT Press, 2002), 133–50.

6. See especially Stephen Bann, ed. *The Reception of Walter Pater in Europe* (London: Continuum, 2004).

6

STEFANO EVANGELISTA

Pater's Novels

We tend to think of Pater primarily as an essayist and a craftsman of small forms. However, his two novels – *Marius the Epicurean* (1885) and *Gaston de Latour* (1888, 1896) – stand at the very heart of his work as aesthetic writer. In terms of both form and style, the novels took on the original features of the imaginary portrait genre with which Pater engaged from the publication of 'The Child in the House' (1878) to the end of his career. They are set in a past historical period that is evoked with all-absorbing intensity by blending fictional and essayistic techniques; they centre on the developing consciousness of young male protagonists who are both quintessential *of* their time and deeply exceptional in their powers of perception. The difference with the portraits is that the novels blow up the miniature work onto a much larger canvas. Indeed, Pater conceived *Marius* and *Gaston* as part of a trilogy of novels 'of a similar character; dealing with the same problems, under altered historical conditions'.[1] Together, the three novels were to provide an ambitious and intensely personal overview of European history focusing on epochs of transition: the transition from paganism to Christianity in the case of *Marius*, the Reformation for the unfinished *Gaston*, and the first dawn of Romanticism in the English late eighteenth century for the third planned novel that never saw the light of day.

Mirroring the fate of their own actual or unwritten characters, Pater's novels came into being in a charged moment of transition in the history of the novel form. One year before *Marius*, Henry James channelled some of the tenets of Paterian aestheticism in his influential essay 'The Art of Fiction' (1884). James ironically captured the need to break away from the mid-Victorian realism of Charles Dickens and William Makepeace Thackeray, which he found well-executed but also naïve and indicative of a complacent attitude towards form: with those writers 'there was a comfortable, good-humoured feeling abroad that a novel is a novel, as a pudding is a pudding, and that this was the end of it'.[2] By contrast, James wanted English novelists to enter a more ambitious phase inspired by French models. He argued that the modern novel needed 'a theory' and, above all, 'a consciousness of itself', by which he meant that novels ought to be upfront about their own artfulness.[3] Just like painters, novelists were artists who strove to achieve a unified composition based on expert handling of their material: literary language. And just like paintings, for James, novels should not aim to amuse or instruct but rather to convey an artistic ideal. It was now the business of novelists to extricate their art from the stronghold of middlebrow and puritanical prejudices that had held it hostage for far too long.

In France itself, the 1880s started with the sensational popular success of Emile Zola's naturalist novels. The rise of the naturalist school to which he belonged, however, was checked by the arrival of new symbolist tendencies that rejected plot-rich, gritty realism in favour of psychological analysis and that moved the focus from social criticism to questions of form and style. Paul Bourget's *Essais de psychologie contemporaine* (1883) marked a watershed in this shift in taste. Bourget, who put forward an extremely influential theory of decadent style later mediated into English by Havelock Ellis,[4] argued that decadence would replace naturalism as a defining phenomenon of the literary culture of the *fin de siècle* – a diagnosis that seemed to prove accurate the following year with the publication of J.-K. Huysmans's iconic decadent novel *À rebours* (1884).

Pater was as familiar as James was with the literary debates that were taking place in France and with some of their key players. Bourget, for instance, a mutual friend of Pater and James, sent Pater a copy of his *Essais*, which Pater praised as providing 'more stimulation of thought than any book I have read for some time past'.[5] This exchange took place just months before the appearance of *Marius*. One year after James's plea for the aesthetic reform of the English novel and the publication of Huysmans's 'breviary of decadence', as Arthur Symons famously dubbed *À rebours*,[6] Pater's *Marius* embodied the new literary tendencies that were in the air. Predictably, many reacted to its experimental character with scepticism or downright hostility. Others, however – an influential minority – greeted *Marius* with a feeling of exhilaration that can perhaps be hard to fathom today. In his *Confessions of a Young Man* (1888), for instance, the Francophile novelist George Moore recalled the experience of reading *Marius* as a spiritual awakening. He compared Pater's novel to Théophile Gautier's notoriously scandalous *Mademoiselle de Maupin* (1835), a favourite among the young generation of aesthetes, which combined gender bending and art for art's sake. Moore called *Marius* the first work of English prose that gave him a 'genuine pleasure in the language itself', independent of character and plot.[7] For the first time, words took centre stage in a novel – words to which suggestive associations clung 'like the odour of dead roses'.[8] W. B. Yeats concurred that *Marius* was 'the only great prose in modern English'.[9] These very literary readers intuited that Pater's handling of the novel opened a path towards what would come to be called Modernism.

The way out of the aesthetic and ethical comfort zone of the mid-Victorian novel, however, was fraught with danger. Yeats might have swooned over the prose, but he also described *Marius*'s impact in pointedly ambiguous terms: 'It taught us to walk upon a rope, tightly stretched through serene air, and we were left to keep our feet upon a swaying rope in a storm.'[10] The storm to which Yeats alludes is the aesthetic and moral crisis of the *fin de siècle*, overshadowed by degeneration theory and the scandalous downfall of Oscar Wilde. Pater's novels challenged contemporary standards of taste by denying the easy pleasure of novel reading (the Dickensian puddings lampooned by James), indeed by questioning the habits of bourgeois reading altogether. With their decided privileging of interior life over external accident, they can be read, pleasingly and plausibly, as the bud of a new way of writing that will only fully flower in the twentieth century, with Virginia Woolf and James Joyce, Marcel Proust and Marguerite Yourcenar. Yet, Pater's experiments with the novel must also be understood in relation to their present time, as embedded in the late nineteenth century's conflicted sense of its own modernity, the rise of decadence, and a cosmopolitan opening of the English novel towards other European traditions.

The Historical Novel

Marius was Pater's second book. Published eleven years after *Studies in the History of the Renaissance*, when its aftershocks had finally subsided, the novel bore the characteristic marks of the learned and highly wrought style that had made Pater's reputation as the master of literary aestheticism. In terms of contents, too, the novel related closely to the philosophical discussion of the Conclusion, as Pater himself would point out.[11] Indeed, *Marius* can be read as an extended meditation, in fictional guise, on how individuals respond to the seductive but flickering and inconstant appeal of the external world in epochs of cultural crisis. Pater sets the action in ancient Rome in the second century CE, a time of cultural transition when the old pagan world is crumbling and Christianity is on the rise. Readers witness the drama of historical change through Marius's eyes as he journeys from the rural environment of his boyhood home steeped in old pagan traditions, to the city of Pisa, where he attends a Platonic academy, and then finally to Rome, where he becomes a sort of private secretary to the Emperor Marcus Aurelius and also befriends a community of early Christians who are forced to operate in semi-clandestine mode.

Pater follows the typical structure of the *Bildungsroman* genre, portraying the formation (*Bildung*) of his protagonist through a series of significant encounters that shape his developing consciousness: his fellow-student Flavian helps him to discover epicureanism, the so-called philosophical emperor Marcus Aurelius introduces him to cynicism, and the soldier Cornelius and his friend Cecilia disclose the mysterious world of the early Christian Church. Pater does not simply register the impressions of the hyper-aesthetic protagonist. He concentrates on the workings of sensations (a keyword in the novel, highlighted in the subtitle) as Marius absorbs the different systems of thought, places, and social doctrines to which he is exposed:

> [Marius] has a strong apprehension, also, of the beauty of the visible things around him; their fading, momentary, graces and attractions. His natural susceptibility in this direction, enlarged by experience, seems to demand of him an almost exclusive pre-occupation with the *aspects* of things; with their aesthetic character, as it is called – their revelations to the eye and the imagination [. . .]. As other men are concentrated upon truths of number, for instance, or on business, or it may be on the pleasures of the appetite, so he is fully bent on living in that full stream of refined sensation.[12]

This passage shows how Pater goes back to some of the key terms and images of the Conclusion: the perpetual motion of the physical world, the stream of sensations, the redemptive power of the eye, the birth of the aesthetic subject. In redeploying and qualifying those same ideas within the dense philosophical fabric of the novel, Pater's aim is to rescue aestheticism from trivialising depictions in the popular culture of the early 1880s, such as Gilbert and Sullivan's operetta *Patience* (1881) and George du Maurier's caricatures of affected dilettanti in *Punch*.

Key to Pater's defence of aestheticism in *Marius* is the way that the novel deals with history. The painstaking research that went into the making of *Marius* results in many erudite and sometimes lavish descriptions of architecture and material objects that bring the past to life with archaeological precision. Vivid visual portraits of the Roman world are complemented by disquisitions of literature, religion, and social customs, where Pater directly engages with a vast archive of ancient sources. Pater's many learned quotations create a patina of bookishness that envelops the novel, contributing to the feeling that *Marius* is simultaneously a fiction and a book about books. The intellectual content is amplified by the fact that the novel teems with scenes of learning, reading, mentoring, lecturing, and intellectual exchange.

In an extreme instance Marius witnesses a conversation between the Syrian rhetorician Lucian – a real second-century author – and one of his students, Hermotimus, which is in fact an abridged translation of one of Lucian's actual philosophical dialogues. With a touch of scholarly perversity, Pater devotes an entire chapter to displaying a source which, in terms of sheer plotting, seems to provide little more than a digression.

This 'Conversation Not Imaginary', as Pater terms it in his chapter title, is characteristic of his way of having his fictional characters interact with actual historical personalities (Marcus Aurelius, his wife Faustina, Lucius Verus) and figures from literary history (Lucian, Cornelius Fronto, Apuleius). The notion of the imaginary conversation evoked here echoes Pater's original concept of the imaginary portrait. Like the short tales, the novel uses fictional devices such as character to carry out 'real' acts of criticism, which complement the type of knowledge provided by historical monographs and scholarly books. For instance, by having the fictional Marius work on Marcus Aurelius's *Meditations* and going to hear Fronto lecture on rhetoric, Pater weaves into his narrative an extended commentary on the production and historical impact of their ideas.

An even more daring example is Marius's boyhood friend Flavian, an invented character to whom Pater attributes the authorship of a real Latin poem, the *Pervigilium Veneris*, of which we know very little in terms of authorship and time of composition. Such juxtapositions of the real, as evidenced by textual sources, and acts of imagination project the reader into an unsettling zone where scholarship and literary artistry are porous. Wilde, one of Pater's most attentive readers, would seize on this aspect of Pater's work when he made the paradoxical suggestion that criticism should be practised as a form of art. In 'The Critic as Artist' (1891), an essay in which he references Pater multiple times, Wilde also provocatively states that 'The one duty we owe to history is to rewrite it.'[13] This is the habit of dangerous thinking that Pater started in *Marius* perhaps despite of himself – the great ethical void, to go back to Yeats's image of tightrope-walking, in which the aesthetic experiments of the novel placed its receptive early readers.

Even if the meditative tone of *Marius* is a far cry from Wilde's provocative aphorisms, the novel does encourage us to reject the idea that history can be fixed into a stable narrative. Marius's own death, the end point of the narrative, is also the high point of the novel's radical scepticism: the reader is left in doubt as to whether Marius has really embraced the Christian faith or whether his identity as a Christian convert is something that has been imposed upon him by the people who take care of him during his last illness. Where do acts of interpretation turn into fragments of truth? What does it mean to know the past, especially the remote past of classical antiquity, beset as that is by absences and lacunae? By posing such questions, *Marius* suggests that feeling and the emotions also have an important role to play in the production of historical knowledge.

In fact, one of the concerns of the book is to recover the elusive presence of queer affect – a topic of great interest to Pater from 'Winckelmann' onwards. Like many of Pater's male characters and indeed many of the artists he writes about in his essays, Marius shows the traits of a queer sensibility: his emotional development goes from his 'friendship at first sight' with the beautiful and dandified Flavian (63) to his attraction for the strapping masculinity of Cornelius ('the very person of Cornelius was nothing less than a sanction of that reverent delight Marius had always had in the visible body of man', 203) to his infatuation with the spiritualised femininity repre-sented by Cecilia. If we go back to the quotation above about the importance of impressions and the '*aspect* of things', we can start to see how Marius's self-conscious difference from 'other men' who devote their life to science, business, or hedonistic pleasure can be mapped upon the new understanding of homosexuality as a social and cultural identity that was taking root during Pater's lifetime. Dustin Friedman includes Pater among a number of late nineteenth-century aesthetes, male and female, who elaborated an early version of an affirmative model of queerness that stressed its creative and intellectual advantages.[14] Marius's fictional queerness, delicately delineated though it is, enables the novel to suggest that non-normative sexuality can provide a distinctive and valuable vantage point on cultural and literary history.

The Decadent Novel

The Latin world depicted in the novel is a society already haunted by the past. The Roman city of Pisa, as Marius experiences it in his boyhood, is a 'partly decayed pensive town' (60). From there, on a festive day, Marius and Flavian make a boat trip to the site of an old Greek colony which had once been a thriving centre in pre-Roman times and of which nothing remains now but some 'rude stones' and 'a handful of silver coins' (96); in the shadow of the massive ruins, the two young men come to feel the powerful charm of the death of civilisations. The atmosphere of belatedness that permeates the novel is nowhere more strongly felt than in the city of Rome, which Pater filters through the consciousness of Marius on his first visit:

> That old pagan world, of which Rome was the flower, had reached its perfec-tion in the things of poetry and art – a perfection which indicated only too

surely the eve of decline. As in some vast intellectual museum, all its manifold products were intact and in their places, and with custodians also extant, duly qualified to appreciate and explain them. And at no period of history had the material Rome itself been better worth seeing – lying there no less consummate than that world of pagan intellect which it represented in every phase of its darkness and light. (132)

Second-century Rome is already a museum – a space for the preservation of the past such as Victorian travellers might recognise, complete with its own guides and a sort of proto tourist industry of which Marius partakes. The novel disappoints readers' expectations that travelling to the past might bring us face to face with a higher truth: the Rome that Marius saw, Pater tells us, is 'more like the modern Rome than the enumeration of particular losses might lead us to suppose' (133). Later characterised as a 'city of tombs, layer upon layer of dead things and people' (147), Rome as Pater conceives it embodies an organicist view of history in which civilisations are caught in perennial cycles of birth and destruction; what counts as alive in the present is nothing more than stratified dead matter from the past.

Pater's image of Rome as a flower in full bloom that is inevitably doomed to fade resonates with George Moore's decadent impression of the novel as emanating 'the odour of dead roses'. Indeed, Pater's characterisation of a world on 'the eve of decline' relies on the nineteenth-century cultural historiography of decadence established by Edward Gibbon's *The History of the Decline and Fall of the Roman Empire* (1776–89) and Désiré Nisard's *Études de moeurs et de critique sur les poètes latins de la decadence* (1834). These critics had influentially portrayed the first centuries of the Christian Era as suffering a loss of the formal perfection and moral integrity associated with classicism. When it comes to describing the literature of the time, too, Pater focuses on the crisis of classicism:

> The popular speech was gradually departing from the form and rule of literary language, a language always and increasingly artificial. While the learned dialect was yearly becoming more and more barbarously pedantic, the colloquial idiom, on the other hand, offered a thousand chance-tost gems of racy or picturesque expression, rejected or at least ungathered by what claimed to be classical Latin. (88)

In this description of the fertile complexity of second-century Latin, Pater echoes Gautier and Huysmans, who had both defended Latin decadence from its detractors by stressing its stylistic novelty and the richness of its literary culture. Gautier, for instance, had defined decadent style as 'constantly pushing back the boundaries of language, borrowing from every kind of technical vocabulary, taking its colours from every palette, its notes from every keyboard, forcing itself to articulate thought at its most inexpressible'.[15] Similarly, the protagonist of Huysmans's *À rebours* scorned the easy appeal of classical Latin literature in favour of the much more sophisticated flavour of the writers of the early Christian Era.

In France, the debate on Latin decadence created a platform to discuss controversial current trends in modern literature. Gautier's comments, for instance, occur in an introduction to the posthumous 1868 edition of Charles Baudelaire's poetry collection *Fleurs du mal* (1857), where he defended Baudelaire's departures from classical French poetry. In *Marius*, Pater does something similar in the English context. By projecting readers back to the scene of decadent literary history in the making, as experienced by his characters, the novel contains a close critical study of decadent style and, at the same time, suggests that that style might be a source of inspiration for modern writers. *Marius*, in this respect, is both a novel about decadence and a decadent novel.

Anticipating the ideal of the literary artist as scholar that Pater was shortly to put forward in the essay on 'Style',[16] Flavian – a budding writer – responds to the crisis of classicism by cultivating an all-absorbing preoccupation with form: he devises a philological model of literary composition based on recovering 'the exact value and power of words' (88) that resonates with Bourget's theory of the fundamental importance of the single word for decadent style. His friend Marius, in the meantime, finds a literary hero in Apuleius, author of the linguistically exuberant second-century *Metamorphoses*, the only Latin novel that has come down to us in its entirety. Marius will get to meet Apuleius at a sumptuous literary banquet held in the writer's honour in a villa outside the capital. In a chapter that is entirely dedicated to the banquet, Pater gives us a lavish description of decadence in action. The location itself is tellingly dominated by the ruins of the villa of Cicero, the writer who is perhaps most closely associated with Latin classical style. However, there is little by way of classical restraint in the scene that presents itself to Marius: a giant synaesthetic spectacle made up of elaborate costumes, exotic perfumes, music, dance, food, and 'choicest literary curiosities' that the fashionable invited guests circulate around the dinner table (220). Apuleius himself gives an impromptu after-dinner performance consisting of 'carved ivories of speech [. . .] as with a fine savour of old musk about them' (222). Pater emphasises the famous writer's studied performance when it comes to both literary style and self-presentation, describing him as having 'a piquancy in his *rococo*, very African [*sic*], and as it were perfumed personality' (222). He even compares Apuleius's affected looks to those of the courtesans who are provided for the guests' post-dinner entertainment, with their 'large wigs of false blonde hair' (222–23).

Significantly, both Apuleius's cameo appearance and Flavian's stylistic experiments are haunted by the spectre of 'artifice' (93), a concept that hostile critics of decadence routinely seized on as an instrument of moral condemnation. According to such critics, the laboured self-consciousness of decadent style – what Arthur Symons would call its 'over-subtilising refinement upon refinement'[17] – was a symptom of overindulgence. It distracted both writers and readers from the important business of morality that ought to be at the heart of literature. Pater alerts readers to the pitfalls of a decadent cult of artificiality. However, he circumvents negative moral arguments by insisting that decadence should rather be approached through the prism of aesthetics, as a set of strategies to interrogate literary language and experiment with the style and form of the novel.

The Cosmopolitan Novel

In the modern as in the ancient world, the question of decadent style is imbricated in the cultural geopolitics of empire. Like late nineteenth-century Britain and France, second-century Rome was in the centre of a vast imperial network that facilitated the global circulation of people, texts, and ideas. Pater is alert to how empires rely on institutionalised violence and the oppression of marginalised people to maintain their power: in a chapter in which Marius plays the unwilling witness to massive spectacles of animal cruelty in the Colosseum, he turns the table on his modern readers, reminding them of the opprobrium of the modern slave trade and of how easy it is for the individual to find moral excuses for 'legal crimes' (170). At the same time, he is interested in how empire creates the conditions for productive forms of cultural contamination. It is no coincidence that the two Latin writers who have the greatest presence in the novel, Apuleius and Lucian, came respectively from North Africa and the Middle East. Indeed Lucian, who absorbed Hellenic culture from an early age in his native Samosata (a city on the upper Euphrates in today's Turkey), wrote all his works in classical Greek. By contrast, Apuleius's decision to write in Latin is described by Pater as a very self-conscious effort to get close to an idiom of the people that was otherwise scorned by the learned upper classes (Apuleius transfigures this everyday Latin by dotting it with neologisms and archaisms).

The linguistic richness of the literature of this period fascinated Pater. He captures it in the novel by making Marius an exceptionally attentive student of language: at various points we see him struggle with the early Greek prose of Heraclitus (107) and declare a personal 'vocation' to the careful study of words (122). However, Pater's attention to the multilingual reality of the

Roman world goes well beyond the spheres of literature and rhetoric. He draws attention, for instance, to the complex etiquette that regulated the use of Latin and Greek among various classes of Roman society from the army to the imperial household. So, for instance, Marcus Aurelius is said to be in the habit of using Greek for his learned conversations but, on their first meeting, he addresses Marius 'more familiarly, in Latin, adorned however, or disfigured, by many a Greek phrase, as now and again French phrases have made the adornment of fashionable English' (155). The question of whether spoken and written styles are improved or spoilt by foreign expressions recurs also in the letters between the Emperor and his friend, the old rhetorician Marcus Cornelius Fronto:

> Fronto seeks to deter his pupil from writing in Greek. – Why buy, at great cost, a foreign wine, inferior to that from one's own vineyard? Aurelius, on the other hand, with an extraordinary innate susceptibility to words – *la parole pour la parole*, as the French say – despairs, in presence of Fronto's rhetorical perfection. (160)

As this passage shows, the practice of switching between languages is not limited to the transactions that take place in the ancient world. It also marks the narrator's voice, which often casually interpolates, like here, foreign words from modern as well as classical languages, mostly French and German. Such instances, combined with the narrator's frequent allusions to the present, show that the multilingual practices of Latin late antiquity are also very much part of modern novelistic style as Pater conceives it. Throughout the narrative, Pater dots his English with foreign words and expressions, marked out in italics, like the French '*parole pour la parole*' in the extract above, which is in fact a far less idiomatic or obvious formula than the narrator would have us believe. *Marius* is the most linguistically cosmopolitan of Pater's works. The visible presence of multilingualism on the page weakens the authority of English – indeed, of any one single language – as a self-sufficient system of representation: Pater shows that the most subtle and original forms of knowledge are often generated between languages, through acts of exchange, transition, and translation.

This is why translation plays such a crucial role in *Marius*'s cosmopolitan style. In an influential reading of literary decadence, Linda Dowling has suggested that, in *Marius*, Pater writes literary English as if it were a classical language. This move had far-reaching consequences according to Dowling, because it went against the link between national language and national identity theorised by the German philosopher Johan Gottfried Herder, which had had a shaping influence on European Romanticism. More radically, it enabled *Marius*'s readers to glimpse the idea that, like

Latin, English, too, was 'quite literally a dead or moribund language', and therefore that English civilisation and the British Empire were also, like ancient Rome, doomed to an inevitable future collapse.[18] One of the stylistic strategies that Pater uses to create the sense of kinship between English and Latin identified by Dowling was to give his English a translational quality, the feeling that the novel was not a linguistic creation that arose autonomously from the imagination of the writer but rather that it was enmeshed in multiple practices of translation. Latin words and phrases constantly bubble up onto the surface of Pater's prose, often accompanied by his translations or paraphrases, as though the English was little more than a veil stretched over a thick Latin-language substratum.

These shorter snippets are complemented by two extended acts of translation: a compressed version of Lucian's *Hermotimus*, as we have seen, and a complete translation of the tale of Cupid and Psyche from Apuleius's *Metamorphoses*. The highly wrought mythic tale of love and desire is the longest and most famous of a series of inset stories that interrupt Apuleius's fantastic narrative, which sees the protagonist, Lucius, transformed into an ass. Pater calls it 'a true gem' and 'a concentration of all [Apuleius's] fine literary gifts' (70) and he underscores its preciousness by featuring it in an outrageously fine edition, wrapped in yellow like scandalous nineteenth-century French novels, perfumed with sandal-wood oil and decorated with ivory. Pater pauses his narrative in order to reproduce Apuleius's inset tale in full, so that translation becomes also a form of imitation, the modern fiction mirroring the digressive structure of the ancient novel. Moreover, as Marius and Flavian read Apuleius's story at the same time as the novel's readers (respectively in the original and in Pater's English version), Pater presents translation and novelistic writing as synchronic and harmonious practices. The act of translation thus becomes an organic part of the process of making fiction, opening the English novel to cosmopolitan and translinguistic practices that constantly urge the reader to look beyond the provincial focus of the English tradition.

The Unfinished Novel

Pater's cosmopolitanism makes significant demands on readers, who have to negotiate the book's surplus of learned references and foreign-language quotation. For all that, *Marius* was a successful book, which went into a second, cheaper edition on its year of publication and then into a third in 1892. Its success inaugurated a new period of productivity and confidence for Pater as an author of fiction, reflected in the quick successive publication of *Imaginary Portraits* (1887) and his second novel *Gaston de Latour*, which he started serialising in *Macmillan's Magazine* in June 1888. However, after only five instalments, Pater stopped publication either because, as numerous critics have pointed out, the perfectionist author found himself unable to keep up with the unforgiving schedule of serial publishing (*Marius* had appeared directly in book form) or because the formal complexity and undercurrents of decadent eroticism that he had unleashed in the narrative brought him to an impasse.[19] In any case, a first book version of the incomplete novel was only published after Pater's death, in 1896 (this included a further chapter that had meantime appeared in the guise of an independent essay, 'Giordano Bruno', in the *Fortnightly Review* in August 1889). Further draft chapters were added to the text later in the twentieth century.

Like Marius, the titular character in *Gaston* is first and foremost an impressionable subject who is highly receptive to the sensations of the outside world – a pliable self that Pater uses as a prism to evoke the literary and aesthetic sensibility of a troubled epoch in French history, around the time of the Wars of Religion. Gaston's physical and interior journey triggers a series of evocative essayistic descriptions of the cities and changing landscapes of sixteenth-century France, to which Pater devotes the same care that he had given to the portrayal of second-century Italy in *Marius*. And again just like *Marius*, *Gaston* stages several fictional encounters with actual books and writers that give Pater the opportunity to discuss literary history and questions of style. The most important is with Ronsard's Odes, which causes an almost spiritual awakening in the protagonist, providing him with 'the key to a new world of seemingly boundless intellectual resources' (50). Through Ronsard, Gaston comes to appreciate the value and power of 'words, single words' (56) – a familiar aesthetic epiphany for readers of Pater. Most importantly, he glimpses there a way of reconciling classicism with modernity of form, a recurrent interest for Pater from *The Renaissance* onwards.

Gaston gets to meet Ronsard in person but the key encounter in the novel is with another author: Montaigne, the philosopher/writer who is regarded as the father of the modern essay. This episode, to which Pater devotes nearly two chapters, has a strongly self-reflexive quality in the context of the essayistic novel. Pater concentrates on Gaston's impressions of the domestic life of the great writer, who is tellingly described as 'a lover of style' (81), which is said to be marked by 'a certain homely epicureanism' (81). Gaston visits Montaigne when the *Essais* are still in a state of 'protoplasm' (81), as Pater writes, borrowing a new scientific concept that captures the organic evolution from notes and snippets of dialogue to text. By acting as the philosopher/writer's conversation partner, Gaston becomes part of the making of the finished text. In fact, we are told that when Gaston read the published *Essais* years later, 'he found there many a delightful actual conversation re-set, and had the key we lack to their surprises' (82). The fifth chapter of *Gaston*, 'Suspended Judgement', in which Pater conveys a digest of the conversations of the two men that took place over a period of nine months, is a tissue of quotations from the *Essais*, which Pater stitches together, repurposing the originals and carving his own individual path through Michel de Montagne's thought. Here too Pater makes extensive use of translation – mostly of Charles Cotton's seventeenth-century English versions of Montaigne – in order to stretch the limits of the novel form, playing with fragments and landing readers in an ambiguous zone between quotation, paraphrase, and interpretation, where the boundaries of texts and the supposed autonomy of the individual voice dissolve.

Unfinished and textually complex though *Gaston* is, the strong elements of thematic and stylistic continuity with *Marius* highlighted here prove that Pater certainly approached the novel with a theory and a high degree of self-consciousness, to go back to the terms of James's 'Art of Fiction': his novelistic practice is informed by an experimental blend of fiction and criticism, a self-reflexive engagement with style and a cosmopolitan ambition in terms of subject matter and frame of reference that Lene Østermark-Johansen has aptly labelled Pater's European imagination.[20] The fragmented quality of *Gaston* has meant that critics then and now have paid less attention to it than to *Marius*. However, students of Pater should rather take on the challenge of understanding how the novel embodies the concept of the unfinished beyond the accident of its mutilated form. Borrowing an image from Montaigne, Pater talks repeatedly of 'undulancy'. *Gaston* focuses our attention on the fluctuating form of the text, the provisional nature of knowledge and the sceptical rejection of closure that are some of the most powerful concerns of Pater's work.

Notes

1. Pater, letter to Carl Wilhelm Ernst, 28 January [1886], in *The Collected Works of Walter Pater*, eds. Lesley Higgins and David Latham (Oxford and New York: Oxford University Press, 2019–ongoing), vol. 9, *Correspondence*, ed. by Robert M. Seiler (2023), 177.
2. Henry James, 'The Art of Fiction', *Longman's Magazine*, 4 (September 1884), 502–521 (502).
3. James, 'The Art of Fiction', 502.
4. Havelock Ellis, 'Huysmans', in *Affirmations* (London: Walter Scott, 1898), 158–211 (180).
5. Pater to Paul Bourget, 2 January [1884], in *Collected Works*, vol. 9: 150.

6. Arthur Symons, 'J. K. Huysmans', *Fortnightly Review*, 51 (March 1892), 402–414 (412).
7. George Moore, *Confessions of a Young Man* (London: Swann Sonnenschein, 1888), 291.
8. Moore, *Confessions*, 291.
9. William Butler Yeats, *Autobiographies* (New York: Macmillan, 1927), 373.
10. Yeats, *Autobiographies*, 373.
11. See Pater, *The Renaissance: Studies in Art and Poetry*, ed. Hilary Fraser (Oxford: Oxford University Press, 2025), 197. Pater omitted the controversial Conclusion from the second edition (1877) of *The Renaissance*, but he restored it to the third edition (1888), feeling that *Marius* had helped to deflect some of the controversy it had caused.
12. Walter Pater, *Marius the Epicurean* (London: Penguin, 1985), 187. Further references to this work are made parenthetically in the text.
13. Oscar Wilde, 'The Critic as Artist', in *The Complete Works of Oscar Wilde*, ed. Ian Small (Oxford: Oxford University Press, 2000–ongoing), vol. 4, *Criticism: Historical Criticism, Intentions, The Soul of Man*, ed. by Josephine M. Guy (2007), 147.
14. Dustin Friedman, *Before Queer Theory: Victorian Aestheticism and the Self* (Baltimore: Johns Hopkins University Press, 2019), 7.
15. Théophile Gautier, 'Charles Baudelaire', in *Decadence: An Annotated Anthology*, Jane Desmarais and Chris Baldick, eds. (Manchester: Manchester University Press, 2012), 79.
16. Cf. 'Style', in *The Complete Works of Walter Pater* (London: Macmillan, 1910), vol. 5 (*Appreciations*), 12.
17. Arthur Symons, 'The Decadent Movement in Literature' [1893], in *The Symbolist Movement in Literature*, ed. by Matthew Creasy (Manchester: Carcanet, 2014), 169–83 (169).
18. Linda Dowling, *Language and Decadence in the Victorian Fin de Siècle* (Princeton NJ: Princeton University Press, 1986), 111.
19. Gerald Monsman, 'Critical Introduction', in *The Collected Works of Walter Pater*, vol. 4 (*Gaston de Latour*, ed. by Gerald Monsman, 2020), 2. Subsequent references to *Gaston* will be to this edition and will be made parenthetically in the text. Monsman provides a full account of the novel's complex textual history.
20. Lene Østermark-Johansen, *Walter Pater's European Imagination* (Oxford: Oxford University Press, 2022).

7

LENE ØSTERMARK-JOHANSEN

Pater's Short Fiction

In March 1888 Henry James submitted the proofs of a volume of essays on contemporary fiction to Frederick Macmillan with the suggestion that the volume carry the title *Partial Portraits*.[1] He had already published two books with Macmillan & Co., Ltd with the word 'portrait' in the title: the novel *Portrait of a Lady* (1881) and *Portraits of Places* (1883), a collection of European and American travel writing.[2] A proposed title of *Half-Length Portraits* had been abandoned because of the existence of another book of that name,[3] but James was evidently keen to view his literary criticism in dialogue with visual portraiture, as he confessed to Frederick Macmillan:

> I have thought of 20 things (Portraits Reduced, Figures Reduced, Faces and Figures, Smaller than Life, Essays in Portraiture, Likenesses, Appreciations &c. &c – somehow they all sound – don't they? – like advertisements or *signs*:) & this [*Partial Portraits*] seems, on the whole, the least objectionable. It preserves the idea of the portrait, which is necessary, & conveys in a graceful & not obtrusive double meaning, both that the picture is *not* down to the feet, as it were, & that the appreciation is favourable – which in every case it happens to be.[4]

This letter testifies, as do more generally also James's *Notebooks*,[5] to the author's extreme care when it came to names and titles. By viewing his criticism as literary portraiture, James aligned himself with Charles Augustin Sainte-Beuve, who between 1827 and 1846 had published some 150 literary essays under the heading '*Portraits*': *Critiques et portraits* (1839), *Portraits des femmes* (1844), *Portraits littéraires* (1844), and *Portraits contemporains* (1846). Merging criticism with life-writing, Sainte-Beuve often let his subjects speak, allowing their own texts to form the core of his portraits while leaving the function of the critic as a framing device. James regarded himself as an appreciative critic; among his list of discarded titles, we find, interestingly enough,

Appreciations, the very title Walter Pater would employ for the volume of essays on English literature he published with Macmillan in 1889.[6] Whether Pater would also think of his brief title as an 'advertisement' is hard to know, but at a, perhaps not entirely conscious, level, he and James were challenging the ways in which the term 'portrait' could be used in a literary context at the end of the nineteenth century. Less than a year before James's letter to Macmillan, Pater had published a volume of four short pieces of fiction with Macmillan under the title *Imaginary Portraits*.

The range of literary genres for which James had employed the term 'portrait' suggests the intrinsic complexity associated with portraiture: James's novel had portrayed the gradual fossilisation of his female protagonist Isabel Archer in the world of art; in his topographical writing he attempted to capture the individual spirit of place, its *genius loci*, while in his literary criticism he portrayed the style, *oeuvre*, and career of a fellow writer. Portraiture could blend the subjective with the objective, the fictional with the factual, and even in the concluding words of Macmillan's reply to James's letter – 'I suppose people will say that a portrait ought to be *im*partial!'[7] – do we find the acknowledgement that portraiture is a slippery art form. The uncertainty of 'I suppose' followed by the distancing device of 'people' and the verb 'ought to' (with the full awareness that reality is often different) make it perfectly obvious that impartiality in portraiture is not always realisable, and that certainly partiality ought to be questioned.

Like James, Pater was a Macmillan author. His first book, *Studies in the History of the Renaissance* (1873), had appeared there and all subsequent volumes, including the multi-volume posthumous *De Luxe Edition* (1900) and the *Library Edition* (1910), would be published by Macmillan. From the late 1870s onwards, nearly all his short fiction appeared in *Macmillan's Magazine*; four of his pieces were compiled in volume form under the title *Imaginary Portraits* in May 1887, and another volume of portraits would most likely have appeared if it had not been for Pater's sudden death in 1894. Although Pater may not deserve the full credit for launching the fashion for literary portraiture at Macmillan, he applied the term 'Imaginary Portrait' to his short fiction from the very beginning and suggested that the reader dealt with his fiction as if it were a painting. On 17 April 1878 he sent a letter to George Grove, editor of *Macmillan's Magazine*, together with the manuscript of his first piece, subsequently published under the title 'Imaginary Portraits. I. The Child in the House':[8]

Dear Mr. Grove,

I send you by this post a MS. entitled 'The House and the Child,' and should be pleased if you should like to have it for *Macmillan's Magazine*. It is not, as you might perhaps fancy, the first part of a work of fiction, but is meant to be complete in itself; though the first part of a series, as I hope, with some kind of sequence in them, and which I should be glad to send *you*. I call the MS. a portrait, and mean readers, as they might do on seeing a portrait, to begin speculating: what came of him?

Very sincerely yours,
W.H. Pater.[9]

Pater suggests that we break the frame by going beyond the frozen moment captured in portraiture, giving us perhaps even a hint of his own experiences in the art galleries as a spectator rarely content with the finality of portraiture. Instead, he is tempted to invent a life, a sequence to what is contained within the portrait. The apparently effortless transition from the finite and material to the realm of the imaginary is embedded in this brief letter, as is the notion of sequence. The manuscript is on the one hand complete in itself, yet also the first in a series of similar portraits, almost like the pictures in a portrait gallery.[10] During the remaining sixteen years of his life Pater published eight such Imaginary Portraits in the short form of some 6,000 to 8,000 words, while another five to six manuscript drafts for portraits remain in different stages of completion.[11] Each portrait revolved around an individual figure, usually a young male, destined for an early death. The tragic ending is alluded to at the beginning of most of the portraits, so Pater's speculative approach ('what came of him?') should be directed at the ways in which these short lives unfolded before they were rapidly cut short, 'on this short day of frost and sun'. As Pater's friend Emilia Dilke observed in her review of the 1887 volume, 'the problem of life seems insoluble', a profound observation which may well hold the key to the death-driven structure of all of Pater's portraits.[12]

Pater set his portraits against a range of historical European backdrops – Ancient Greece, Medieval Italy, Renaissance France, golden-age Holland, Rococo Germany, or Romantic England – and most of his short fiction provides us with portraits of places and historical periods as well as portraits of persons.[13] He and James were, in other words, sharing a relatively broad view of the application of the term 'portraiture'. Pater's Imaginary Portraits are not merely short pieces of fiction but creative history writing, travelogue, and criticism, in close interrelationship with the essays and reviews he was composing in the 1880s and 1890s. The cross-pollination of his prose and his fiction is considerable, and the portraits should not be seen in isolation from the rest of his *oeuvre*.

Pater and *Macmillan's Magazine*

With his editorship of *Macmillan's Magazine* (1868–83), George Grove was transforming the journal in several ways: the magazine which Alexander Macmillan had founded in 1859, at first intended as an English counterpart to the French *Revue des Deux Mondes* with the title *The World of Letters*, originally had a heavy literary agenda.[14] This was already suggested by the magazine's title page with its portraits of King Alfred, Chaucer, Shakespeare, and Milton, framed by acorns and oak leaves. The literature of the past provided the framework for the literature of the present. With the Milton scholar David Masson as editor from 1859 to 1868, the presence of the past was evident in the contents list. Grove reduced the proportion of essays on foreign politics and literature, and turned from publishing long novels in many instalments to shorter pieces of fiction, and the short story as a relatively recent literary genre began to manifest itself in the pages of *Macmillan's Magazine*.[15] Grove shifted the contributors' background from a heavily Cambridge-dominated circle of contributors (rooted in the Macmillan connection to Trinity College) to a new majority of Oxford men. When one looks at the table of contents for the issues of the magazine in the mid-1880s, the name of 'Walter H. Pater' figures quite regularly as a contributor.[16]

As Ann Parry points out, Grove was also stressing a pan-European agenda, with essays about European educational institutions and articles about a new united Europe in the wake of the Franco-Prussian War of 1870–71.[17] Pater's proposed series of Imaginary Portraits fitted well with Grove's new editorial policy, as he was exploring the development of the European self from Antiquity to the present, stressing the European aspect while downplaying national characteristics. In his very choice of geographical locations and historical periods, Pater was often choosing liminal sites in historical war zones where, at a horizontal level, geopolitical factors left national identity in a state of constant flux ('Sebastian van Storck', 'A Prince of Court Painters', 'Duke Carl of Rosenmold', 'An English Poet') or where, at a vertical level, Roman Antiquity was rising to the surface, allowing paganism to upset and interfere with Christianity ('Denys l'Auxerrois', 'Apollo in Picardy'). The weft and warp of a pan-European culture across time makes itself felt in most of Pater's short fiction, subtly challenging the nineteenth-century rise of the nation state. Indeed, Pater is implicitly inviting us to consider how German his Carl is, how French his female narrator in 'A Prince of Court Painters' is, and whether his English poet is actually all that English. Topography matters in his portraits – just notice how many of his protagonists are tied to a geographical location already in the title: 'Denys l'Auxerrois', 'Apollo in

Picardy', 'Duke Carl of Rosenmold', 'Tibalt the Albigense'. Person and place are inextricably intertwined for Pater, and his Imaginary Portraits could in most cases easily have carried as a subtitle the Jamesian *Portraits of Places*.

The term 'Imaginary Portraits' teased and confused Pater's readers, some of whom sensed that not everything in his fiction was entirely imaginary. The historical French Rococo painter Antoine Watteau was one of the protagonists of Pater's 'A Prince of Court Painters'; the Jewish philosopher Baruch de Spinoza had an important walk-on part in 'Sebastian van Storck', and when reading about a resurrected Dionysian figure in Burgundian Auxerre in an evocative account permeated with topographical description, Eleanor Price exclaimed in *The Spectator* that 'we have no clue where imagination ends, and fact begins'.[18] Pater would undoubtedly have been pleased by this reaction; was he himself identical with the nineteenth-century narrator-traveller who had hallucinatory experiences involving the return of a medieval Dionysian figure in a Burgundian town? Two of Pater's younger disciples, Vernon Lee and Arthur Symons, retraced the narrator's steps to Auxerre and wrote their own evocative accounts of the place in homage to Pater, revealing how they had absorbed his very special conflation of myth, gothic story, autobiography, and travel writing.[19]

One of Pater's other reviewers, Selwyn Image, was aware of how lightly Pater carried his learning in the Imaginary Portraits. As he pointed out,

> A careless, or ignorant, or unsympathetic reader may pass from end to end of his writings, and never recognize the knowledge and the realization of knowledge, which underlie them, but which are never suffered to parade themselves. Perhaps it would be impossible to compare two writers more unlike one another than Mr Pater and Lord Macaulay: but their comparison for a moment is singularly to the point, in order to illustrate what I am here saying. Lord Macaulay was a man who had accumulated in his mind a store of facts which was astounding: and there they are on every page of his brilliant essays thrown in our faces, as it were, sentence after sentence. How the man must have read! We cry: and what a memory! But of Mr Pater's reading we do not think; he gets himself too completely out of the way; it is only by and by, when we come to criticize what we have been reading, that the sense of how much must have gone to produce these admirably full and accurate impressions, these slight but significant hints, these deeply searching judgments or suggestions, begins to dawn on us.[20]

Image points out what became abundantly clear to the present writer when in 2014 and 2019 she made the first annotated critical editions of the *Imaginary Portraits*: the density of reference, to historical and political events, to works of art, religious controversies and philosophical movements in Pater's short fiction is astonishing, revealing his profound understanding of European culture across time and nationhood, the result of the prodigious and extensive reading of a lifetime.[21] Occasionally, the editor found herself caught in the dilemma of whether Pater would really have wanted her to reveal his sources or whether there were veiled references or quotations which he would have preferred to have gone unannotated. The academic treasure hunt of uncovering yet another reference might seem to go against Pater's deliberately allusive style and coded language, directed at those in the know, and yet his short fiction can be enjoyed at many levels. *Macmillan's Magazine* was, after all, a family magazine, and *Imaginary Portraits* was frequently reprinted in 1890, 1901, 1902, 1903, 1905, 1907, and 1908, so that by the time the volume appeared in the 1910 Library Edition, some 8,500 copies already existed in print.[22] By 1910, *Imaginary Portraits* was the volume that had been translated into more foreign languages than any of Pater's other texts. Thus a French (1899), a Czech (1907), a Russian (1908), and a Polish (1909) translation existed, to be followed by an Italian one in 1913. The European afterlife of the *Imaginary Portraits* has remained vibrant, with a new French translation in 1930, a Castilian one in 1942, two more Italian translations in 1944 and 1994, and a German and a Dutch translation in 1946 and 1998, respectively.[23]

Cross-Pollination between Fiction and Criticism

Pater was a notoriously slow writer, and the many unfinished manuscripts now at the Houghton Library suggest that he had several writing projects in different genres running alongside one another.[24] It is therefore also very likely, I think, that the portraits had a long gestation period and developed alongside his essays and reviews over several years. There are obvious thematic or stylistic links between clusters of portraits and essays which may serve to underline Eleanor Price's observation that 'we have no clue where imagination ends, and fact begins'. Pater would explore many of the same issues in different genres, through historical and fictitious figures, and his short fiction therefore benefits from being studied in conjunction with the essays with which they entered into a dialogic relationship.

Within a few months of each other, 'The Child in the House' and Pater's essay on Charles Lamb appeared.[25] Both dealt with childhood recollections, with the development of the aesthetic sensibility, degrees of autobiographical writing, and with the house as a receptacle of memories. They served as different modes of exploring the romantic self, with what Pater called 'the Montaignesque' element in literature whereby the author gives a partial portrait of himself in his writing. On a very different note, the cluster of Pater's Dionysian writings – 'A Study of Dionysus: The Spiritual Form of Fire and Dew', 'Denys l'Auxerrois', 'The Bacchanals of Euripides' – present the reader with different renditions of the complex double nature of Dionysus connected with the Eleusinian mysteries, as fertility god and a deity tied to the Underworld. The study of the Euripidean play explored the effects of the unleashing of powerful forces in a small community which Pater transferred to Burgundian France in 'Denys l'Auxerrois'. Pater's two-sided deity added the ancient and nineteenth-century modernity of a tortured soul to the chief god of revelry, celebrated in Renaissance and baroque painting.[26] The theme of mental darkness continued in Pater's studies of a range of melancholy solipsists who renounced the world and withdrew into philosophising in the seventeenth and nineteenth centuries: 'Sebastian van Storck', 'Sir Thomas Browne', and the consumptive Swiss philosopher Henri-Fréderic Amiel. Pater reviewed Mary Ward's translation of 'Amiel's Journal Intime' during the same spring as he was completing his imaginary portrait and his essay on the doctor of Norwich.[27] Pater's early concern with childhood and male education was taken up again in the early 1890s in his imaginary portrait 'Emerald Uthwart' and his study of Spartan warrior culture 'Lacedæmon'.[28] Both texts are studies of communities of young men undergoing education, implicitly inviting a comparison between ancient and nineteenth-century schooling, while considering the importance of the presence of the classical authors in the modern world. His essay on Northern Italian art, 'Art Notes in North Italy', was, we gather from a letter to Arthur Symons, intended as a 'prologue to an Imaginary Portrait with Brescia for background',[29] the unfinished portrait of 'Gaudioso the Second' which took its source of inspiration in an altarpiece by Moretto da Brescia in the National Gallery.[30] In both texts the resurrection of paganism in the Italian Renaissance and a certain flirtation with the clerical life make themselves felt; inspired by Moretto's portrait of a bishop, Pater took the opportunity to consider priest-hoods, ancient and modern.

Pater's Imaginary Portraits cannot simply be classified as 'short fiction'; there is far more to them than that. Already in June 1887 Oscar Wilde questioned the very notion of the 'imaginary', preferring to rename them 'Imaginative Portraits' on the grounds that they constituted a 'series of philosophic studies, in which the philosophy is tempered by personality'.[31] By changing the adjective from 'imaginary' to 'imaginative', Wilde was shifting the focus to Pater's methods of engaging with philosophical ideas and schools, as imaginative rewritings or recreations of something already existent. Praising the perfection of form in Pater's portraits, Wilde was partly referring to the texts' stylistic qualities, but he was also thinking of the way in which Pater, as Symons would put it, had given 'concrete form to abstract ideas'.[32] His protagonists became the embodiments of philosophical schools or general attitudes to life, although in most cases, as Emilia Dilke had concluded, 'the problem of life seems insoluble'. Most of Pater's writings are pervaded by an extraordinary, almost obsessive, focus on persons.[33] History, topography, philosophy, and beauty reside in the person, and no matter whether Pater studies the Renaissance spirit, Medieval monastic orders, or modern education, his starting point is the person. An 'intellectual impressionist',[34] an 'artist and thinker',[35] was how Wilde and Symons, Pater's two young disciples, would hail him in their reviews of the *Imaginary Portraits*, stressing mind, perception, invention, and style as some of the essential qualities of the four texts in the volume. Their own writings would take the Imaginary Portrait into new ventures, in their merging of satire, pastiche, criticism, gothic story, and autobiography, always with a pictorial twist. Wilde's writings of the late 1880s and early 1890s – 'Pen, Pencil, and Poison: A Study in Green' (1885), 'The Remarkable Rocket' (1888), 'The Portrait of Mr W. H.' (1889), *The Picture of Dorian Gray* (1890) – and Symons's *Spiritual Adventures* (1905) bring Pater's genres into the twentieth century when also the Modernists, most noticeably Virginia Woolf, would develop the form.[36] It is no coincidence that Pater's Imaginary Portraits constitute the opening chapter of Max Saunders's extensive study of modernist autobiografiction.[37]

Among Pater's contemporaries, and indeed among his subsequent critics, there has been considerable disagreement as to the extent to which his Imaginary Portraits were autobiographical or not. Emilia Dilke, who was a close friend of Pater's since his youth, saw all the portraits as different states of Pater's own mind, explorations of what he would have been like, had he lived in seventeenth-century Holland, eighteenth-century Germany, etc. Seeing the portraits as attractive studies in moods and atmospheres with the Paterian ego at the centre, Dilke pointed to the evanescent Paterian self, a figure in a cracked mirror which is there one moment and gone the next in pursuit of the insoluble problem of life.[38] Gerald Monsman, the twentieth-century critic who has written most extensively about the Portraits, very consistently continued the autobiographical reading of Pater's fiction,[39] while Saunders, by adding the complexity of modernist autobiografiction to his readings, has continued this tradition, albeit with far less of a Freudian slant than Monsman. Martine Lambert-Charbonnier placed the Paterian selves in their historical and cultural context,[40] and Stephen Cheeke has most recently connected the Portraits with the Pateresque, with his style of writing, and the self as a persona, a mask which both reveals and conceals at the same time,[41] reminding us, of course, of Henry James's pointed description of Pater shortly after his death in a letter to Edmund Gosse as 'the mask without the face'.[42]

'Charming', 'attractive', 'beautiful', and 'sad' were the adjectives which Pater's contemporary critics pinned on the Imaginary Portraits when they were first published, paying attention also to Pater's prose style, to the pieces as works of art in their own right. In the case of Arthur Symons, one of Pater's most perceptive critics, his signed review of the 1887 volume abounded in pictorial language as he spoke of 'the silvery-grey coolness of A Prince of Court Painters', 'the chill, more leaden grey of Sebastian van Storck', 'the more variously-tinted canvas of Duke Carl of Rosenmold', stressing his view of the pieces as works of art, poems in prose, closely aligned with the polished verse of Théophile Gautier and the art of the painters Albert Moore and Jean Louis Ernest Meissonier.[43] Rather than reading the portraits as veiled autobiography, Symons insisted on their artiness, on their formal and stylistic perfection, in contrast to Pater's recently completed novel *Marius the Epicurean* (1885), and invited his readers to embrace their artifice. By framing Pater's texts entirely within an aestheticist and formalist context, Symons freed the Imaginary Portraits from any kind of moral reading by turning, almost in a Wildean manner, the mirror at the reader rather than at the writer. The concluding words of his review in *Time* let the portraits speak for themselves:

> In truth, Mr Pater is no moralist, and alike as an artist and as a thinker, he feels called upon to draw no moral, to deduce no consequences, from the failures or successes he has chronicled to a certain culminating point. 'There is the portrait,' he seems to say; 'all I have been writing is but as so many touches toward that single visible outline: there is the portrait!'[44]

An outline, giving us only the contours of the person sketched, needs filling in, and although Symons was fully aware of the etymology of the French word *portrait*, *trait pour trait*, literally 'feature by feature', he was pointing out how Pater in his artificiality was deliberately distinguishing himself from the detailed character-drawing of mid-nineteenth-century realist fiction. In Pater's fiction there are hardly any physiognomical portraits of characters requiring Victorian face-reading; indeed, the physical appearance of most of his protagonists remains elusive, perhaps best summed up by the handsome Sebastian van Storck, who refuses to have his likeness captured in paint, in spite of living in the very midst of a Dutch burgher culture where portraiture is omnipresent. Most of Pater's characters are not 'real' and were never meant to be, and Symons did well to point this out to an audience in search of the real. He submitted his review to Pater in a letter and Pater replied that he had read it carefully and 'on the whole with much pleasure', acknowledging that it struck him as 'the work of a really critical mind and a well-skilled pen' for which he felt grateful.[45] This was probably as high a praise as could be gained from Pater, always with a touch of reserve, in acknowledgement of the young reader, critic, and follower who better than most had grasped the 'pictorial turn' Pater was bringing to the relatively new genre of the English short story.

Pater's immediate success with *Macmillan's Magazine* was very different from that of Thomas Hardy, another writer of fiction with a distinctly pictorial mind and style, who had been courting the Macmillans since 1868 without much success.[46] Only from May 1886, as Pater was publishing his Imaginary Portraits, did Hardy's *Woodlanders* make it into serialisation in the magazine, and his *Wessex Tales* appeared in volume form from Macmillan in 1888. The erotic passion and complicated romantic relationships between men and women, which characterised so many of Hardy's texts, were too controversial for the editor to whom A. C. Swinburne (who never made it to *Macmillan's Magazine*) referred as 'the chaste Macmillan'.[47] The undercurrent of homoeroticism which pervaded Pater's series of Portraits of handsome young male protagonists appears to have eluded the editors; it certainly did not escape readers like Oscar Wilde, who professed his preference for Pater's Sebastian, patron saint, not just of the delivery from pestilence but also since the renaissance a popular queer icon. And Wilde's detection of Pater's Duke Carl as a thinly veiled portrait of the recently deceased Ludwig II of Bavaria brought the focus on the effeminate man with no conventional love interests out even more clearly. Yet Pater's artifice and literary style, perhaps together with his choice of historical and geographical settings, helped to slur the controversial eroticism between narrator and protagonist in several of the portraits and landed the majority of the Portraits safely in a family magazine year after year. In the course of 1892 and 1893 he was branching out to other periodicals, like the *Contemporary Review*, the *New Review*, and *Harper's New Monthly Magazine*, while William Canton, editor of the *Contemporary Review*, was also attempting to lure him to contribute to his other magazine, *Good Words*. Yet the strong bond to *Macmillan*'s seems to have persisted: 'Many thanks for your kind suggestions on the matter of publishing. I do not think I could leave Macmillan except for very substantial reasons', he confessed to Canton towards the end of 1893.[48]

Pater's first portrait was also to be his last revised portrait: 'The Child in the House' appeared in a special limited edition from the Daniel Press in Oxford in June 1894, about a month before his death. Sold at a charitable event at Worcester College Oxford, it soon became a collectors' item, and the many unfinished portraits in the Houghton Library at Harvard University bear witness to Pater's fondness for the genre, which undoubtedly appealed to his imagination in so many ways.[49] After his death in late July plans were afoot to put together a commemorative volume for him, and one of the authors approached by the proposed editor, Arthur Symons, was none other than Henry James. James, who, as he had confessed to Edmund Gosse, had had 'fifty minds to go to [Pater's] funeral', yet not 'the fifty-first which might have carried ... [him] there'[50] was equally evasive when it came to contributing to the memorial volume:

> the only thing I can fancy myself writing about Pater would be a thing for which absolute freedom of literary portraiture would be indispensable ... the sort of thing his memory would render imperative is a sort of thing that I am able to attempt to produce but rarely and that I never produce with any facility – only with mortal slowness and infinite pains. It ought to be very, very good and I shouldn't, calculably, have time to make it good enough.[51]

James's literary portrait of Pater may be the ultimate imaginary portrait. In the end, nothing came of Symons's volume; other contributors may well have shared James's hesitation. The respect for Pater as a writer which James's letter reflects testifies to the sophisticated level to which he had brought literary portraiture by the end of the century. Not even a partial portrait would have done Pater full justice.

Notes

1. The volume contained essays on R. W. Emerson, George Eliot, Anthony Trollope, R. L. Stevenson, Alphonse Daudet, Guy de Maupassant, Ivan Turgenieff, and George du Maurier, together with an essay on Constance Fenimore Woolson.
2. Serialised in *Macmillan's Magazine* from October 1880 to November 1881, the novel was subsequently published in volume form.
3. Gibson Craig, *Half-Length Portraits* (London: Sampson Low, 1876). See Rayburn S. Moore (ed.), *The Correspondence of Henry James and the House of Macmillan, 1877–1914* (Basingstoke: Macmillan, 1993), 134–135.
4. James to Frederick Macmillan, 21 March 1888, quoted by Moore, *Correspondence*, 135.
5. See Leon Edel and Lyall H. Powers (eds.), *The Complete Notebooks of Henry James: The Authoritative and Definitive Edition* (Oxford: Oxford University Press), 1987.
6. See Charles Martindale, Lene Østermark-Johansen and Elizabeth Prettejohn (eds.), *Walter Pater and the Beginnings of English Studies* (Cambridge: Cambridge University Press, 2023).
7. Quoted in Moore, *Correspondence*, 136.
8. 'Imaginary Portraits. I. The Child in the House', *Macmillan's Magazine*, 38 (August 1878): 313–21. This is Pater's first documented use of the term.
9. Pater to George Grove, 17 April 1878 in Robert Morris Seiler (ed.), *The Book Beautiful: Walter Pater and the House of Macmillan* (London: Athlone Press, 1999), 83. Of Pater's subsequent Portraits, only the unfinished 'An English Poet'

also carried the term in the title. See 'Imaginary Portraits 2: An English Poet', *Fortnightly Review*, 129 (April 1931), 433–448 (composition date 1878–80).

10. 'I am very pleased to hear of your continued memory of and interest in my projected series of Imaginary Portraits, one of which I have now seriously on hand.' Pater to John Miller Gray, November 1881, *Correspondence. The Collected Works of Walter Pater*, vol. 9, ed. Robert M. Seiler (Oxford: Oxford University Press, 2023), 131.

11. For the complete portraits, see Walter Pater, *Imaginary Portraits. The Collected Works of Walter Pater*, vol. 3, ed. Lene Østermark-Johansen (Oxford: Oxford University Press, 2019); for the short fiction in manuscript, see the various fragments in the Houghton Library at Harvard University, Houghton bMS Eng. 1150.

12. Emilia Dilke in an unsigned review in the *Athenaeum* (25 June 1887), 824–25. Quoted in R. M. Seiler (ed.), *Walter Pater: The Critical Heritage* (London: Routledge & Kegan Paul, 1980), 165–167 (167).

13. See Lene Østermark-Johansen, *Walter Pater's European Imagination* (Oxford: Oxford University Press, 2022) for a discussion of the portraits within a European context.

14. See George J. Worth, *Macmillan's Magazine, 1859–1907* (Aldershot: Ashgate 2003), 9.

15. See Ann Parry, 'The Grove Years 1868–1883: A "New Look" for "Macmillan's Magazine"', *Victorian Periodicals Review* 19:4 (Winter 1986), 149–157 (151).

16. Parry, 150.

17. Parry, 153.

18. Eleanor Price, [unsigned review], *Spectator* (16 July 1887): 966–7, quoted from Seiler, *Critical Heritage*, 167–72 (170).

19. Vernon Lee, 'Dionysus in the Euganean Hills: Walter H. Pater in Memoriam', *Contemporary Review*, 120 (1 July 1921): 346–353; Arthur Symons, 'The Magic of Auxerre' (1924), in *Wanderings* (London: J. M. Dent & Sons, 1931), 178–82.

20. Selwyn Image, signed article, *Century Guild Hobby Horse* 3 (January 1888), 14–18; quoted from Seiler, *Critical Heritage*, 182–86 (186).

21. *Imaginary Portraits*, ed. and intr. Lene Østermark-Johansen, MHRA Critical Texts (London: Modern Humanities Research Association, 2014); *Imaginary Portraits*, ed. Lene Østermark-Johansen (Oxford: Oxford University Press, 2019).

22. Print runs and exact publication dates can be found in Seiler, *The Book Beautiful*, 181–82.

23. See the timeline in Stephen Bann (ed.), *The Reception of Walter Pater in Europe* (London: Continuum, 2004), xviii–xxvi.

24. See Edmund Gosse's obituary 'Walter Pater: A Portrait', *Contemporary Review* 66 (1894): 795–810.

25. 'Imaginary Portraits. I. The Child in the House', *Macmillan's Magazine* 38 (August 1878): 313–321; 'Charles Lamb: The Character of the Humourist', *Fortnightly Review* 24 (1 October 1878): 466–474.

26. 'A Study of Dionysus: The Spiritual Form of Fire and Dew', *Fortnightly Review* 20 (1 December 1876): 752–772; 'Denys l'Auxerrois', *Macmillan's Magazine* 54 (October 1886): 413–423; 'The Bacchanals of Euripides', *Macmillan's Magazine* 60 (May 1889): 63–72. A version of the Euripides essay was most likely in draft

form by 1877, when Pater proposed to include it in a subsequently abandoned anthology to be published with Macmillan. See Laurel Brake, 'After *Studies*: The Cancelled Book', in Laurel Brake, *Print in Transition, 1850–1910: Studies in Media and Book History* (Basingstoke: Palgrave, 2001), 213–24.

27. 'Sebastian van Storck', *Macmillan's Magazine* 53 (March 1886): 348–60; 'Amiel's "Journal Intime"', *Guardian* (17 March 1886), in *Essays from the Guardian*, 19–37; 'Sir Thomas Browne', *Macmillan's Magazine* 54 (May 1886): 5–18.

28. 'Emerald Uthwart', *New Review* 6 (June 1892): 708–22, *New Review* 7 (July 1892): 42–54; 'Lacedæmon', *Contemporary Review* 61 (June 1892): 790–808.

29. Letter to Arthur Symons 18 October 1890, *Correspondence*, ed. Seiler, 264.

30. 'Art Notes in North Italy', *New Review* 3 (November 1890): 393–403; 'Gaudioso the Second', Houghton bMS Eng. 1150 (8). For an annotated transcript of 'Gaudioso', see Gerald Monsman, 'Pater's Portraits: The Aesthetic Hero in 1890 (Part I)', *Expositions* 2:1 (2008): 83–102.

31. Oscar Wilde, [unsigned review], *Pall Mall Gazette* 11 June 1887, 2–3. Quoted from Seiler, *Critical Heritage*, 162–65 (163).

32. Arthur Symons, [signed review], *Time* 6 (August 1887), 157–62. Quoted from Seiler, *Critical Heritage*, 175–182 (179).

33. See Stephen Cheeke, 'Walter Pater: Personality and Persons', *Victoriographies* 5.3 (2015): 234–50. See also Stephen Cheeke's chapter, 'Private Pater' in the present volume.

34. Wilde, [unsigned review], 164.

35. Symons, [signed review], 181.

36. See Elisa Bizzotto, 'The Imaginary Portrait: Pater's Contribution to a Literary Genre', in Laurel Brake, Lesley Higgins, and Carolyn Williams (eds.), *Walter Pater: Transparencies of Desire* (Greensboro, NC: ELT Press, 2002), 213–23.

37. See Max Saunders, *Self Impression: Life-Writing, Autobiografiction, and the Forms of Modern Literature* (Oxford: Oxford University Press, 2010).

38. Emilia Dilke in an unsigned review in the *Athenaeum* (25 June 1887): 824–25.

39. See Gerald Monsman, *Pater's Portraits: Mythic Pattern in the Fiction of Walter Pater* (Baltimore, MD: Johns Hopkins University Press, 1967); Monsman, *Walter Pater's Art of Autobiography* (New Haven, CT: Yale University Press, 1980); Monsman, 'Pater's "Child in the House" and the Renovation of the Self', *Texas Studies in Literature and Language* 28:3 (Fall 1986): 281–295.

40. Martine Lambert-Charbonnier, *Walter Pater et les 'portraits imaginaires': Miroirs de la culture et images de soi* (Paris: L'Harmattan, 2004).

41. See Stephen Cheeke, '"Pateresque": The Person, The Prose Style', *Cambridge Quarterly* 46:3 (2017): 251–69; Cheeke, 'Walter Pater and Personification', *Essays in Criticism* 70:3 (2020): 325–50.

42. James to Gosse on 13 December 1894, reprinted in Seiler, *Critical Heritage*, 293.

43. Symons, [signed review], in Seiler, *Critical Heritage*, 180.

44. Symons, [signed review], 181.

45. Pater to Symons, 9 August 1887, *Correspondence*, ed. Seiler, 196.

46. See 'Appendix I: Chronology of the Writing of Hardy's Fictional Prose' in Simon Gattrell, *Hardy the Creator: A Textual Biography* (Oxford: Clarendon Press, 1988), 227–46. For Hardy's pictorialism, see J. B. Bullen, *The Expressive*

Eye: Fiction and Perception in the Work of Thomas Hardy (Oxford: Oxford University Press, 1986).

47. Quoted in Worth, *Macmillan's Magazine*, 37.
48. Pater to William Canton, 7 November 1893, *Correspondence*, ed. Seiler, 315.
49. See Lene Østermark-Johansen, 'The Daniel Press Edition of Walter Pater's Last Book', *Journal of Pre-Raphaelite Studies* 25 (Fall 2016): 73–86.
50. Henry James to Edmund Gosse 10 August 1894, quoted in Robert Morris Seiler (ed.), *Walter Pater: A Life Remembered* (Calgary: University of Calgary Press, 1987), 171.
51. Henry James to Arthur Symons on 7 September 1894, quoted in Seiler, *A Life Remembered*, 171–72 (172).

8

GILES WHITELEY

Pater and Philosophy

Recalling Pater's reputation in Oxford in the 1860s, John Nichol remarked: 'it was said [...] that his speculative imagination seemed to make the lights turn blue.'[1] Silently quoting Shakespeare's *Richard III*, the Faustian imagery suggests the scent of the otherworldly, as though there were something diabolical going on in his chambers at the 'dead midnight'.[2] What was it that marked Pater's philosophy out as so radical and potentially dangerous?

Nichol would have been well aware of the young aesthete's burgeoning reputation. Nichol had founded the Old Mortality Society in 1856, a kind of literary and philosophical club at Oxford, alongside the poet Algernon Charles Swinburne. Pater joined the Society in 1863, and read a paper on the topic of 'Subjective Immortality' on 20 February 1864, just over a fortnight after he had been elected to a Fellowship at Brasenose College. Auditors that day likely would have included the author John Addington Symonds, Charles Shadwell, who became Pater's literary executor, Ingram Bywater, a classicist and one of Pater's closest friends, as well as future philosophers, William Wallace and Edward Caird, both of whom would become leading figures in the movement of British idealism, like another member of the Society, T. H. Green, another of Pater's friends and his neighbour when both lived on Oxford's Bradmore Road.

One attendee recalled Pater's paper as a 'hymn of praise to the absolute',[3] but some felt these hymns inappropriate. Another auditor, Samuel Brooke, characterised it as 'one of the most thoroughly infidel productions it has ever been our pain to listen to'.[4] Pater's title alluded to the French positivist philosopher Auguste Comte's idea that the subject could be memorialised after their death by those that survive them, attaining a measure of 'subjective immortality', if not the kind of afterlife promised by Christianity. Apparently, Pater extrapolated the idea into an early version of his aesthetic philosophy, 'advocat[ing] "self-culture" upon eminently selfish principles', and for what Brooke considered 'a most unsatisfactory end':

To sit in one's study all [day?] and contemplate the beautiful is not a useful even if it is an agreeable occupation; but if it were both useful and agreeable, it would hardly be worth while to spend so much trouble upon what may at any time be wrested from you. If a future existence is to be disbelieved the motto 'Let us eat and drink for to-morrow we die', is infinitely preferable.[5]

Brooke was incensed, offering a reply in his own paper a week later, in which he 'endeavoured to the best of [his] power to shew the absurdity of that belief put prominently forward by W. H. Pater [...] "that a future state is impracticable"'.[6] Religious conservativism clearly had much to do with Brooke's outrage, as it would when Pater's name become more widely known following the 1873 publication of *Studies in the History of the Renaissance* with its infamous Conclusion, which the Bishop of Oxford lectured against from his pulpit. But as one graduate of Brasenose recalled, by 1864 Pater was already 'vaguely celebrated' for having a 'new and daring philosophy of his own, and a wonderful gift of style'.[7]

New and daring it may have been, but was it 'philosophy'? Brooke's attack on Pater also questioned his philosophical credentials:

Pater is said to [be the?] best philosopher in Oxford, yet if what Pater affirms is to be understood intelligibly we can only say that Oxford is a very unfortunate place, and that philosophers must be very deluded people. If a man cannot make an original remark, if he cannot cut out a new figure he will hack and carve the old ones. Pater seldom makes what may be considered a really original remark, but he is fond of criticizing original remarks, and drawing fine distinction between identical conceptions.[8]

This is high praise and damning at once. Reputed the 'best philosopher in Oxford', Brooke promotes Pater over contemporaries like Green, Caird, and Wallace, whose brand of idealism, forged during the same period, would go on to redefine British philosophy in the last decades of the century. But more cutting is the suggestion that Pater was too heavily reliant upon those eminent names which preceded him – a *critique* and pedant without originality, and perhaps even something of a plagiarist.

Pater saw the history and practice of philosophy somewhat differently to Brooke. A couple of years later, in his first published essay on 'Coleridge's Writings' (1866), he subtly addressed the thorny issue of the English poet's plagiarism from the German turn-of-the-century philosopher Friedrich Schelling. '"There can be no plagiarism in philosophy"', Pater opines, quoting the Romantic writer Heinrich Heine on the topic of Schelling's own plagiarism from the Italian sixteenth-century philosopher, Giordano Bruno; since certain ideas reoccur as 'constant tradition[s] in the history of thought', they can be seen to embody 'permanent type[s] of the speculative temper'.[9] So whereas Brooke accused Pater of rehashing the greatest hits of the past, he would have recognised a story of reworking and revision. Even Plato, a philosopher who ranked as Pater's 'favourite' according to his friend, William Sharp,[10] could be accused of the same: 'as in many other very original products of human genius', in Plato 'the seemingly new is old also, a palimpsest, a tapestry of which the actual threads have served before'. From a certain perspective, any new idea is conceivable as a revival of earlier ones, refracted into different contexts. In his cyclical vision of historical repetition, in which ideas endlessly returned throughout the intellectual history of mankind, 'nothing but the life-giving principle of cohesion is new'.[11]

For Pater, 'in the creation of philosophical literature, as in all other products of art, form, in the full signification of that word, is everything, and the mere matter is nothing' (*Plato and Platonism*, 3). Writing about Plato, Pater is reflecting on the form in which philosophy is delivered, but the idea is part also of his more general meditation on the intertwining of content and style. For Pater, it is form which animates content, just as every philosophical idea by necessity demands its own perfect formal expression. Little wonder that he patiently investigates the ways in which philosophy is a crucial element in shaping aesthetic appreciation and individual lives. In what follows, I give an overview of this lifelong project of self-discovery, addressing four separate aspects in thinking about Pater and philosophy. First, I address Pater's reading of philosophy, and the importance of this reading to his intellectual development; secondly, I consider how Pater engaged with the work of three prominent figures in the history of philosophy, Heraclitus, Plato, and Hegel; thirdly, I consider the ways in which Pater's treatment of philosophy is part of his wider commitment to interdisciplinarity, and how his engagements with philosophers and their ideas shape diverse and perhaps unexpected aspects of his writings; and finally, I sketch out and evaluate the philosophical significance of Pater's own aestheticism.

Pater's Reading of Philosophy

How seriously we take Pater as a philosopher depends on what one thinks counts as philosophy in the first place. Deriving from the ancient Greek word φιλοσοφία, philosophy is etymologically *the love of wisdom*, and Pater's voracious reading habits testify to this love. Arriving at Queen's College, Oxford, in 1858, he immersed himself in the wisdom of the past two millennia of Western thought, with his college friend Rainier McQueen recalling the undergraduate Pater sitting up 'all night reflecting on τὸ ὄν' [existence or being].[12] In 1860, he began private tuition with Benjamin

Jowett, Regius professor of Greek, who had been the driving force for a number of reforms in the *Literae Humaniores* syllabus in the previous decade, establishing Plato, previously studied only as an auxiliary to Aristotle, as central to the Oxford curriculum. Jowett was responsible also for introducing modern idealist philosophy in private to his tutees, who also included Green, Caird, and Wallace. By Pater's time, successful undergraduates would be expected to have a grounding in the history of philosophy, versed not only in Plato and Aristotle but also in the pre-Socratics, Bacon, Locke, Mill, and, increasingly, Kant, and nineteenth-century German philosophy.[13]

Pater was not only informed by but also formed by his reading in the history of philosophy, as part and parcel of his developing identity as an educator and writer. As Richard Wollheim put it, 'by the standards of his time, though barely of ours, Pater lived the life of a professional philosopher'.[14] Certainly, he was helped professionally by his philosophical expertise: when Pater was awarded his Fellowship, it was 'thanks chiefly [...] to his knowledge of German philosophy, and especially of the systems of Schelling and Hegel'.[15] For some like Brooke, this marked Pater out as an 'infidel', but in point of fact, his expertise in Hegel anticipated the direction in which British philosophy would be headed in the following years: Pater was at the vanguard of new philosophical trends. Once in post, Pater lectured widely on philosophical subjects – between 1872 and his resignation of his tutorship in 1883, he delivered lectures on Plato and Aristotle, but also on general topics: moral philosophy, the history of philosophy, the history of Greek philosophy, Bacon's *Novum Organum*, and 'Philosophical Questions'.[16] Plato was that figure to whom he returned consistently, lecturing on him again in 1891–92 as he was writing *Plato and Platonism* (1893), a work which invented the then new – today familiar – genre of the introductory text book to a philosopher.[17] But Plato notwithstanding, Pater also knew the importance of variety. 'The theory or idea or system which requires of us the sacrifice of any part of this experience [...] has no real claim upon us', he famously opined in the Conclusion: for Pater, we should never find ourselves 'acquiescing in a facile orthodoxy, of Comte, or of Hegel, or of our own'.[18]

The two names are notable: Comte, the founder of positivism, whose ideas were represented in the mid-Victorian period by influential thinkers such as Frederic Harrison, and Hegel, the absolute idealist whose dialectical method continued to dominate the German philosophical scene even as Pater wrote, four decades after his death. This rhetorical rejection took Comte and Hegel's names as shorthand for opposing poles of the nineteenth-century philosophical spectrum. For Pater, any 'orthodoxy' lacks intellectual authenticity, revealing a '*bêtise* and a slavish capacity of being duped',[19] risking the individuality of the subject, the development of which was the ultimate driving idea behind his own aesthetic philosophy. It is far better to be 'for ever curiously testing new opinions and courting new impressions' (*Renaissance*, 199), in order to come to self-realisation as an individual.

Little wonder, then, that the list of different philosophers Pater discusses is extraordinary, even by the standards of the nineteenth century when authors tended to be more diverse in their reading and less specialised in their professionalism. Such variety speaks to Pater's fear of atrophy, an obsessive compulsion to be forever on the intellectual move. In his writing we find discussions of Protagoras, Pythagoras, Heraclitus, Zeno, Anaximander, Plato, Aristotle, Plotinus, Aristippus, Epicurus, Lucretius, Apuleius, Marcus Aurelius, Aquinas, Augustine, Bacon, Hobbes, Boehme, Ficino, Machiavelli, Descartes, Bruno, Berkeley, Leibniz, Spinoza, Shaftsbury, Hume, Pascal, Locke, Mill, Bentham, Reid, Voltaire, Hamilton, Lessing, Kant, Novalis, Schiller, Schleiermacher, Fichte, Schelling, Amiel, Cousin, Comte, and Hegel. Billie Andrew Inman's research into Pater's library borrowings during the period shows he read even more widely than this, consulting other writers whose names never made it into published work but with whom he engaged in unpublished manuscripts and lectures.[20] Pater also kept up to date with contemporary philosophical scholarship, through the work of Oxford colleagues such as Bywater, Jowett, and Lewis Campbell, and a number of recent German books on the history of philosophy.

Heraclitus, Plato, Hegel

Given the prodigal bounty of Pater's reading and interests, it can be reductive to over-emphasise certain figures in Pater's intellectual development, as Kate Hext has rightly argued.[21] To focus too greatly on single influences risks obscuring the breadth and depth of Pater's philosophical interests and debts. With this having been said, however, focusing on certain leitmotifs in Pater's writing as influenced by a few of the names to which he returned insistently across his work can be instructive, if admittedly providing only a partial portrait of how he approached the study of philosophy and its use in his writings. Three such indicative names are those of Heraclitus, Plato, and Hegel.[22]

Pater had been reading the pre-Socratic philosophy of Heraclitus at least since 1859, but it was around 1873 that the name of the ancient Greek philosopher began to take a central stage. When Pater revised material from his essay 'Poems by William Morris', first published in *The Westminster Review* in October 1868, for inclusion as the Conclusion to

The Renaissance, he added a quotation from Heraclitus, drawn from Plato's *Cratylus*, as an epigraph: 'Everything is in motion; nothing at rest' (*Renaissance*, 197). William Shuter has suggested that the addition was only an 'afterthought', appended late in the writing process as material was reworked for the book,[23] but the epigraph nevertheless became an element in the book's reception. The issue was that, whereas the earlier essay had appeared anonymously, *The Renaissance* was published under Pater's name, proudly announcing his heritage as a 'Fellow of Brasenose'. From this moment onwards, Pater and his aestheticism became associated with a Heraclitean philosophy of the flux.

According to Heraclitus, the physical world was in constant motion, a flux of material forces in perpetual change. In citing him so prominently before his own Conclusion, these ideas contextualised Pater's own philosophy that 'to burn' with a 'hard, gem-like flame' constituted 'success in life' (*Renaissance*, 199). In response, the art critic Sidney Colvin claimed Pater promoted 'a Hedonism – a philosophy of refined pleasure'.[24] The charge stuck, even if Pater himself maintained that 'words like "hedonism"' were among 'the worst examples of what are called "question-begging terms"' (*Marius the Epicurean*, 1: 162). Indeed, Pater supposedly complained, 'I wish they would not call me a hedonist. It gives such a wrong impression to those who do not know Greek'.[25] Having removed the Conclusion from the 1877 second edition of *The Renaissance*, he reinstated it in the 1888 third edition with the proviso that he had dealt more fully with the thoughts suggested by it in his historical novel *Marius the Epicurean* (1885), published three years earlier. There, Heraclitus had featured prominently as an early influence on the intellectual development of its protagonist. Reading his philosophy closely, Marius finds in Heraclitus a very different kind of figure than the 'popular' one with whom Pater had been bundled together in 1873, a philosopher who noted in the flux an expression of 'the divine reason, maintained throughout the changes of the phenomenal world' (*Marius*, 1: 141). In emphasising the role of this 'reasonable order' (*Plato and Platonism*, 12), Pater offered a retort to those who characterised his aestheticism as solely hedonistic, showing the ways in which an emphasis on sensory phenomena might go hand in hand with moral philosophies.

In this skirmish, we find that reading and rereading Heraclitus involved the recovery of a more historically authentic vision of his philosophy and its place in the ancient Greek world. Such an attempted and precise recovery is indicative of many of the rhetorical moves in Pater's work post-1873. In this case, Pater's engagement was mediated through Plato, who was a constant touchstone throughout his writing. To be sure, Plato's idealism, in which the material world is understood as imperfect reflections of another perfect realm of the Forms, could occasionally be the subject of discomfort for Pater, who asks why we would choose to 'change the colour or curve of a rose-leaf' for Plato's 'colourless, formless, intangible, being' (*Appreciations*, 67). But such discomfort was compensated by more attractive aspects of Plato's philosophy and the central role of beauty in his aesthetics. Here was an idealism which prioritised not only the spirit but also the body, the sensuous element in life. In Plato, the ideal world was linked indissolubly to the material one, shaping the philosopher 'into a seer who has a sort of sensuous love of the unseen' (*Plato and Platonism*, 130).

Pater may have had additional reasons for his interest in Plato. Alongside others at Oxford during the period, he found in Plato an accommodating space for the cultural negotiation of homoerotic desire.[26] While Pater was keen to accentuate the significance of '*ascêsis*' or discipline in Plato's philosophy (*Plato and Platonism*, 50), which critics have discussed in relation to the backdrop of homophobic sentiment and the passing of the 1885 Criminal Law Amendment Act,[27] it is notable that he was interested in dialogues such as the *Symposium* and *Phaedrus*, as much as in Oxford set-texts such as the *Republic*. Against the more conservative interpretations of colleagues such as Jowett, Pater emphasised the ways in which Plato had made the love of beautiful male bodies an essential moment in the philosophical journey of the subject.[28] In Pater's reading, Plato's 'sensuous lover' becomes 'a lover of the invisible', and the philosopher a 'lover of the Ideas' (*Plato and Platonism*, 155). The appreciation of sensual beauty becomes a crucial philosophical moment, be that the beauty of the work of art or the (male) lover.

In this reading of Plato, Pater's method was 'historic', as it had been in his reading of Heraclitus, situating philosophies within 'the group of conditions, intellectual, social, material' which produced them (*Plato and Platonism*, 5). In the opening passages of *Plato and Platonism*, Pater credits Hegel with the philosophical underpinnings of the 'historic method', and he had long been taken with the German's idealist philosophy. Hegel was a crucial presence in Pater's 1867 essay on the German art historian Johann Joachim Winckelmann, later included in *The Renaissance*. There Pater reiterates and adopts Hegel's progressive history of art, which divided aesthetics into three stages, beginning with the Symbolic period of the Egyptians, passing through its pinnacle in the Classical period with Greek sculpture, and on to its lesser forms in the art and literature of the so-called *Reflexionkultur* of the Romantic period (see *Renaissance*, 169–96). For Hegel, this historicist approach to aesthetics is justified by his central contention that 'art is the sensible appearance of the Idea'.[29] Hegel holds that the artwork expresses the philosophical Idea in material form, so that it may be appreciated sensibly, revealed in beauty. Art captures the essence of the immaterial in the material, petrifying it in a kind of perfect instant or 'exquisite interval', as Pater puts it in 'Winckelmann' and again in the Conclusion (*Renaissance*, 186, 197). Like Hegel, Pater holds that aesthetics, as the philosophy of art, links the sensible or material with the conceptual or immaterial. In this way, Hegel's idealism as well as Plato's lay at the heart of Pater's reconsideration of the place of the body and sensible appreciation in philosophical thought.

Pater was not immune to the attractions of Hegel's dialectical method, so flexible and capacious, or his teleological progressivism, in which all aspects of past, present, and future life could be explained as a moment onwards towards the coming-to-self-consciousness of the individual subject and World-Spirit. But he was also suspicious of any system which pretended to account so neatly for the vagaries of existence. Unlike many of his Oxford peers among the British idealists, Pater also read Hegel against the grain. Some of Pater's unpublished manuscripts dating from the 1880s, composed during the writing of *Marius*, show that he simultaneously entertained two very different readings of Hegel. The first manuscript on 'Moral Philosophy' gives us Hegel the thinker of the 'greater reason', an idea which Marius becomes attached to in the first half of Pater's novel, linking to his approach to Heraclitus. In this tradition, the lives of individuals are understood as moments which partake in a Hegelian 'absolute' over and above it, which they reflect and which justifies those lives. Such a philosophy spoke to Pater's own desire for security and a sense of home, a common theme throughout his writings. But Pater could not neatly square Hegel's panlogicising tendencies with that emphasis of the sensuous which first drew him to his philosophy. His problem with Hegel was that absolute idealism sought to incorporate everything into the single Idea, dissolving or 'sublating' (German: *Aufheben*) difference into unity. This is a point which Pater develops in the second unpublished manuscript from the period, treating the 'History of Philosophy', in which Hegel is read as a sceptical, critical, or destructive philosopher, far removed from the figure which the British idealists were promoting.[30]

The topics of these two unpublished manuscripts are significant, and not only to his reading of Hegel. They testify not only to Pater's deep engagement with issues in the history of philosophy from the classical period to the contemporary but also to the originality of his vision and the ways in which his magpie-like tendency to combine insights from across history allowed him to constantly sidestep philosophical 'orthodoxy'.

Interdisciplinary Philosophy

In this context, it is perhaps surprising to remember that, with the exception of his last book on *Plato and Platonism*, Pater published no other essays explicitly focused on philosophy: his writing was, at least ostensibly, on other subjects. Yet this is also telling: in Pater's hands, philosophy skirts the boundaries between disciplines. Such an idea is in keeping with Pater's writing in general, in which he approaches every subject from an interdisciplinary perspective. For instance, his essay on Prosper Mérimée (1890) begins by situating the French Romantic author historically, first alongside Napoleon, and then Heine's comments on the Revolution. While Mérimée's first novellas dated to well over a decade after Napoleon's fall, Pater uses the philosophical climate to draw comparisons. After Immanuel Kant's criticism, Pater writes, the mind's 'pretensions to pass beyond the limits of individual experience seemed as dead as those of old French royalty' (*Miscellaneous Studies*, 1). As such, Kant's philosophy becomes one way in which to understand Romantic-era 'désillusionné', linking the Revolution, Napoleon, Heine, and Mérimée alike. This is indicative of the sort of dense network of philosophical allusion which occurs on nearly every page of his writing. Pater's writing constitutes a 'diaphanous' intermingling of sources, through which he draws a rich image of the mind or the age under particular scrutiny.

Perhaps Pater's greatest investigation of these themes, in which philosophical ideas are seen to ground an individual's experience of the world, came in his only completed novel, *Marius the Epicurean*. Subtitled *His Sensations and Ideas*, Pater is interested in the relationship between physical experiences and philosophical conceptions throughout the novel. Set in second-century Rome, Pater documents the intellectual journeys of its protagonist: his early religious practices, his formative reading in Heraclitus, Aristippus and Plato, his flirtations with stoicism and audiences with Marcus Aurelius, Fronto, and Apuleius, before later encountering new philosophical ideas filtered through the prism of early Christianity. These webs build up Marius's intellectual 'environment', through which Pater's protagonist first develops and then radically re-evaluates his Epicurean philosophy of 'New Cyrenaicism'. Pater was likely thinking in part of an anonymously penned attack on the 'Modern Cyrenaicism' of his *Renaissance*, published years beforehand,[31] and offers something of a reply in his novel, suggesting such critics were guilty of mischaracterising both Pater's aestheticism and the historical sources, and proposing a more rounded vision of Epicureanism.[32] As such, while Marius's intellectual environment is grounded in historic times, given the history of attacks on his own thought, it also bears comparison to Pater's own. As his friend and neighbour, the novelist Mrs Humphrey Ward noted, 'no one can fail to catch the autobiographical note' in *Marius*.[33] The novel portrays how reading philosophy is intrinsic to Marius's identity, informing his decisions and his experiences and forming that life. The same may be said for Pater.

But if Pater investigates the ways in which a subject's philosophical background and approach beneficially impacts the living of their life in *Marius*, then elsewhere in his work, he occasionally finds subjects whose philosophies are the efforts of 'sickly thought' (*Appreciations*, 68). In his imaginary portrait 'Sebastian van Storck' (1886), Pater sketches the life of a young Dutch philosopher modelled on the rationalist Baruch Spinoza. Initially, Sebastian seems to be another model of the successful bridging of philosophy and life, his tutor remarking that his 'theorems will shape life for him, directly'.[34] But Sebastian's philosophy is characterised by an intellectual 'coldness', a retreat from life: written in the 'hard, systematic' geometrical style of the Dutch philosopher upon whom he is modelled, Sebastian rejects the sensuous world which was Pater's own domain, in favour of 'intellectual disinterestedness' and 'unimpassioned mind', suppressing the subject (*Imaginary Portraits*, 108). In this portrait, Pater portrays Sebastian as anticipating a number of Spinoza's ideas in quotation or paraphrase, but de-emphasises the quality of 'joy' which lies at the cornerstone of Spinozism. Regardless of whether or not Pater was aware that this was itself a partial portrait of Spinoza's philosophy – closer to Arthur Schopenhauer's pessimism than the Dutchman's joyful wisdom[35] – in this narrative, Sebastian's life is seen to be lifeless. The imaginary portrait concludes with his committing a kind of suicide, making a final '"equation" between himself and what was not himself' (*Imaginary Portraits*, 112).

Pater uses this fictional portrait to investigate the pernicious possibilities that a mistaken philosophical position might have in the misdirection of a given life. Indeed, Pater holds that there is no greater sin, in either or philosophy or life, than Sebastian's 'ideal of a calm, intellectual indifference' (*Imaginary Portraits*, 107). Pater had already railed against 'indifference' as early as his essay 'Diaphaneitè', read to the Old Mortality Society in July 1864 (*Miscellaneous Studies*, 220). Indifference is also critiqued in *Marius* in the form of Marcus Aurelius's stoical philosophy, exemplified in his dispassionate response to the brutal spectacles of the Colosseum (*Marius*, 1: 258). Pater would return to the topic in detail in its unfinished sequel, *Gaston de Latour*, set during the French Wars of Religion. There, philosophical 'indifference' is associated with moral 'indifference', with Pater drawing uncomfortable comparisons between Bruno's philosophy and the partisan butchery of the St Bartholomew's Day massacre.[36] Throughout his fiction, Pater shows us examples not only of those who do philosophy well but of those who do it badly – who fall facilely into orthodoxy or whose philosophies promote a colourless, repressive, or joyless vision of the world. If Pater's philosophy began as an aestheticism aimed at capturing the moment of beauty as a way of life, the later Pater was at pains to show that this philosophy amounts not to hedonism, solipsism, or nihilism, as his critics chaffed, but advocated an active engagement with the real world in all its vitality.

Aestheticism, Ethics, and the Philosophy of Life

Recalling Brooke's early dismissal of the young aesthete, we may ask whether or not a true philosopher must have some claim to originality in their own right? In point of fact, however, *pace* Brooke, we find that Pater can lay a realistic claim to originality in his aesthetic philosophy. To be sure, aestheticism had its philosophical ancestors, resting on ideas drawn from the Greek investigation of the power of αἰσθητικός (sensory perception) and German eighteenth-century thinkers such as Alexander Baumgarten, who founded the modern discipline of aesthetics. Likewise, Pater was not the originator of nineteenth-century aestheticism, reliant in particular on recent developments in French thought driven by Théophile Gautier, who coined the phrase '*l'art pour l'art*', and Charles Baudelaire. Yet Pater, who translated the idea of 'art for art's sake' into striking new terms for his English readers, arguably stands as aestheticism's greatest exponent. It was in his writing that aestheticism was given its most rigorous and 'philosophical' exposition.

The time was ripe for such an exponent: by the mid-nineteenth century, the idea of the autonomy of the aesthetic was attractive, offering a potential retort to the ways in which art had been instrumentalised across history. For centuries, art had been reduced to a medium which supposedly existed only to convey messages and offer up moral lessons. During Pater's own time, the utilitarianism of figures such as John Stuart Mill had dominated the mid-Victorian philosophical scene, reducing art to a question of utility, exorcising its soul and cheapening its splendour. Broadly speaking, the art for art's sake movement responded to utilitarianism by absolving the artwork of its extraneous baggage: its responsibility was to beauty, rather than external systems. But Pater took this logic further, and in his hands, aestheticism developed into a fully fledged philosophy of life.

Pater's development of aestheticist ideas is perhaps most clearly stated in his 1874 essay on William Wordsworth:

> That the end of life is not action but contemplation – *being* as distinct from *doing* – a certain disposition of the mind: is, in some shape or other, the principle of all the higher morality. [...] To treat life in the spirit of art, is to

make life a thing in which means and ends are identified: to encourage such treatment, the true moral significance of art and poetry. Wordsworth, and other poets who have been like him in ancient or more recent times, are the masters, the experts, in this art of impassioned contemplation. Their work is, not to teach lessons, or enforce rules, or even to stimulate us to noble ends[.]

(*Appreciations*, 61–2)

Characteristically, Pater's ideas are developed in an interdisciplinary dialogue with those of the past, and a number of crucial aspects of his philosophy are encapsulated in this passage. First, the focus on the contemplative life highlights the quiet radicalism of his aestheticism. Unlike the so-called 'philosophy of the hammer' of contemporaries like Friedrich Nietzsche, with whom he has often been compared,[37] Pater's 'diaphanous' aestheticism allowed new ideas to appear 'softened, harmonised as by distance, [...] without the noise of axe or hammer' (*Miscellaneous Studies*, 221). Secondly, Pater emphasises the doctrine of aesthetic autonomy, that art is not there for 'lessons', 'rules', or 'noble ends', but exists for its own sake. Thirdly, and most crucially, this aestheticism becomes an ethics: the aim of life is to 'treat life in the spirit of art', which, by extension meant 'to use life, not as the means to some problematic end, but, as far as might be, from dying hour to dying hour, an end in itself' (*Marius*, 1: 240).

This is the affirmative quality to Pater's philosophy which treats life not as a teleological puzzle to be solved but as a space of 'curiosity' and 'desire', a searching out of the beauty of the world in a voyage which is also a process of self-discovery. 'The essential elements [...] of the romantic spirit are curiosity and the love of beauty', Pater opines. It also explains Pater's willingness to find beauty in unlikely locations, or ones hitherto deemed unseemly. There is 'a strange beauty, to be won, by strong imagination, out of things unlikely or remote' (*Appreciations*, 75–6). As such, Pater finds himself 'fascinated' by the aesthetic qualities of the '*macabre*' and death (*Marius*, 1: 65), as had Gautier and Baudelaire before him. Indeed, death is not simply fascinating to Pater but an impetus to his philosophical pursuit of beauty. 'We are all under sentence of death but with a sort of indefinite reprieve', Pater notes, translating Victor Hugo (*Renaissance*, 199). It is precisely the pressing finitude of existence which adds impetus to the aesthete's task. As he puts it in his first imaginary portrait, 'The Child in the House' (1876), in a semi-autobiographical reflection, in Pater the 'desire of physical beauty mingled' with 'the fear of death – the fear of death intensified by the desire of beauty' (*Imaginary Portraits*, 141).

Given Pater's claim that the aim of life is to 'treat life in the spirit of art', then life and art, body and soul, content and form, are not to be understood as separate but identified. As Pater famously opined in 'The School of Giorgione' (1877), '*All art constantly aspires towards the condition of music*', precisely since in music, it is impossible 'to distinguish the matter from the form', substance from style (*Renaissance*, 145). In this context, that 'wonderful gift of style' – upon which his early reputation was partly based and which continued to mesmerise his peers to the end – can be read as a statement not only of Pater's writerly qualities but also as pertaining to his philosophy. In 'Style', Pater creatively reworks the logical philosophy of the mid-Victorian theologian H. L. Mansel, to claim that good writing should be considered the 'means of securing, in each and all of its apprehensions, the unity, the strict identity with itself, of the apprehending mind' (*Appreciations*, 18). As is clear from extant manuscript evidence, and the recollections of those who knew him, Pater constantly polished and refined his style.[38] Read in context, his quest for perfect stylistic expression is at once an attempt to represent his impression of the world and an attempt at self-fashioning. 'Style is the man' (*Appreciations*, 263), Pater argues with Comte de Buffon.

But as we have seen, style cannot be wholly extricated from content, nor content from style. To live life in the spirit of art is to seek out and appreciate beauty and pleasure, but Pater's aestheticism is aware of its responsibility not only to the self but to the other. This is something that Pater made clear in the final paragraph of his essay on 'Style', meditating on the difference between 'good' and 'great' art:

> It is on the quality of the matter it informs or controls, its compass, its variety, its alliance to great ends, or the depth of the note of revolt, or the largeness of hope in it, that the greatness of literary art depends [...]. Given the conditions I have tried to explain as constituting good art; – then, if it be devoted further to the increase of men's happiness, to the redemption of the oppressed, or the enlargement of our sympathies with each other, or to such presentment of new or old truth about ourselves and our relation to the world as may ennoble and fortify us in our sojourn here, or immediately, as with Dante, to the glory of God, it will be also great art[.] (*Appreciations*, 36)

The statement struck some of Pater's contemporaries as curious, a profession of apparent Christian orthodoxy from the aesthete seemingly rejecting his youthful iconoclasm. But here there is little orthodox, and Pater's allusion to Dante is in fact only one example of his wider emphasis in the passage on the ways in which art not only gives us pleasure but speaks to the other.

Pater then was indeed an original thinker, not simply hacking at old figures but carving new ones. If his philosophical distinctions are 'fine', and perhaps too fine for some of his critics like Brooke, they open up new possibilities for aestheticism. In his hands, the idea of 'art for art's sake' becomes an ethics. Not simply concerned with optimising the subject's experiences, Pater's philosophy holds that these experiences should fortify the subject physically and spiritually, as one who engages actively and fruitfully with the world beyond the subject. It is through art and living life in the spirit of art that Pater hoped to find his own 'architectural place' in 'the great structure of human life' (*Appreciations*, 36).

Notes

1. William Knight, *Memoir of John Nichol* (Glasgow: Maclehose, 1896), 150.
2. William Shakespeare, *Richard III*, 5.3.180.
3. Thomas Wright, *The Life of Walter Pater*, 2 vols. (London: Everett, 1907), 1: 209.
4. Quoted in Gerald Monsman, 'Old Mortality at Oxford', *Studies in Philology*, 67:3 (1970): 359–389 (370).
5. Quoted in Monsman, 'Old Mortality at Oxford', 370. Although, as Pater later noted, '*Let us eat and drink, for to-morrow we die!* – is a principle, the real import of which differs immensely according to the natural taste, and the acquired judgment, of the guests who sit at the table'. *Marius the Epicurean*, 2 vols. (London: Macmillan, 1885), 1: 156; future references cited parenthetically in the text.
6. Quoted in Monsman, 'Old Mortality at Oxford', 380.
7. Quoted in Arthur Benson, *Walter Pater* (London: Macmillan, 1906), 22.
8. Quoted in Monsman, 'Old Mortality at Oxford', 380.
9. Walter Pater, *Appreciations, With an Essay on Style* (London: Macmillan, 1889), 73–4; future references cited parenthetically in the text.
10. William Sharp, 'Some Personal Reminiscences of Walter Pater', *The Atlantic Monthly*, 74 (1894): 801–14 (810).
11. Walter Pater, *Plato and Platonism* (London: Macmillan, 1893), 3; future references cited parenthetically in the text.
12. Wright, *Life*, 1: 170.
13. See William Shuter, 'Pater as Don', *Prose Studies*, 11:1 (1988), 41–58 (p. 42).
14. Richard Wollheim, *On Art and the Mind* (Cambridge, MA: Harvard University Press, 1974), 158.
15. Wright, *Life*, 1: 210.
16. See Shuter, 'Pater as Don', 43–44.
17. On the generic novelty of *Plato and Platonism*, see *Pater the Classicist*, ed. Stefano Evangelista, Charles Martindale and Elisabeth Prettejohn (Oxford: Oxford University Press, 2017), 259.
18. Walter Pater, *The Renaissance: Studies in Art and Poetry*, ed. Hilary Fraser (Oxford: Oxford University Press, 2025), 199; future references cited parenthetically.
19. Walter Pater, *Miscellaneous Studies* (London: Macmillan, 1895), 7; future references cited parenthetically.

20. See Billie Andrew Inman, *Walter Pater's Reading* (London: Garland, 1981), and *Walter Pater and His Reading, 1874-1877* (London: Garland, 1990).

21. See Kate Hext, *Walter Pater: Individualism and Aesthetic Philosophy* (Edinburgh: Edinburgh University Press, 2013).

22. For discussions of Pater's debts to these three thinkers, see Giles Whiteley, 'Pater's Heraclitus: Irony and the Historical Method', in *Pater the Classicist*, ed. Evangelista, Martindale and Prettejohn, 261-273; on Plato, see Adam Lee, *The Platonism of Walter Pater* (Oxford: Oxford University Press, 2020); on Hegel, see William Shuter, *Rereading Walter Pater* (Cambridge: Cambridge University Press, 1997), 61-77, Anthony Ward, *Walter Pater: The Idea in Nature* (London: Macgibbon and Kee, 1966), 53-77, and Giles Whiteley, *Aestheticism and the Philosophy of Death: Walter Pater and Post-Hegelianism* (Oxford: Legenda, 2010).

23. Shuter, *Rereading Walter Pater*, 8.

24. Robert M. Seiler, ed., *Walter Pater: The Critical Heritage* (London: Routledge, 1980), 53.

25. Quoted by Edmund Gosse, *Critical Kit-Kats* (London: Heinemann, 1896), 258.

26. See Linda Dowling, *Hellenism and Homosexuality in Victorian Oxford* (Ithaca, NY: Cornell University Press, 1994), and Stefano Evangelista, *British Aestheticism and Ancient Greece: Hellenism, Reception, Gods in Exile* (Basingstoke: Palgrave Macmillan, 2009).

27. When incriminating letters regarding Pater's relationship with William Money Hardinge, a male undergraduate, came to Jowett's attention in 1873, the negative impact on Pater's Oxford aspirations was profound: see Billie Andrew Inman, 'Estrangement and Connection: Walter Pater, Benjamin Jowett, and William M. Hardinge', in *Pater in the 1990s*, Laurel Brake and Ian Small, eds. (Greensboro, NC: ELT Press, 1991), 1-20. On the ways in which Pater's writing negotiated new institutional, social, and cultural realities following the passing of the Criminal Law Amendment Act, see Laurel Brake, 'The Entangling Dance: Pater after *Marius*, 1885-1891', in *Walter Pater: Transparencies of Desire*, Laurel Brake, Lesley Higgins and Carolyn Williams, eds. (Greensboro, NC: ELT Press, 2002), 24-36.

28. See Lesley Higgins, 'Jowett and Pater: Trafficking in Platonic Wares', *Victorian Studies* 37:1 (1993): 43-72.

29. G. W. F. Hegel, *Aesthetics: Lectures on Fine Art*, trans. T. M. Knox, 2 vols (Oxford: Oxford University Press, 1975), 1: 111.

30. See Walter Pater, 'Moral Philosophy', bMS Eng 1150 (17), and 'History of Philosophy', bMS Eng 1150 (3), held at the Houghton Library, Harvard University.

31. See Seiler, ed., *The Critical Heritage*, 73-78.

32. Pater famously suppressed the infamous Conclusion to *The Renaissance*, which had so upset his critics from the second edition (1877) for fear it might 'mislead some of the young men into whose hands it might fall', only to reinstate it in the third edition (1888), noting that he had 'dealt more fully in *Marius the Epicurean* with the thoughts suggested by it' (*Renaissance*, 197 n.). Pater reiterated a similar point in his review of Oscar Wilde's *The Picture of Dorian Gray* (1891), whose protagonist, Pater claims, 'fails': 'A true Epicureanism; aims at a complete though harmonious development of man's entire organism. To lose the moral

sense ... is to become less complex, to pass from a higher to a lower degree of development'. 'A Novel by Mr. Oscar Wilde', *The Bookman*, 1 (1891): 59–60 (59).

33. Seiler, ed., *The Critical Heritage*, 131.

34. Walter Pater, *Imaginary Portraits*, ed. Lene Østermark-Johansen (Oxford: Oxford University Press, 2019), 98; future references cited parenthetically in the text.

35. See Billie Andrew Inman, '"Sebastian van Storck": Pater's Exploration into Nihilism', *Nineteenth-Century Fiction* 30:4 (1976), 457–476 (458).

36. Walter Pater, *Gaston de Latour*, ed. Gerald Monsman (Oxford: Oxford University Press, 2019), 105, 112, 120–121.

37. The parallel has proved especially attractive owing to Pater's interest in the 'darker side' of the god Dionysus in his 1876 essay: see Walter Pater, *Classical Studies*, ed. Matthew Potolsky (Oxford: Oxford University Press, 2020), 107. Nietzsche's own treatment of Dionysus appeared four years earlier in *The Birth of Tragedy* (1872).

38. See Gosse, *Critical Kit-Kats*, 263–264.

9

MICHAEL D. HURLEY

Pater and Religion

Pater's relationship with religion was neither simple nor stable. His views were subtle and evolved over the course of his life, and tracking them is made all the more difficult by the fact that he rarely addressed the matter directly. While religion is an important theme in his imaginative portraits, his only completed novel (*Marius the Epicurean*), and his scholarly reviews and studies of art and literature, he was unusual in his time and class for neither keeping a diary nor being much of a letter writer; he left no journals or notebooks, either. We do not therefore have the benefit of a sustained, confessional account. 'Not easily or surely', Edmund Gosse cautions in his early biographical 'Portrait' (1903), 'shall we divine the workings of a brain and conscience scarcely less complex, less fantastic, less enigmatical, than the face of the Mona Lisa herself'.[1] The lesson is well taken, though it should not be exaggerated. Henry James went too far in his quip to Gosse that Pater was 'the mask without the face'.[2]

Pater's Formation

There was a tradition in the Pater family that sons would be brought up Roman Catholic, and daughters, Anglican. But Pater's father ceased to be a Catholic before he married, and his wife went on to raise all their children Anglican. As a young boy, Pater embraced the pomp and ceremony of it all, the costumes and processing, including the chance of play-acting the role of priest. Later, when he attended King's School, Canterbury, his religious education was more rigorous and intense, and he won two school prizes for Ecclesiastical History. Nor was his interest in religion merely scholarly. He was personally affected by his encounters with influential figures associated with Tractarianism, notably John Keble, and by the school's intimate connections with its cathedral. Pater's heavily autobiographical imaginative portrait, 'Emerald Uthwart' (1892), paints a psychologically suggestive scene: 'in that place, religion, religious system' was liable to 'overpower' the 'boyish mind', with its 'great church, its customs and traditions'.[3]

Pater acknowledged the power of the historical church in other writings too, notably in three important but incomplete (and still unpublished) essays: 'Moral Philosophy', 'Art and Religion', and 'The Writings of Cardinal Newman'.[4] These essays emphasise the value of custom and tradition as collective wisdom to check 'our capricious [. . .] subjectivity', 'like the authority of parents idealised'.[5] 'To have Dante or Augustine against us', he shakes his head at the brute presumption, 'is too great a price to pay for liberty or even a tangible measure of present improvement'.[6] The way he pins his argument, with reference to particular heroes of the Christian imagination, is consistent with the argument of the essay as a whole: ethical truth, he wagers, is not best explored through abstract systems, but rather as poets and novelists have done, through 'the concrete facts of human experience'. Uthwart, we are told, had not merely witnessed religious customs: they 'touched him from first to last'. Their influence was 'a thing immeasurable', and ultimately unknowable: 'a secret; a thing, you might say, "which no one knoweth, saving he that receiveth it"' (Pater, 'Emerald Uthwart', 221).

While some of Pater's contemporaries claimed, and some scholars still claim, that he was only 'fascinated' by the 'apparatus of religion', that 'his preference had been for ritual as theatre',[7] his aestheticism is not so simply stated. He loved beauty for its own sake, but he also believed it was the most compelling means of mediating truth. Good art may be merely pleasing, but for it to be 'great', he argues in his important intervention on 'Style' (1888), it must be also 'true'.[8] By extension, he cared not only for the sensuous appeal of religious practice but also for its truth-content, even if he was at different stages in his life disconcertingly uncertain about what that might mean. The biographical fact of the matter – frequently overlooked by those evaluating his aesthetic commitments – is that by the end of his degree at Oxford, he had decided to take holy orders. The only reason he did not in the end become ordained in the Church of England was that his candidacy was blocked by one of his old school friends with whom he had fallen out, who wrote to the Bishop of London to say he was unsuitable. Even after that disappointment, he was determined to live a religious life, as a Unitarian minister, an idea he only abandoned as late as 1864.

Squinting back at Pater from the twenty-first century, it can be hard to see him as anything other than a prototypical Oxford prof. But it is well to note that even after he abandoned his hopes of entering the Church his life in academia was by no means an inevitability. Although clearly a very able undergraduate who impressed his tutors, he was awarded a second-class degree in *Literae Humaniores*, and it took him two years and several failed attempts before he was elected to a Fellowship in Classics at Brasenose, the College's first non-clerical Fellowship. Nor did his election see him then settle down as a don. He remained something of an outsider at Oxford, not least because, as a journalist, he had found an audience outside the university. It has been said that his stints at different periodicals 'resulted in work *expressive* of those periodicals – their politics, the nature of their readership (men, or men and women; religious or free thinkers)'.[9] It is a plausible observation, but journalism also drew out from him certain views, very much his own, that he would otherwise likely have kept private. This is especially the case early in his career, when he published anonymously.

In the years immediately after he was made a Fellow at Brasenose he published three unsigned reviews for the *Westminster* – 'Coleridge's Writings' (1866), 'Winckelmann' (1867), and 'Poems by William Morris' (1868) – all of which in different ways declared his heterodoxy. The first essay rejects dogmatic morality and religion in favour of 'surrendering human life to the relative spirit'.[10] 'Hard and abstract moralities are yielding to a more exact estimate of the subtlety and complexity of our life', he opines: 'every formula less living and flexible than life itself'. While 'the dominant tendency of life is to turn ascertained truth into a dead letter – to make us all the phlegmatic servants of routine' – he instead promotes a 'relative spirit, by dwelling constantly on the more fugitive conditions or circumstances of things'. Determined to break through 'a thousand rough and brutal classifications', he commends a mode of ethical agility offering 'a delicate and tender justness in the criticism of human life' (Pater, 'Coleridge', 66, 105, 104–5). The affront to contemporary moral codes is obvious, but the essay was also a reply to Matthew Arnold's classicism (which pits absolute rule over the relativising, modern spirit associated with romanticism), and his conviction that art and artistic criticism might have a salvific function.

The second *Westminster* essay is notable for the sympathy it extends to Winckelmann's Hellenism, which is 'wholly Greek, and alien from the Christian world', but also – following the logic of this affinity, which is ultimately more than intellectual – his homoeroticism, 'his romantic, fervent friendships with young men'.[11] Once again, passion and ardour, rather than external laws or principles, are presented as the index for the authenticity of the writer, and the warrant for his authority. The same essay approves of what it calls the 'pagan grandeur' of the Roman Catholic religion, while disapproving of 'the Protestant principle in art' that had cut Germany off from 'the supreme tradition of beauty' (Pater, 'Winckelmann', 197).

The third essay corrals in a similar fashion, this time taking its cue from Victor Hugo's admonition that 'we have an interval and then we cease to be': 'our one chance is in expanding that interval', Pater advises, by 'getting as many pulsations as possible into the given time'. In this respect, he looks above all to 'the poetic passion, the desire of beauty, the love of art for art's sake': 'for art comes to you professing frankly to give nothing but the highest quality to your moments as they pass, and simply for those moments' sake.'[12] Pater's emphatic turn towards individual experience is set against any 'religious or philosophical idea'. But the shock of his polemic is only really felt once the essay is lightly revised, and gathered up with the other two, as part of his first book, *Studies in the History of the Renaissance* (1873). That book – which repurposes the penultimate paragraph of his essay on Morris for its climactic Conclusion, its now-infamous injunction to burn always with 'this hard gemlike flame' as the marker of 'success in life' – bears Pater's name and institutional standing, which is in no small part why it proved so controversial. The chaplain of his College made this point lucidly at the time, writing to Pater directly after the publication of *The Renaissance*:

> I am aware that the concluding pages are [...] taken from a review of Morris's poems published in 1868 in the *Westminster Review*. But that article was anonymous, whereas this appears under your own name as a Fellow of Brasenose and as the mature result of your studies in an important period of history. If you had not reprinted it with your name no one would, I presume, have had a right to remonstrate with you on the subject, but now the case appears to be different [...].[13]

Anonymity afforded Pater the cover and confidence to *essay*, such that we may ask whether he would have been willing to write such a book if he had, from the outset, sought to do so under his own name and as an acknowledged member of the university establishment. In any event, as things turned out, the reception of *The Renaissance*, together with the discovery of some compromising letters revealing his homosexuality, left him professionally stymied at Oxford, so that he always thereafter had one eye beyond its beaten bounds.[14] In 1883 he actually resigned his tutorship, taking a house in London, only living in his College rooms during the weekdays of full term.

Artistic Sensibility

The Renaissance is a good place to begin thinking about Pater's views on religion, as the first but also perhaps the most inflammatory thing he would ever launch into the public square under his own name. The full story starts earlier, however. The influence of John Ruskin's *Modern Painters* (1843–60), for instance, which he read while still a schoolboy, was a seminal moment, for directing his attention away from art as an object of beauty towards its power to stimulate transcendent experiences. He took further encouragement in this direction from his humanistic learning at Oxford, so that by the time he was elected to the 'Old Mortality' in 1864 (a weekly essay society in Oxford), he was well on his way. He read at least two theologically contentious papers in the very first year of his membership of the society: 'Diaphaneitè' (1864) and 'Subjective Immortality' (1864).

The latter essay is lost but appears to have included a forceful denial of the afterlife. The former was published posthumously and stages a description of Pater's great friend, Shadwell, as an archetype of the aesthetic hero. Another member of the Old Mortality, S. R. Brooke, recalls Pater's contribution that evening (20 February 1864) as 'one of the most thoroughly infidel productions it has ever been our pain to listen to'.[15] The scandal arose from Pater's advocating of 'self-culture' on 'eminently selfish principles', in which respect Brooke's particular choice of disapprobation, 'infidel', is suggestive. Apparently, Pater should know better. Lord David Cecil described him as 'too odd a mixture' ever to have been a 'typical don'. The man who wore a sober dark broadcloth paired that signal of respectable Victorian professionalism with a tie of brilliant apple-green silk. He was that rare hybrid, 'the scholar-artist',[16] with a temper torn between 'the scholarly spirit', which is intellectual and impersonal and refers its judgements to reason and fact, and 'the artistic', which is sensuous and personal and refers its judgements to standards of feeling and imagination (Cecil, *Walter Pater*, 4).

Cecil's important insight is that Pater was not merely a scholar *and* an artist. He was, dynamically, both at the same time: a creative critic, with a vision of beauty at once intellectual and sensuous. Relatedly, Pater's writings on almost any topic, no matter how refined or recherché, inevitably include speculations of an artistic sort, on what the ideas under inspection mean for human beings. When not discussing religious questions directly, then, he very often addresses them indirectly, as a working out of what it means to live a good life. His autobiographical imaginary portrait, 'The Child in the House', dramatises the vibrant capaciousness of this vision of religion as an expression of human experience, within a single, overbrimming sentence:

> His way of conceiving religion came then to be in effect what it ever afterwards remained – a sacred history indeed, but still more a sacred ideal, a transcendent version or representation, under intenser and more expressive light and shade, of human life and its familiar or exceptional incidents, birth, death, marriage, youth, age, tears, joy, rest, sleep, waking – a mirror, towards which men might turn away their eyes from vanity and dullness, and see themselves therein as angels, with their daily meat and drink, even, become a kind of sacred transaction – a complementary strain or burden, applied to our

every-day existence, whereby the stray snatches of music in it re-set themselves, and fall into the scheme of some higher and more consistent harmony.

(Pater, 'The Child in the House', Appreciations, 194)

Religious Impulse

What, then, does Pater mean when he writes of aesthetic appreciation – of 'experience itself' – as 'the end' of life, with the primary and perpetual goal of being to seek out and 'maintain', to 'burn always' with 'this ecstasy'? There is an obvious sense in which religion, or any form of dogmatic moral code, might be an impediment to engaging intensely with beauty on these terms, for its own sake. But Pater himself spent the better part of his career seeking to invert this presumption, looking primarily to Plato as his authority. That is not to say his later work was merely a clarification of his earlier position; while there is continuity in his thinking, it also evolves. It is only in a highly qualified sense that the world view of *Marius the Epicurean* (1885), for instance, can be squared with *The Renaissance*, given the emergent wisdom of that novel; namely, that for all the value and truth of the ancient world, 'the highest Platonic dream is lower than any Christian vision'.[17] And beyond any explicit moralising or metaphysics within the novel, whether or not we decide that Marius has ultimately converted to Christianity, or shown 'the necessity for religion' in general, we are invited to admire his final self-sacrifice.[18] It is far from obvious how such radical selflessness can find a counterpart in the ethics of *The Renaissance*, given the primacy it affords to self-cultivation.

Counterintuitively, though, the very same Conclusion in which he seems to forsake religion might also contain the key to unlocking his religious sympathies. For there are different modalities for 'sacrifice' as a virtue. If to burn always with a hard, gemlike flame, to maintain an ecstasy, is success in life, then it follows that 'The theory or idea or system which requires of us the sacrifice of any part of this experience, in consideration of some interest into which we cannot enter, or some abstract theory we have not identified with ourselves, or of what is only conventional, has no real claim upon us' (Pater, *Renaissance*, 199). By extension, Pater approaches religion as ratified by the experience it yields, whether as a re-historicised paganism or through the revival of mysticism and sacramentalism associated with the Oxford movement.

Pater might in that sense be said to anticipate the Harvard psychologist-turned-philosopher William James, whose *Varieties of Religious Experience* (1902) eschews theological doctrine, dignifying instead 'the religious impulse' itself; that is, 'the feelings, acts, and experiences of individual men', 'so far as they apprehend themselves to stand in relation to whatever they may consider the divine'.[19] Whereas James's psychological account of religion invites sheer subjectivity, however, Pater's agnosticism fights shy of the atheistic conceit that religion is no more than the projection of our individual minds. He presses something more like Blaise Pascal's distinction between the God of the philosophers and the God of Abraham and Isaac.

Pater was much preoccupied with Pascal; the very last thing he ever wrote was, it so happens, a lecture on his *Pensées*.[20] Determining that Pascal was 'not a sceptic converted, a returned infidel', Pater negates the apparent negativity of his reputation: *not* being a sceptic means being positively open to possibilities, as *not* being a returned infidel (that word which was used against Pater himself by S. R. Brooke) strains to an even more radical recuperation, urging the idea of being unexpectedly faithful after all. Pater elaborates his logic by describing, very precisely, an account of Pascal 'as if at the very centre of a perpetually maintained tragic crisis, holding the faith steadfastly but amid the well-poised points of essential doubt all around him and it'. 'It is no mere calm supersession of a state of doubt by a state of faith', Pater is keen to emphasise: 'the doubts never die, they are only just kept down in a perpetual agonia.'[21]

Pater's sketch of Pascal's spiritual *agonia* is unexpectedly poignant, perhaps because it sounds like it might also be Pater's own personal confession and *apologia*. While Pater's first book set the hares of aestheticism running, it was in his penultimate, *Plato and Platonism* (1893), collected from lectures rather than periodical essays, that he argued most fully for how an aesthetic and religious life might after all be reconciled. What's spiritual in us is fed by experience: 'men's souls are, according to Plato's view, the creatures of what men see and hear.'[22] Looking especially to the third and tenth books of *The Republic*, Pater adduces Plato's claim for the 'close connexion between what may be called the aesthetic qualities of the world about us and the formation of moral character, between aesthetics and ethics' (Pater, *Plato and Platonism*, 269). That is why Plato relied largely on aesthetic education for the ethical formation of the young when it came to imagining the formation of the citizens of his Perfect City. Pater goes so far as to suggest Plato 'anticipates the modern notion that art as such has no end but its own perfection, – "art for art's sake"' (Pater, *Plato and Platonism*, 268).

By no means flying from reality, then, as an amoral or even immoral self-indulgence, Pater elevates the aesthetic life – the 'great fact of experience' – into a means of right knowledge and conduct (Pater, *Plato and Platonism*, 268). It remains to be shown, nonetheless, whether what he commends is right belief as well as right conduct; religious orthodoxy, that is, as well as mere orthopraxy. Certainly, Keats' famous equation – 'beauty is truth, truth beauty' – does not, for Pater, appear to work in both directions.[23] Whereas a moral system may be commended if it turns out to be beautiful, he did not think it appropriate to apply a moral system to art to *determine* its beauty. Aesthetics is the standard for ethics, but the opposite does not always follow. As he most famously staked out this logic within *The Renaissance*, the driving consideration is not first of all objective but reflexive: 'What is this song or picture, this engaging personality presented in life or in a book, to *me*? What effect does it really produce on me?' (Pater, 'Preface', *Renaissance*, 73). *Appreciations* (1889), his very last book – albeit collected from earlier essays (two from the 1860s, five from the 1870s, and four from the 1880s) – re-emphasises this central position of the self. The very title of the book announces the fact. Its headline accent on 'appreciations' is a tacit but emphatic riposte to Arnold's influential approach to art and literature as a mode of disinterested 'criticism'.

When it comes to tracing continuities in Pater's view of religion, it should also be said that his writing is suffused with religious symbolism and sympathy from start to finish: in his imagery and allusions, in his belief in art's transcending power, and in his idea of the 'divine spark' within each individual (Pater, 'Sir Thomas Browne', *Appreciations*, 160). These are more than dispensable features of his thinking. They are not accidentally derivative from religion. They work within and through his writing, operatively as well as ornamentally, long after his early religious fervour had been overtaken by his later aestheticist polemics. 'Pater's interest in ecclesiastical matters was never really dead', Gosse recalls, even after he abandoned the idea of becoming a priest or minister; 'it soon began to revive' (Gosse, 'Walter Pater: a Portrait', 252):

> When I had known him first he was a pagan, without any guide but that of the personal conscience; years brought gradually with them a greater and greater longing for the supporting solace of a creed. His talk, his habits, became more and more theological, and it is my private conviction that, had he lived a few years longer, he would have endeavoured to take orders and a small college living in the country. (Gosse, 'Walter Pater: a Portrait', 256)

Gosse's 'private conviction' that, had he lived longer, Pater would have taken holy orders after all, or if not then perhaps converted to Roman Catholic, was evidently shared by several of Pater's other friends too. Latterly, he reviewed for a Church of England paper (the *Guardian*) and was also said to regularly attend church services. The revolutionary spirit of youth yielded to the moderating temper of maturity, expressed in his evolving attitude towards Christianity, but also – to switch religious register – in his retreat from Dionysus, and 'the gods and goddesses of disorder', in favour of 'a strikingly militant Apollonianism'.[24]

That Pater's increasingly conservative instincts ushered his religious commitments is telling, but risks simplification. While *Plato and Platonism* makes a strident case for order in an unruly word, it is after all within his final collection of essays, *Appreciations*, that we find some of his most sharply sceptical sentiments on religion; not least, when describing the monasticism of the Middle Ages as being, 'in many of its bearings, like a beautiful disease or disorder of the senses' (Pater, 'Aesthetic Poetry', *Appreciations*, 217). Amplifying his objection, he notes that 'a religion which is a disorder of the senses must always be subject to illusions' (Pater, 'Aesthetic Poetry', 217). He is here talking about religion as it found expression in a particular time and place, far removed from his own. That this time and place was, however, one often valorised in his own moment as an ideal to be revived through full-blooded Catholicism surely troubles any neat narrative that he was in his last years bound for Rome. The essay where these comments appear, 'Aesthetic Poetry', was a re-branded version of his 1868 review of William Morris's poems that had appeared in *The Renaissance*, but the fact that he chose to repurpose it in 1889 is suggestive of the extent to which his impatience with institutional religion was alive in his later years too.

Honest Doubt

The deeper one plumbs the depths of Pater's religious views, the murkier things become. Or rather, the clearer it becomes that the whole subject of religious faith itself resists the tidy, binary categories of belief versus unbelief, conviction versus scepticism. If he tended, over the decades of his youth and his maturity, first towards, then away from, then back once more to Christian orthodoxy, there appears always to have been, as Gosse well describes it, a 'perennial conflict in his members, between his exquisite instinct for corporeal beauty on the one hand and his tendency to ecclesiastical symbol and theological dogma on the other': 'He was not all for Apollo, nor all for Christ, but each deity swayed in him, and neither had that perfect homage that brings peace behind it' (Gosse, 'Walter Pater: A Portrait', 270).

Pater himself was careful to hedge his own position when he confessed that he was not 'wholly of the remnant'.[25] Whatever 'wholly' means, whatever fraction might be parsed from his phrasing, Pater's sympathies for religion and aestheticism were not only ambivalent and entangled, but also on the move. Whatever 'equipoise' the Victorian age might have enjoyed, socially, economically, or politically (a thesis that continues to invite endorsement as well as criticism),[26] philosophical accounts and personal experiences of religion in the period were widely and urgently in flux,[27] and Pater was among those caught up within the very centre of that intellectual-affective maelstrom.

Pater's life was animated by an abiding, unresolved meditation on the nature of belief itself. Recent scholarship on the late nineteenth century has exposed the inadequacy of the so-called 'secularisation thesis', which posits a simple falling away of faith in the period, newly recognising the ways in which 'honest doubt' is a more complex matter than the sheer antithesis of faith:[28] how doubt may in fact be a positive expression of a restless desire for a living faith, as against that which had in many cases been denuded into mere doctrine.[29] Pater's own commitments can certainly be read in that way.[30] His emphasis on the phenomenology of belief led him to attempt 'more seriously than anyone before him in England to understand the Greek gods as gods, not as long-dead divinities but as living spirits'.[31] But that very same emphasis led him to think about Christianity as having a life beyond its sedimented strictures too. The way Pater thus bridged ancient and modern religion in his thinking is remarkable, not least for the extent to which the emergent Victorian 'science' of religious anthropology, and the contemporary philosophies of religious scepticism exemplified by Nietzsche, by contrast typically approached pagan religion in ways that undermined the potency and credibility of the Christian faith.

Without wishing to overstate the extent to which Pater's views might after all be accommodated within a Christian scheme, there is an instructive sense in which his insistence on the value of experience within belief converges with that towering religious figure of the period, Cardinal John Henry Newman, whose *An Essay in Aid of a Grammar of Assent* (1870) stakes out the difference between what he calls 'real' as against 'notional assent': the latter coming by way of abstract inference; the former, through experience. It is not clear how far if at all Pater might have been borrowing Newman's operative word in his own writings, but there are certainly several suggestive occurrences where 'assent' appears. Here he is echoing the essential logic of Newman's *Grammar*, that Christianity warrants belief not as a special case but for very much the way we believe any number of things in our everyday lives – for being more plausible than not:

> To my mind, the beliefs, and the function in the world, of the historic church form just one of those obscure but all-important possibilities which the human mind is powerless effectively to dismiss from itself, and must wisely accept, in the first place, as a workable hypothesis. The supposed facts on which Christianity rests, utterly incapable as they have become of any ordinary test,

seem to me matters of very much the same sort of assent we give to any assumptions, in the strict and ultimate sense, moral.[32]

This passage comes from a letter Pater sent to the novelist and social reformer Mary Augusta Ward, following her review of *Marius*, which like many of his 'imaginary portraits' worries over the matter of how we believe – the act of belief itself – as against the theological niceties of dogmatic principle. Here is how he approaches the same subject in 'The Child in the House':

> There were times when he could think of the necessity he was under of associating all thoughts to touch and sight, as a sympathetic link between himself and actual, feeling, living objects; a protest in favour of real men and women against mere grey, unreal abstractions; and he remembered gratefully how the Christian religion, hardly less than the religion of the ancient Greeks, translating so much of its spiritual verity into things that may be seen, condescends in part to sanction this infirmity, if so it be, of our human existence, wherein the world of sense is so much with us, and welcomed this thought as a kind of keeper and sentinel over his soul therein.
>
> (Pater, 'The Child in the House', 187)

What a suggestive phrase: 'a protest in favour of real men and women against mere grey, unreal abstractions'. Pater posits an implicit tautology. Abstraction is the definition of unreality – and the opposite of what's 'actual', which is what's mediated through 'feeling'. Is 'the world of sense is so much with us' perhaps also an allusion to Wordsworth's famous protest against the spiritually alienated soul of the nineteenth century, 'The world is too much with us'? It certainly conjures something of the same defiant exasperation that would 'rather be / A Pagan suckled in a creed outworn',[33] if it would mean that existence might be awoken once again to the numinous.

While Pater is very much the champion of Romantic, Hellenic paganism that celebrates an embodied experience over the intellectual abstraction offered by a certain brand of Christianity, he, like Wordsworth, only flirts with paganism, knowing it to be, as he shows most vividly in *Marius*, a 'creed outworn'. Yet he cannot quite commit to Christianity, either; not entirely. Returning to Ward, it is revealing to read his 1888 review of her novel *Robert Elsmere*. This story of an Anglican clergyman who loses his faith and so quits his priesthood is taken up by Pater first as a mark of Elsmere's intellectual honesty. It is a positive trait, though that commendation is quickly countered by the claim that 'the main issue of the "religious question" is not precisely where Mrs. Ward supposes'.[34]

Pater does not contest that a man such as Elsmere ought not to be a clergyman. Whatever inevitable doubts a clergyman must have in this 'doubting age', to be a priest he must nonetheless feel, 'on the whole, the preponderance in it of those influences which make for faith'. For all the stringency of this principle, his language of 'preponderance' accommodates proportion, as he also goes on to avow the difficulty of having any kind of faith at all: 'It is his triumph to achieve as much faith as possible in an age of negation.' The penultimate step in Pater's argument is to assert that 'it is the positive not the negative' of belief that might justify the priest's position ('We have little patience with those liberal clergy who dwell on nothing else than the difficulties of faith and the propriety of concession to the opposite force') (Pater, 'Robert Elsmere', 66–67).

The reason Pater has dwelt on the potential relativity of faith – caught between positive belief and negative doubt – is that he wishes to insist on the virtue as well as the necessity of epistemological pragmatism that can find its appropriate balance:

> Had he possessed a perfectly philosophic or scientific temper he would have hesitated. This is not the place to discuss in detail the theological position very ably and seriously argued by Mrs. Ward. All we can say is that, one by one, Elsmere's objections may be met by considerations of the same genus, and not less equal weight, relatively to a world so obscure, in its origin and issues, as that in which we live. (Pater, 'Robert Elsmere', 67)

Descending from abstraction to the human scale allows us 'to recognize our doubts, to locate them, perhaps to give them practical effect'. The point is philosophical and pragmatic, but 'It may be also a moral duty to do this' (Pater, 'Robert Elsmere', 67–68). Hesitating is not, in this context, to haver. It means holding firm, by resisting both the complacency of uninspected piety and the bigotry of peremptory scepticism, which is 'the purely negative action of the scientific spirit' (Pater, 'Robert Elsmere', 68). Honest doubt indeed.

Whatever else might be said about religious faith, it is, Pater would have us see, 'so great and complex a question' that it demands more from us than could ever find adequate expression through the grey and unreal and abstract rubrics of either religious dogma or scientific data (Pater, 'Robert Elsmere', 67). In that Platonic spirit, his 'retreat' into beauty was, by design, generative: a 'protest' 'in favour of real men and women', 'as a sympathetic link between himself and actual'. Knowing he could not himself achieve what Newman called 'certitude',[35] he came only as far as the threshold of the 'actual'; he hesitated. His commitment to beauty was not an alternative religion, nor was it irreligious. It was the intermedial modality by which he sought 'to achieve as much faith as possible in an age of negation'.

Notes

1. Edmund Gosse, 'Walter Pater: a Portrait', in *Critical Kit-Kats* (London: Heinemann, 1903), 271.
2. Percy Lubbock (ed.), *The Letters of Henry James* (London: Macmillan, 1920), vol. 1, 227–8.
3. Walter Pater, 'Emerald Uthwart', in Charles Lancelot Shadwell (ed.), *Miscellaneous Studies* (London: Macmillan and Co., 1895), 220.
4. See Gerald Monsman's account in his appendix notes to *Marius the Epicurean*, ed. Monsman (Kansas City, KS: Valancourt Books, 2008), 329–338.
5. Pater, 'Moral Philosophy', Houghton Manuscript, MP, 13v.
6. Pater, 'Moral Philosophy', Houghton Manuscript, MP, 25v.
7. J. Mordaunt Crook, *Brasenose: The Biography of an Oxford College* (Oxford: Oxford University Press, 2008), 273.
8. See Michael D. Hurley, 'Form, Matter, and Metaphysics in Walter Pater's essay on "Style"', in *Walter Pater and the Beginnings of English Studies*, Charles Martindale, Lene Østermark-Johansen, and Elizabeth Prettejohn, eds. (Cambridge: Cambridge University Press, 2023).
9. Laurel Brake, *Walter Pater* (Plymouth: Northcote House, 1994), 17.
10. Pater, 'Coleridge', *Appreciations* (London: Macmillan and Co., 1889), 104. This essay was originally printed anonymously in *The Westminster and Foreign Quarterly Review*, 29 (1 January, 1866): 106–131.
11. Pater, 'Winckelmann', *The Renaissance: Studies in Art and Poetry*, ed. Hilary Fraser (Oxford: Oxford University Press, 2025), 171, 176. This essay was originally printed anonymously as 'Winckelmann' in *The Westminster Review*, 31 (January 1867): 80–110.
12. [Pater], 'Poems by William Morris', *The Westminster Review*, 34 (1 October, 1868): 312.
13. John Wordsworth to Walter Pater, 17 March 1873, Lawrence Evans, ed., *Letters of Walter Pater* (Oxford: Clarendon Press, 1870), 13. I am grateful to Samuel Webb for alerting me to this letter.
14. See Brake, *Walter Pater*, 12–13.
15. *Sam Brooke's Journal, The Diary of a Lancing Schoolboy* (Lancing, 1953), quoted in Gerald C. Monsman, 'Old Mortality at Oxford', *Studies in Philology*, 67, no. 3 (July, 1970): 359–389 (371).
16. Lord David Cecil, *Walter Pater: the Scholar-Artist* (Cambridge: Cambridge University Press, 1955), 3.
17. Pater, *Marius the Epicurean* (Kansas City: Valancourt Books, 2008), 197.
18. Pater allegedly told a friend that he wrote Marius in order 'to show the necessity for religion': Thomas Wright, *The Life of Walter Pater*, 2 vols. (New York, 1907), 87.
19. William James, *The Varieties of Religious Experience: A Study in Human Nature* (London: Longmans, Green, 1920), 31.
20. See Hyden Ward, '"The Last Thing Walter Wrote": Pater's "Pascal"', in *Pater in the 1990s*, Laurel Brake and Ian Small, eds. (Greensboro, NC: ELT Press, 1991), Ch. 11.
21. Pater, 'Pascal', *Miscellaneous Studies* (London: Macmillan, 1895), 71.
22. Pater, *Plato and Platonism* (London: Macmillan, 1910), 271.

23. John Keats, 'Ode on a Grecian Urn', *Keats: The Complete Poems* (London: Longman, 1970), 537.

24. See Robert Keefe and Janice A. Keefe, *Walter Pater and the Gods of Disorder* (Athens: Ohio University Press, 1988), 14, 12.

25. Pater confessed this in the unfinished manuscript, 'Art and Religion'; see [Walter Pater], 'Art and rel[igio]n', bMS Eng 1150 (11), Houghton Library, Harvard University, 11.

26. See Martin Hewitt, ed., *An Age of Equipoise? Reassessing mid-Victorian Britain* (Aldershot: Ashgate, 2000).

27. See Dominic Green, *The Religious Revolution: The Birth of Modern Spirituality, 1848–1898* (New York: Farrer, Strauss, and Giroux, 2022).

28. In *In Memoriam A.H.H.*, Tennyson wrote that 'There lives more faith in honest doubt, / Believe me, than in half the creeds'; Alfred, Lord Tennyson, *In Memoriam* (London: W.W. Norton, 2004), 71.

29. See Michael D. Hurley, *Faith in Poetry: Verse Style as a Mode of Religious Belief* (London: Bloomsbury, 2017).

30. See Sara Lyons, *Algernon Swinburne and Walter Pater: Victorian Aestheticism, Doubt and Secularisation* (London: Legenda, Modern Humanities Research Association and Maney, 2015).

31. Robert Fowler, 'Pater and Greek Religion', in *Pater the Classicist: Classical Scholarship, Reception, and Aestheticism*, Charles Martindale, Stefano Evangelista, and Elizabeth Prettejohn, eds. (Oxford: Oxford University Press, 2017), 241.

32. Mrs. Humphry Ward (Mary Arnold Ward), *A Writer's Recollections* (London: W. Collins Sons, 1918), 210.

33. William Wordsworth, 'The World Is Too Much With Us, Late and Soon', *The Poetical Works of Wordsworth* (Boston: Houghton Mifflin, 1982), 349.

34. Pater, 'Robert Elsmere', *Essays from 'The Guardian'* (London: Macmillan, 1910), 66.

35. See Ch. 7, 'Certitude', in John Henry Newman, *An Essay in Aid of a Grammar of Assent* (Oxford: Clarendon Press, 1985), 210–259.

MATTHEW POTOLSKY

Pater on Ancient Art and Mythology

Although his work ranges over periods from antiquity to the present, by training and profession, Pater was a classicist. He received his university degree from Queen's College, Oxford, in *Literae Humaniores*, a rigorous course of study that required mastery of ancient Greek and Latin and included readings in classical literature, history, and philosophy. After finishing his degree, Pater was elected to a non-clerical fellowship at Brasenose College, Oxford, in 1864, where he was charged with tutoring undergraduate students in classical languages and literature, delivering lectures at the college, and later offering university lecture courses on classical subjects, including Plato, Aristotle, and the history of Greek art. Even after he resigned from his tutorial position in 1883 to focus on completing *Marius the Epicurean* (1885), he continued to lecture on Plato and Aristotle at Oxford and to receive papers from students. He counted among his teachers, colleagues, friends, and students some of the most prominent scholars of classical philosophy, literature, and archaeology, and he was familiar with the most important intellectual developments in the field.[1]

Literae Humaniores had traditionally emphasised the study of Latin, but in the 1840s, under the influence of Pater's tutor Benjamin Jowett, the curriculum shifted its focus to Greek authors and subjects, reflecting (and in turn prompting) a broader shift among British intellectuals, who began to find their models in Athens and Sparta rather than Rome.[2] Pater was no exception and, apart from *Marius the Epicurean*, which is set in the Rome of Marcus Aurelius, the bulk of his writings on antiquity concern Greece. This does not mean that he necessarily shared the majority view of Greek culture at the time. As Frank Turner has shown, influential Victorian figures like Matthew Arnold and George Grote saw the ancient Greeks as paragons of intellectual clarity and grace, whose works held important lessons for contemporary readers and potential answers for pressing social problems.[3] In *Culture and Anarchy* (1869), Arnold famously contrasted what he called the Hellenic tradition of 'sweetness and light' with the rigorous morality of the

Hebraic tradition.[4] The image of Greece that Arnold promotes reflected the influence of the eighteenth-century German art historian Johann Joachim Winckelmann, whose writings on ancient art all but invented classical Greece as it came to be defined in the nineteenth century.[5] For Winckelmann, the keynotes of Greek culture were embodied in two German words: *Heiterkeit*, meaning serenity and cheerfulness; and *Allgemeinheit*, meaning broadness of mind and intellectual outlook. These qualities governed the reception of ancient Greece among Victorian intellectuals. Figures like Homer, Socrates, and Sophocles were believed to have looked on even the most distressing elements of life with serene wisdom and a breadth of understanding that could place individual suffering into a larger perspective. Classical tragedy turned the most painful emotions into the highest art; the pure white forms of Greek sculpture rendered the unclothed human form chaste.

Pater was sympathetic to this understanding of the classical world, but beginning in the mid-1870s, he began to explore darker and more subversive aspects of ancient Greek culture. In the myths of Demeter and Dionysus, he found expressions of sorrow that lent emotional depth to the cheerful light that Victorians saw in antiquity. Building on descriptions of lost works by the ancient Greek traveller Pausanias, he tinted the white surfaces of ancient sculpture with myriad variegations. He found erotic resonances in familiar works and transcendent beauty in the archaic and obscure as well as in the classical. In his telling, Greek art and thought emerge from and wrestle with older Asian influences.

Pater's highly original vision of ancient Greece was informed by nineteenth-century developments in the fields of classics and archaeology, and his works draw upon and often critically engage with the methodological advances and new archaeological discoveries described in the works of German scholars like K. O. Müller, Ludwig Preller, and Johannes Overbeck, as well as in those of British contemporaries like E. B. Tylor, F. Max Müller, Charles Thomas Newton, and Andrew Lang. He never saw himself purely as a scholar, however, and the information he draws from such sources is always transformed in his writings by a passionate commitment to the aesthetic. So, although they often have the sheen of traditional scholarship, Pater's writings on antiquity are shaped by a self-consciously Romantic sensibility.[6] Shawn Malley usefully calls his approach 'archaeological aestheticism'.[7] These writings are peppered with allusions to Romantic poets like William Wordsworth, John Keats, Percy Shelley, and William Blake and to classicising contemporary writers and artists like Algernon Charles Swinburne and Simeon Solomon. Identifying neither with the ideal-ised Greece of Arnold and Grote nor with the dry 'scientific' methodology of the scholars, Pater treated antiquity as a challenging alternative to the status quo, a potential threat to the daylight world.

Perhaps the clearest instance of this challenge comes in Pater's attention to gender and sexual dissidence in the materials he discusses. Here again, Winckelmann is a key influence, though in this case for his frequent praise of male beauty and passionate friendships with young men, rather than for his depictions of Hellenic serenity. In his 1867 essay 'Winckelmann', Pater implies that the study of ancient art for his subject is an erotic as well as an archaeological pursuit, something the German art historian's scholarly and popular followers tended to gloss over, writing: 'he fingers those pagan marbles with unsinged hands, with no sense of shame or loss'.[8] Stefano Evangelista has characterised the essay as 'a pioneering psychological study of how sexual preferences colour artistic taste and intellectual life'.[9] Pater's attention to the erotic resonances of classical taste was part of a larger turn in Victorian Oxford. As Linda Dowling has demonstrated, Jowett's introduction of Plato and other Greek thinkers to the Oxford curriculum had the unintended effect of exposing students to the full diversity of Greek eros, in which homosexual relationships were not only permitted but exalted as the highest form of love.[10] When Pater comments on the 'effeminacy' of Dionysus or mentions homoerotic texts like Plato's *Phaedrus* or *Lysis*, he is implicitly challenging contemporary gender and sexual norms. And when he praises the 'variegation' of Greek art, he is alluding to the Greek word *poikilia*, which was often used as a term of same-sex endearment in Victorian Oxford.[11] The new respect accorded Greek culture in the period gave these kinds of observations a veneer of respectability in a culture increasingly hostile to homosexual relationships. Many other queer Victorian writers, from Oscar Wilde to John Addington Symonds, also used discussions of Greek culture to defend non-normative desires. Women writers, largely excluded from the university study of classics, turned this subversive reading of antiquity to their own ends, often taking Pater as their intellectual lodestar, as Yopie Prins has shown.[12] They, too, were drawn to the dark side of Greek culture, seeing it as another kind of challenge to contemporary gender ideology.[13] Arguably, this eroticised classicism was Pater's most important contribution to later writers.

Pater's discovery of a different antiquity – dark, emotive, sensual – bears comparison with that of his near-contemporary Friedrich Nietzsche, who was also revolutionising classical studies in the 1870s. Although it is unlikely that the two thinkers knew each other's work, there are many parallels between their writings, something Patrick Bridgwater speculates may be traced to common scholarly sources.[14] Both find explosive new perspectives hiding in the shadows cast by the light of the ancient world. In *The Birth of*

Tragedy (1872), his first book, Nietzsche argues that the 'Apollinian' calm and clarity lauded by nineteenth-century classicism were in fact built upon a 'Dionysian' substrate that embodied 'a terrifyingly profound view of the world and the most acute sensitivity to suffering'.[15] Long seen as an epitome of Grecian serenity, tragedy is driven by Dionysian energies that are shaped, ordered, and rationalised by the Apollinian. The subsequent rise of Greek rationalism, Nietzsche argues, represents a case of degeneration rather than progress, a denial of the Dionysian elements at the root of the culture.

Pater's challenge to contemporary verities about antiquity is less dramatic than Nietzsche's but it shares the German philosopher's insistence that Greece gives modernity something more than white marble forms and rational debate. Not unlike Nietzsche, Pater builds his account of antiquity on a foundational opposition, derived in this case from the geography of Greece rather than its gods. In 'The Marbles of Aegina' (1880) he describes a clash between two tendencies, the Ionian and the Dorian, which shapes nearly every aspect of ancient Greek life, and, in Gerald Monsman's words, structures the 'whole of Pater's world view'.[16] 'All through Greek history', Pater writes in this essay, 'we may trace, in every sphere of the activity of the Greek mind, the action of these two opposing tendencies, – the centrifugal and centripetal tendencies, as we may perhaps not too fancifully call them'.[17]

The opposition between the Ionian and the Dorian was familiar in classical scholarship. It refers to two regions with longstanding Greek settlements that often found themselves at odds. The Ionian tendency found its ancient home in the 'Asiatic' Greek settlements on the western coast of present-day Türkiya, while the Dorian tendency was centred in the more 'European' confines of the Peloponnesian Peninsula and the island of Crete (145). Pater frames this opposition in two original ways, however. First, rather than seeing the opposition in terms of geography or ethnic identity, he understands it as aesthetic and intellectual: the Ionian and the Dorian are styles of thought and expression, not inherent qualities of a population or a race. Second, whereas his scholarly sources tended to see the Dorian as the original tendency and the Ionian as a later flourish, Pater insists that the Ionian precedes the Dorian, and that the Dorian seeks to tame and subject it to control. While the Ionian is associated with motion, colour, individuality, and freedom – variegation in all its aesthetic and erotic senses – the Dorian is associated with order, discipline, uniformity, and reason.

The Ionian or centrifugal tendency, as Pater characterises it in 'The Marbles of Aegina', is always 'flying from the centre, working with little forethought straight before it, in the development of every thought and fancy; throwing itself forth in endless play of undirected imagination'

(145). In aesthetics, the Ionian delights in 'brightness and colour, in beautiful material, in changeful form everywhere', while in politics,

> it rejoices in the freest action of local and personal influences; its restless versatility drives it towards the assertion of the principles of separatism, of individualism, – the separation of state from state, the maintenance of local religions, the development of the individual in that which is most peculiar and individual in him.   (145–6)

The Dorian or centripetal tendency, by contrast, aims at 'a severe simplification everywhere, in society, in culture, in the very physical nature of man' (146). It sees the human mind as 'the most absolutely real and precious thing in the world, enforces everywhere the impress of its sanity, its profound reflections upon things as they really are, its sense of proportion' (146). Pater sees the Dorian as a correction or limitation of the Ionian. For Plato, he notes, the Dorian offers a 'cure' for the Ionian tendencies in Athenian government, which is 'what made the unity of Greece impossible' (146). While the Ionian tendency encourages individualism and separateness, the Dorian 'links individuals to each other, states to states, one period of organic growth to another, under the reign of a composed, rational, self-conscious order, in the universal light of the understanding' (146). The mortal enemy of variegation, it finds beauty solely in '*composition*': structure over freedom, rationality over creativity, universality over variety (146; italics in original). Democratic Athens, as Pater suggests in *Plato and Platonism* (1893), is the 'perfect flower of Ionian genius', while authoritarian Sparta is the 'perfect flower of Dorian genius'.[18]

The word 'Asiatic' in Pater's description deserves some comment. Consistent with then-familiar distinctions in classical scholarship, Pater uses the word to refer primarily to the cultures of Persia, Asia Minor, and the Middle East: Asia as the Greeks were likely to engage with it in their trading relationships, imperial clashes, and travels around the Mediterranean basin. In many ways, this use is characteristic of the Orientalist discourses that, as Edward Said has noted, collapse the many cultures of the East into a single 'other' to Europe.[19] Despite his association of Asia with centrifugal 'motion' and creativity, for example, Pater also gives voice to scholarly commonplaces about the 'frozen' development of Egyptian or Assyrian art and the inability of Asian artists (unlike their 'European' counterparts) to depict the human form. He uses words like 'languid' and 'voluptuous' to describe Ionian qualities, evoking another kind of immobility (128). In brief discussions of Japanese art from his essays on Greek sculpture he notes, similarly, that while artists from Japan carry 'a delicacy like that of nature itself into every form of imitation' of natural objects, they fail when they try to depict 'the sacred human form'.

Modern Japanese art is developmentally frozen, resembling 'the earliest stages of Greek art' rather than the contemporary arts of Europe, a characterisation common at the time (130).²⁰ In other cases, Pater uses the word 'Asiatic' to refer to Greek thinkers and artists, not actual Asian traditions. Both the Ionians and the Dorians were Greek in origin and identity. Thus, in *Plato and Platonism*, he contrasts Heraclitus, the philosopher of motion and change, who was born in the Ionian Greek city of Ephesus, with Parmenides, the philosopher of unity, a native of the Dorian colony of Elea in modern-day Italy. The two philosophers represent contrasting 'tendencies' in the Greek mind, not a difference of culture.

But Pater's Asia is more than a mere echo of contemporary scholarly commonplaces or an instance of unwarranted cultural appropriation. Always fascinated with cultural contact, Pater is quick to acknowledge key Asian influences on Greek culture, tracing many of the distinctive qualities of early Greek art to styles drawn from Assyrian, Egyptian, and Phoenician works. 'We may, perhaps, forget sometimes', he comments in 'The Beginnings of Greek Sculpture',

> thinking over the greatness of its place in the history of civilisation, how small a country Greece really was; how short the distances onwards, from island to island, to the coast of Asia, so that we can hardly make a sharp separation between Asia and Greece, nor deny besides great and palpable acts of import-ation, all sorts of impalpable Asiatic influences, by way alike of attraction and repulsion, upon Greek manners and taste.   (127–8)

Pater here reminds his readers that Greece was but one culture among many in the region, and a latecomer at that. More powerfully still, he uses the term 'Asiatic' to draw attention to the value of those qualities repudiated by the classical: the archaic, the popular, the local, the colourful, the heterogeneous, and the erotic. To be sure, Pater is alive to the importance of both tendencies in Greek life, and it would be wrong to characterise him, as many of his contemporaries did, purely as an advocate of the Ionian, a modern-day Heraclitus disguised as an Oxford don. As William Shuter has argued, Pater's late works tend to criticise the Asiatic 'expressions of mobility' that the early works celebrated, showing a preference instead for stillness and rest.²¹ In *Plato and Platonism*, for example, where he includes a revised version of the passage delineating the Ionian and the Dorian tendencies, Pater adds that the Ionian needs Dorian restraint: 'The Greek spirit! – it might have become a hydra ... a monster; the hand developing hideously into a hundred hands, or heads'.²² In a chapter entitled 'Lacedaemon' in the same book, Pater writes admiringly of Spartan order, discipline, and approval of same-sex relationships – a characterisation that subtly blends both tendencies.

Still, given the praise of Dorian virtues in Victorian discussions of ancient Greece, Pater is eager to find traces of the Ionian wherever he can, troubling both the Arnoldian vision of 'sweetness and light' and the scholarly reduction of Greek art to dry facts. His sympathy for the Ionian comes across in many ways in his writings on classical subjects. He is drawn, to take one example, to images of travel, often describing scenes from antiquity as if through the eyes of a foreign visitor. The gods that interest him are itinerant, wandering among humans rather than dwelling on Olympus. He draws attention to the afterlife of the classical tradition, frequently adapting the German poet Heinrich Heine's 1853 story about the wanderings of Greek deities in Europe, 'The Gods in Exile'. Such images demonstrate the persistence of the Ionian, constituting an implicit argument for the value and necessity of what comes before, falls outside of, or has been absorbed into and neutralised by the praise of all things 'classical'.

Consider the two essays on the Greek myths of Demeter and Dionysus from the mid-1870s, which would have an important influence on the uses of myth among twentieth-century Modernists like James Joyce and T. S. Eliot. Written in the wake of *The Renaissance*, and at one point slated to appear, alongside pieces on Romantic writers, in a book entitled *Dionysus and Other Studies* that Pater withdrew from his publisher at the last minute, the essays epitomise two broadly 'Ionian' qualities of the myths and their history.[23] First, they foreground the primitive and the local, tracing the emergence of both myths to the observations of peasants working in fields. Building on Romantic ideas about the value of folk culture and anonymous stories, Pater sees such observations as crucial raw material for the later systematising work of poets and priests. Second, the two essays are fascinated by 'variegation' in all the senses of that word, from their exploration of the depths of Greek emotional and erotic experience to their interest in the multiple versions of each myth. Demeter and Dionysus emerge from the essays as kaleidoscopic figures, whose attributes multiply as Pater tells their stories, rather than settling down into a single eternal image. Both gods were themselves itinerant: Demeter wanders from Olympus to Eleusis and Dionysus from India and the Arab world to Greece and then north to Thrace. Like the myths, the gods themselves are always in motion.

'The Myth of Demeter and Persephone' was presented as a lecture in 1875 and then published in two parts in the prominent journal *The Fortnightly Review* in 1876. The goddess of grain and the harvest, Demeter lost her child Persephone to Hades, lord of the Underworld, who carried her away while she was picking flowers in a field. Furious with the refusal of the other gods to help her, she leaves Mount Olympus and goes to the countryside disguised as an old woman, refusing to allow the crops to grow until her daughter is returned to her. Hades relents but persuades Persephone to eat some pomegranate seeds before she returns to earth, binding her to the Underworld and making it necessary that she spend one season every year there.

As Pater frames it, the story of Demeter challenges Victorian verities about ancient Greece in several ways. Building on a critique he first broached in 'Winckelmann', the essay replies to Arnold's 'Pagan and Medieval Religious Sentiments' (1865), an essay that, as David DeLaura has noted, served as an important 'foil' for Pater's 'special reading of Greek culture'.[24] Arnold argues that Greek religion is concerned only with the outward and 'pleasure-giving' aspects of the world and, unlike Christianity, had no room for true sorrow.[25] As Pater shows, sorrow is central to the Demeter myth. In her grief at the loss of her child, the goddess anticipates the most famous image of sorrowful motherhood in Christian iconography: the Virgin Mary grieving over the body of Christ. The myth also demonstrates for Pater the profound importance of the poor, women, and local beliefs in Greek life, against conventional attention to 'great men' like Plato and Pericles. He traces Demeter from her early service as an explanation for seasonal change to her role as the central figure in the Eleusinian Mysteries, the most important mystery religion in ancient Greece. Although, he writes, it is 'Alien in some respects from the genuine traditions of Greek mythology', the myth nevertheless 'asserted its interest' over the Greeks and soon 'took a complex hold' on their minds, 'becoming finally the central and most popular subject of their national worship' (59). Likewise, Demeter herself is at first an outsider among the Olympian gods, who is forced to conceal her divinity and wander among humans, but who ultimately succeeds in her quest. In addition to challenging Arnold's characterisation of Greek religion, then, Pater's account of the Demeter myth promotes a new model of Hellenism sensitive to the contributions of cultural outsiders.[26]

'A Study of Dionysus: The Spiritual Form of Fire and Dew' is, if anything, even more invested in the centrifugal Ionian tendency than the Demeter essay. Dionysus, the god of wine, is multiple in almost every aspect of his story, as Pater conveys it. At once human and divine – the product of a liaison between Zeus and the mortal Semele – he belongs among the Olympians but, like Demeter, dwells on the earth, surrounded by minor nature deities and human followers (the maenads), who together constitute 'a little Olympus outside the greater' (91). He is born twice: the first time prematurely, when his mother dies after Zeus grants her wish to see him in his proper form; and the second time when his divine father sews the infant into his leg until he is ready to be born again. He is associated, according to Pater, with both fire

149

(the lightning of Zeus) and dew (the fountain of the nymphs who raised him). His worship is connected both to the country and the city. First understood as a ruddy nature god, linked to the vine and the harvest, he later becomes delicate and effeminate, mingling with 'urbane young men' at elaborate banquets (105). In the country, he is represented by phallic puppets and the rough spirit of comedy, while in Athens, as Nietzsche also observed, he becomes the inspiring god of tragic theatre. Finally, Dionysus embodies two emotions. As the god of wine and the harvest, he is the source of intoxication and enthusiasm, of poetry, music, and the revelling of the maenads: the experience 'of passing out of oneself through words, tones, gestures' (95). But he also has a melancholy streak, manifested in his relationship to tragedy and in his longing for his dead mother. This melancholy comes out most strongly in the myth of winter Dionysus: Dionysus Zagreus, by which 'a certain perceptible shadow comes growing over the whole story' (108). This version of Dionysus sees the god hunting in the forests, consuming human flesh, and being torn apart by his followers, only to be born again the following season.

In both myth essays, Pater draws upon the speculations of German classical scholars and Victorian anthropologists, who argued that myths are personifications of 'the phenomena of the outside world', creations of peasants as they observe the 'changes in physical things' over time (64). In another gesture towards the Romantic tradition, he borrows his special term for this process, 'spiritual form', from Blake. Demeter and Persephone are the 'spiritual form' of the growth of grain and the changes in the seasons, while Dionysus is the 'spiritual form' of the growth of vines and of the movement of water and fire. Once personified, the gods take on independent life and come to represent deeper meanings. Dionysus, for example, is originally 'the soul of the individual vine', but later embodies 'the soul of the whole species, the spirit of fire and dew, alive and leaping in a thousand vines', and later still the spirit of tragedy (93). The process begins early in the history of myth, but in Pater's conception does not end in antiquity. The myth essays are rife with allusions to Renaissance and modern artworks, which demonstrate the persistence of the gods in later culture and help bring out elements of Demeter and Dionysus that conventional classical scholarship cannot always capture.

Although Pater does not use the terms consistently in the two essays, the development of myth as he describes it recalls the disciplining of the Ionian by the Dorian tendency. What begins in an encounter with the 'Ionian' experience of change in nature – seasons, growth, physical transformation – becomes fixed through the 'Dorian' labour of poets and priests, who synthesise different versions of the story and channel a variety of local traditions into regular forms of worship. In the essay on Demeter, Pater outlines three developmental stages in this process, drawing on (but also modifying) a similar account of myth proposed by John Ruskin and German classical scholars.[27] In the first or 'mystical' stage, a still-unwritten myth passes 'from mouth to mouth', changing in external details but preserving 'certain primitive impressions of the phenomena of the outward world' (64). Myriad popular ideas about the growth of grain and grapes, rooted in local communities, collect around the definitive form of the gods. The second stage sees the poets take hold of the myth, 'fixing its outlines, and simplifying or developing its situations' (64). With this stage, Demeter and Persephone, often confused in archaic versions of the story, become two distinct characters, and Demeter's anger becomes part of a connected narrative. Pater calls the third stage 'ethical', pointing to the way the gods become 'abstract symbols ... of moral or spiritual conditions' (64). Demeter emerges as a symbol for 'divine grief', and Persephone as the goddess of death, whose yearly return inspires mystical meanings (65). Reason takes over from the popular imagination, creating fixed (Dorian) doctrines where there were once scattered (Ionian) impressions. But while the development of the myths seems to document the triumph of the Dorian, Pater's very way of telling the story preserves something of their Ionian origins. Never privileging a single, authorised version of the myths, as I mentioned above, he recounts different variations without insisting on the priority of any, leaving readers with an impression of constant change rather than fixity. Dowling has noted, moreover, that Pater's use of the word 'ethical' seems to have more in common with the aesthetic than with ethics in its philosophical sense, bringing the late developments of the myths back to their origins in impressions and imagination.[28]

Pater first elaborated on the opposition between the Ionian and Dorian tendencies to account for the development of Greek art, and the three essays on sculpture make that opposition paramount. Pater based these essays on a lecture course on Greek art and the writings of Pausanias that he offered at Oxford in 1878. The first two essays, 'The Beginnings of Greek Sculpture' and 'The Marbles of Aegina', were published in three instalments in *The Fortnightly Review* in 1880, while the third, 'The Age of Athletic Prizemen', was published in the *Contemporary Review* in 1894, though it also derives from the lecture series. Several unpublished fragments from the 1890s suggest that Pater was planning a book on Greek sculpture that never came to fruition.

The extant essays show how Greek sculpture moved from its Ionian and 'Asiatic' origins in the decorative arts, especially variegated metalwork, to a Dorian and 'European' focus on representations of the human form – a more concrete version of the way local impressions become personified gods with stories and symbolic meanings in the history of myth. A brief excursus on the art of sculpture in 'A Study of Dionysus' succinctly anticipates this argument. Sculpture, Pater writes there, arises from 'a romantic *Streben*' (the German word for 'struggle') by which artists mould the 'floating essence' of Greek perceptions about nature and human character into a 'palpable and limited human form' carved in stone. 'On the one hand, was the teeming, still fluid, world, of old beliefs', the Ionian variegation of individual impressions, ideas, and feelings. 'On the other hand', Pater continues,

> was that limiting, controlling tendency, identified with the Dorian influence in the history of the Greek mind, the spirit of a severe and wholly self-conscious intelligence; bent on impressing everywhere, in the products of the imagination, the definite, entirely conceivable human form, as the only worthy subject of art. (103)

Pater's claims about sculpture draw on the aesthetic philosophy of G. W. F. Hegel, who, in his *Lectures on Aesthetics* (1835), argues that the arts show the increasing influence of mind and reason over representation. With what Hegel calls 'classical' art (embodied in Greek sculpture), reason finds its self-image in sculptural depictions of the human form: 'the external human form is alone capable of revealing the spiritual in a sensuous way'.[29] Pater adapts Hegel's account of classical art to his own opposition between the Ionian and the Dorian, but also challenges Hegel's valorisation of artistic rationality by attending closely to the variety, colour, and decorative character of early Greek art, which is not wholly erased by the Dorian tendency. Although they may appear to be 'the most abstract and intellectualised of sensuous objects', Pater writes, even the pinnacles of classical sculpture are 'still sensuous and material, addressing themselves, in the first instance, not to the purely reflective faculty, but to the eye' (114). The Dorian may triumph over early Asiatic influences, but the Ionian continues to exert its pull.

In 'The Beginnings of Greek Sculpture', Pater broadens Winckelmann's received account of Greek sculpture by sorting through existing written evidence and copies of lost works to document the earliest forms of ancient art, and by insisting, for perhaps the first time in nineteenth-century art criticism, on the genuine beauty of archaic art, not just its historical importance.[30] Drawing upon descriptions from Homer's epics (such as the shield of Achilles from the *Iliad*), as well as from Pausanias and the nineteenth-century explorer Heinrich Schliemann, who unearthed the Bronze Age cities of Mycenae and Troy, Pater finds the origins of Greek art, as Lene Østermark-Johansen has written, in 'a world of colored and tactile' objects.[31] The anonymous and mythical artists he discusses are less concerned with the human form than with the 'variegated' qualities that excite the Ionian tendency. Pater gives particular attention to ancient descriptions of craft, documents the importance of foreign influences, and highlights the chryselephantine technique, in which the artist layers gold and ivory over a core of carved cedar wood. The Greek god of metalwork, Hephaestus, is, in Pater's words, 'the "spiritual form" of the Asiatic element in Greek art' (129).

In the second half of 'The Beginnings of Greek Sculpture' and in 'The Marbles of Aegina', Pater documents the emergence of realistic human forms, which replace the variegated metalwork of earlier Greek art. Under the influence of the Ionian tendency, Greek art cannot capture 'the human form as the expression of human soul' (129), but that changes as the Dorian tendency comes to the fore. Pater documents the first evidence of this shift in anecdotes he records about real (not just mythical) artists, styles, and artistic schools. Butades of Sicyon invents the art of portraiture when he tries to comfort his daughter by moulding the face of her absent lover in terracotta; Canachus, creator of a much-imitated figure of Apollo, is one of the first 'personalities' in the history of sculpture (139). 'The Marbles of Aegina' is the earliest essay in the series to discuss an extant artwork. Pater here tracks the increasing realism of Greek sculpture, as it passes from archaic stiffness to the lifelike and expressive human figures in the Aegina marble group, held at the Glyptothek Museum in Munich. Crafted in white marble rather than colourful metal, the group depicts a tale from the *Iliad* that, as Pater tellingly notes, recounts 'a combat between Greeks and Asiatics' over the body of the Greek hero Patroclus (149).

Because his sculpture book was never completed, it is difficult to know how Pater would have imagined the resolution of the 'combat' between the Ionian and the Dorian tendencies in Greek art. In *Plato and Platonism*, he suggests that Plato manages to blend dialectically the influence of Heraclitus and Parmenides by way of the quasi-mythical figure Pythagoras, who embodies both motion and rest. Something similar happens in 'The Age of Athletic Prizemen', where Pater focuses on two realistic sculptures of athletes by the classical artists Myron and Polycleitus. Myron's *Discobolus* depicts an athlete in motion, throwing a discus during competition, while Polycleitus's *Diadumenus* depicts an athlete at rest, fastening a diadem to his head after victory. This pairing might suggest that the 'European' has finally subdued the 'Asiatic' influences that lay at the origins of classical art, but even as he describes the victory of the Dorian, Pater also hints at the stubborn persistence of the Ionian, which will not allow its rival to impose rest universally. As in the myth essays, Pater tells the story of Greek sculpture through manifold examples; while the essays narrate the rise of the Dorian, their variegated form epitomises the continuing attraction of the Ionian. However much the Dorian tendency tries to control it, motion refuses to be stilled, and the 'combat' at the heart of pagan culture continues to resonate even in the purportedly staid confines of Victorian Oxford.

Notes

1. See Isobel Hurst, 'Pater as a Professional Classicist', in *Pater the Classicist*, Charles Martindale, Stefano Evangelista, and Elizabeth Prettejohn, eds. (Oxford: Oxford University Press, 2017), 33–46.
2. See Christopher Stray, *Classics Transformed: Schools, Universities, and Society in England, 1830–1960* (Oxford: Oxford University Press, 1998). See also William F. Shuter, 'Pater, Wilde, Douglas and the Impact of "Greats"', *English Literature in Transition*, 46.3 (2003): 250–278.
3. Frank Turner, *The Greek Heritage in Victorian Britain* (New Haven, CT: Yale University Press, 1981).
4. Matthew Arnold, *The Complete Prose Works of Matthew Arnold*, ed. R. H. Super, 11 vols. (Ann Arbor, MI: University of Michigan Press, 1960–77), 5: 99.
5. See Katherine Harloe, *Winckelmann and the Invention of Antiquity* (Oxford: Oxford University Press, 2013).
6. See Stefano Evangelista, '"Outward Nature and the Moods of Men": Romantic Mythology in Pater's Essays on Dionysus and Demeter', in *Walter Pater: Transparencies of Desire*, Laurel Brake, Lesley Higgins, and Carolyn Williams, eds. (Greensboro, NC: ELT Press, 2002), 107–118.
7. Shawn Malley, 'Disturbing Hellenism: Walter Pater, Charles Newton, and the Myth of Demeter and Persephone', in Brake, ed., *Walter Pater: Transparencies of Desire*, 92.
8. Walter Pater, *The Renaissance: Studies in Art and Poetry*, ed. Hilary Fraser (Oxford: Oxford University Press, 2025), 191.
9. Stefano Evangelista, *British Aestheticism and Ancient Greece* (Basingstoke: Palgrave Macmillan, 2009), 35.
10. Linda Dowling, *Hellenism and Homosexuality in Victorian Oxford* (Ithaca, NY: Cornell University Press, 1994).
11. Linda Dowling, 'Ruskin's Pied Beauty and the Constitution of a "Homosexual" Code', *Victorian Newsletter*, 75 (1989): 1–8.
12. Yopie Prins, 'Greek Maenads, Victorian Spinsters', in *Victorian Sexual Dissidence*, Richard Dellamora, ed. (Chicago: University of Chicago Press, 1999), 43–81.
13. See Tracy Olverson, *Women Writers and the Dark Side of Late-Victorian Hellenism* (Basingstoke: Palgrave Macmillan, 2010).
14. Patrick Bridgwater, *Nietzsche in Anglosaxony* (Leicester: Leicester University Press, 1972), 26.
15. Friedrich Nietzsche, *The Birth of Tragedy*, trans. Ronald Speirs (Cambridge: Cambridge University Press, 1999), 24.

16. Gerald Monsman, *Pater's Portraits* (Baltimore, MD: Johns Hopkins University Press, 1967), 9.
17. Walter Pater, *Classical Studies*, ed. Matthew Potolsky (Oxford: Oxford University Press, 2021), 145. Subsequent references to this edition will be cited parenthetically in the text.
18. Walter Pater, *Plato and Platonism: A Series of Lectures* (London: Macmillan, 1910), 103.
19. See Edward W. Said, *Orientalism* (New York: Vintage), 1994.
20. See Grace Lavery, *Quaint, Exquisite: Victorian Aesthetics and the Idea of Japan* (Princeton: Princeton University Press, 2019).
21. William F. Shuter, *Rereading Walter Pater* (Cambridge: Cambridge University Press, 1997), 2.
22. Pater, *Plato and Platonism*, 104.
23. On the cancelled book, see Laurel Brake, *Print in Transition, 1850–1910* (Basingstoke: Palgrave Macmillan, 2001), 213–24.
24. David DeLaura, *Hebrew and Hellene in Victorian England* (Austin, TX: University of Texas Press, 1969), 245.
25. Arnold, *Complete Works*, 3: 225.
26. Malley, 'Disturbing Hellenism', 103.
27. See Steven Connor, 'Myth as Multiplicity in Walter Pater's *Greek Studies* and "Denys L'Auxerrois"', *Review of English Studies*, 34.133 (1983): 28–42.
28. Linda Dowling, 'Walter Pater and Archaeology', *Victorian Studies*. 31.2 (1988): 218.
29. G.W.F. Hegel, *Hegel's Aesthetics: Lectures on Fine Arts*, trans. T. M. Knox, 2 vols. (Oxford: Oxford University Press, 1975), 1: 433.
30. Elizabeth Prettejohn, 'Pater on Sculpture', in Martindale, ed., *Pater the Classicist*, 230.
31. Lene Østermark-Johansen, *Walter Pater and the Language of Sculpture* (London: Routledge, 2016), 215.

II

NICHOLAS SHRIMPTON

Pater among the Aesthetes

'The Renaissance frosts came, and all perished.'[1] John Ruskin, in the first volume of *The Stones of Venice*, supplied a characteristically vivid formulation of what was, in 1851, the avant-garde account of the cultural history of Western Europe. Twenty-two years later, writing as an 'aesthetic critic', Walter Pater would publish *Studies in the History of the Renaissance*. This book saw the Renaissance, not as a deadly frost but as a vital and vivifying phenomenon. In its earliest phases it had the 'freshness' of youth. It went on to put forth (like a field or a tree) 'an aftermath, a wonderful later growth', full of 'subtle and delicate sweetness'.[2] The reversal of attitude but retention of imagery seems too close to be coincidental. It is not surprising that Pater came to be seen as a key spokesman of the aesthetic movement as it turned against the Medievalist assumptions of a previous generation of artists and critics.

John Morley certainly saw him as that, when he reviewed the book in *The Fortnightly Review* in April 1873. Noting Pater's commitment to 'art for art's sake', he went on to suggest the importance of the question 'What is to give significance and worth to ... life' and of the need to find an answer to it:

> The writer of the essays before us answers it as we have seen, and there is now a numerous sect among cultivated people who accept his answer and act upon it. So far as we know, there never was seen before in this country so distinct an attempt to bring the aesthetical element closely and vividly round daily life ... Dutch farmhouses are systematically swept by brokers, that the vulgarity of ormolu may be replaced by delft, and nankin, and magic bits of oriental blue and white. There is an orthodoxy in wall-papers, and you may commit the unpardonable sin in discordant window-curtains. Members of the sect are as solicitous about the right in tables and the correct in legs of chairs, as members of another sect are careful about the cut of chasuble or dalmatica.[3]

Read carelessly, this could be taken to imply that Pater was the initiator or 'progenitor'[4] of the English aesthetic movement and, with hindsight, it is easy to find anticipations of what Morley calls 'his answer' in Pater's early essays. The insincerity of Winckelmann's conversion to Roman Catholicism was excused, in January 1867, because it was 'only one incident of a culture in which the moral instinct, like the religious or political, was lost in the artistic'[5] and, more explicitly, the review of William Morris's poems in *The Westminster Review* in October 1868 contained the declaration that 'Of this wisdom ... the love of art for art's sake, has most'.[6] But these articles were anonymous and, though some similar things were said in the four signed pieces which Pater contributed to *The Fortnightly Review* between 1869 and 1871 (most specifically the account of Leonardo's 'carelessness in the work of art of all but art itself'),[7] his commitment to aestheticism would only become conspicuous when six of the last seven paragraphs of 'Poems by William Morris' (with their reference to 'the love of art for art's sake') became the final section of the Conclusion to his *Studies in the History of the Renaissance* in February 1873.

By then, indeed, by 1867, the fashion for 'delft, and nankin, and magic bits of oriental blue and white' was, in fact, already well established. When Dante Gabriel Rossetti redecorated his rooms in Blackfriars, after his marriage to Elizabeth Siddal in 1860, he 'had the fireplace covered with real old blue glazed Dutch tiles'.[8] After his move to Cheyne Walk in October 1862, he added Oriental porcelain to his existing collection, possibly encouraged by the Japanese Court at the London International Exhibition. In the same year, in Paris, Louise and Emile Desoye opened their shop in the Rue de Rivoli ('Spécialité des objets du Japon'). When Rossetti visited it in 1864, he was pleased to hear, from Madame Desoye, about his rival James Abbott McNeill Whistler's 'consternation at my collection of china'.[9] The architect William Eden Nesfield formed his 'very jolly collection' in 1862–63.[10] His colleague J. M. Brydon described the 'blue and white Nankin china and Persian plates ... How proud he was ... and how enthusiastic over the flush of blue in his hawthorn jars'.[11] Whistler exhibited his painting *Lange Lijzen of the Six Marks* at the Royal Academy in 1864.

As for 'wall-papers' and 'the legs of chairs', the new art furniture industry was already active in the early 1860s. Morris, Marshall, Faulkner & Company, founded in April 1861, was making its ebonised 'Rossetti' chairs by 1863. It would decorate rooms in St James's Palace in 1866–67 and the Green Dining Room at the South Kensington Museum in 1867–68. Though Arthur Lazenby Liberty would not open his own shop (a key source for aesthetic interiors) until 1875, he was selling many of the same things from 1862 as manager of Farmer & Rogers's Oriental Warehouse. Charles Locke Eastlake's *Cornhill Magazine* article on 'The Fashion of Furniture', in March 1864, noted that 'An attempt has been made ... to form a new school of art furniture',[12] and by 1866 Ruskin could observe, in *The Art Journal*, that 'The introduction of furniture of Art ... is now taking place rapidly'.[13] Eclectic, rather than exclusively medieval (as 'Reformed Gothic', the avant-garde fashion of the previous two decades, had been), aesthetic décor established itself in the 1860s as the domestic manifestation of advanced ideas in art and life.

Accustomed though we are to think of Pater's *Renaissance* as 'a manifesto for aestheticism',[14] in other words, it was not a manifesto in the usual sense of a prospectus or foundational document. Rather, it appeared more than a decade after aestheticism had begun to establish itself in Britain as a mode of artistic, literary, decorative, and critical practice. John Morley did, in fact, acknowledge this lack of priority later in his review, though the point was made more cogently in *The Saturday Review*, whose reviewer observed,

> Since the days of the purists, when Mr Ruskin denounced the Renaissance as hollow and unholy, a singular change has come over the younger generation ... Poetry, painting, and criticism alike – the poetry and pictures of Mr Rossetti, the poetry of Mr Swinburne ... the paintings of Mr Burne Jones, together with divers critical writings such as the work now before us – all tell of a modern renaissance of the old Renaissance ... aspiring through the ministration of the arts to conditions of high mental enjoyment and pure aesthetic culture.[15]

Even in the 1860s the concept was not new. The idea of art for art's sake had emerged in eighteenth-century Germany. Gotthold Ephraim Lessing in his *Laocoön*, in 1766, argued that the term 'works of art' should not be used of statues betraying 'marked traces of aptitude for devotional purposes' because 'in these the Art has not laboured for its own sake, but merely as an aid to religion'[16] and the idea was implicitly encouraged by Immanuel Kant's division of his philosophical system into three distinct sections. The *Critique of Pure Reason* (on logic and epistemology, or truth) was published in 1781, the *Critique of Practical Reason* (on ethics, or the good) in 1788, and the *Critique of Judgement* (on aesthetics, or taste and beauty) in 1790. This sense that beauty could be considered independently, without reference to issues of truth or moral goodness, became, by the end of the century, a disturbing but also exciting belief. Friedrich Schlegel, in his essay 'On the Limits of the Beautiful' in 1794, referred (disapprovingly) to the person who 'lives only for the beautiful, unheeding of the good and true'.[17] Benjamin Constant, in a diary entry for 10 February 1804, recorded a meeting with Henry Crabb Robinson, then studying in Jena with Schelling but invited to Weimar to explain the new German philosophy to Madame de Staël. During their conversation, Robinson introduced him to the theory of '*l'art pour l'art sans but, car tout but dénature l'art*' ['art for art without purpose, for all purpose spoils art'].[18] Madame de Staël, in turn, would insist in *De l'Allemagne* (1813) that 'In separating the beautiful from the useful, Kant clearly proves that it is not in the nature of the fine arts to give lessons'.[19] By 1817 Leigh Hunt could review John Keats's *Poems* as 'poetry for its' own sake' and S. T. Coleridge suggest, in his *Biographia Literaria*, that poetry proposed 'for its *immediate* object pleasure, not truth'.[20]

Pater himself was well aware of the early history of aestheticism, writing in his essay 'Charles Lamb' (1878) that Lamb was a 'disinterested' writer who, 'In the making of prose ... realises the principle of art for art's sake, as completely as John Keats in the making of verse'.[21] But the traditional view, summed up in Horace's famous statement that a good poet *'miscuit utile dulci'* – 'mixed the useful' (or morally instructive) 'with the sweet' (*Ars Poetica* 343) – did not disappear. Instead, for the next forty years, the concept of art for art's sake made significant but occasional appearances as a controversial opinion about which writers often changed their mind. Thomas Carlyle gave an enthusiastic account of the new idea in his 'State of German Literature' essay in the *Edinburgh* in 1827: 'Art is to be loved, not because of its effects, but because of itself; not because it is useful for spiritual pleasure, or even for moral culture, but because it is Art.'[22] Fourteen years later, however, when he restated it in *Heroes and Hero Worship*, he accompanied it with a careful discrimination between true and false beauty. Thomas De Quincey moved in the opposite direction. Having satirised the idea as early as 1827 in his *Blackwood's Magazine* article, 'On Murder Considered as One of the Fine Arts', he would treat it with increasing sympathy in the additions made to that essay in 1839 and 1854.

Unqualified assertions of the concept, in the second quarter of the nineteenth century, were more frequent in France and America. Victor Cousin, back from a visit to Germany during which he had met Schelling and Hegel and keen to introduce his Sorbonne audiences to the new German philosophy, had outlined the theory of *'l'art pour l'art'* in a lecture in 1818. It was soon restated by a new generation of French writers: Victor Hugo in the preface to *Les Orientales* (1829), and Theophile Gautier in his prefaces to *Albertus* (1832) and *Mademoiselle de Maupin* (1835). A decade later, in America, Edgar Allan Poe recommended the idea in 'The Philosophy of Composition' (1846) and 'The Poetic Principle' (1850), though his great phrase 'the heresy of the Didactic' would not achieve its full effect until it was translated (as *'l'hérésie de l'enseignement'*) in Charles Baudelaire's 'Notes nouvelles sur Edgar Poe' in 1857.

Meanwhile, in Great Britain, reviewers were wrestling with the problem of impropriety in the novel, especially in the cases of Edward Bulwer-Lytton and Honoré de Balzac. G. H. Lewes bravely insisted, in the *Foreign Quarterly*

Review in July 1844, that Balzac's artistic merits were 'great enough and rare enough to outweigh his faults'.[23] Bulwer-Lytton defended his controversial novel *Night and Morning* in 1845 by arguing that 'Moral Design ... should be excluded from the aims of the Poet ... his Art should regard only the Beautiful'.[24] The traditional view that good art must be morally good did not, however, die out – on the contrary, it remained (and remains) the orthodoxy. In the second volume of *Modern Painters* (1846) Ruskin set out his 'Theoretic' alternative to the 'Aesthetic' view of art:

> ... the Theoretic faculty, is concerned with the moral perception and appreciation of ideas of beauty. And the error respecting it is the considering and calling it Aesthetic, degrading it to a mere operation of sense ...[25]

Eleven years later Charles Kingsley would caricature aestheticism in the figure of the Keatsian poet Elsley Vavasour in his novel *Two Years Ago*: 'I think he is rather hard on that unlucky poet' was Swinburne's comment.[26] The issue is encapsulated very neatly by Ruskin's response to the two outstanding paintings in the Royal Academy exhibition of 1855. Frederic Leighton's *Cimabue's Madonna Carried in Procession through the Streets of Florence* (a depiction of the public celebration of a work of art) was 'a very important and very beautiful picture'. But it was not the best exhibit. 'The only *great* picture exhibited this year' was John Everett Millais's *The Rescue* (a fireman saving children from a burning building, painted during the campaign to turn the fire brigade from a business run by insurance companies into a universally available public service). Ruskin noted that 'The execution of the picture is ... in some respects imperfect'. Unlike Leighton's painting, however, it was '*very* great' and had 'The immortal element ... in it', clearly for reasons of content.[27] It was great art because it was (in modern terminology) morally and politically correct.

Not until the late 1850s did aestheticism achieve the self-confidence and critical mass which can turn an idea into a movement. Pater would identify William Morris's *The Defence of Guenevere* volume, published in February 1858, as 'the first typical specimen of aesthetic poetry'.[28] Morris had revised the poems collected in that volume during the painting of the Oxford Union murals in 1857 and it was probably the gathering of artists and writers, first in Oxford and then at the Hogarth Club (1858–61) in London, that gave birth to what can be identified as an aesthetic movement. William Michael Rossetti argued in *The Saturday Review*, in May 1858, that 'the essentially artistic quality is the delight in a thing as an *object of sight*'.[29] Dante Gabriel Rossetti began painting *Bocca Baciata* in 1859 and showed it (at the Hogarth) in February 1860. Algernon Charles Swinburne's long poem *Rosamund*, with its similar celebration of a kissed mouth as the symbol of beauty, was begun in February 1858 and published in December 1860. His review of Baudelaire's *Les Fleurs du mal*, in *The Spectator* on 6 September 1862, argued that critics had 'pretty well forgotten that a poet's business is ... to write good verses, and by no means to redeem the age and remould society'.[30] Whistler's *The White Girl* had been shown at the Berners Street Gallery earlier that year. The year 1863 saw the publication of Gilchrist's *Life of Blake* (with its defence of Thomas Griffiths Wainwright on the grounds that 'art has its own truth ... not to be appealed against on any grounds of good deeds')[31] and the appearance of Leighton's *A Girl with a Basket of Fruit (Eucharis)* and *A Girl Feeding Peacocks*. William Michael Rossetti described those two paintings, in his *Fraser's Magazine* review, as 'the art of luxurious exquisiteness; beauty for beauty's sake; colour, light, form, choice details, for their own sake, or for beauty's', and by 1867 Sidney Colvin would be able to identify nine contemporary English painters whose aim 'seems to be pre-eminently beauty', insisting that 'perfection of form and colours – beauty in a word – should be the prime object of pictorial art'.[32] The year 1864 brought Whistler's *Lange Lijzen*, Simeon Solomon's *Sappho and Erinna at Mytelene*, and Edward Burne-Jones's *Green Summer*. The year 1865 saw Rossetti's *The Blue Bower*, George Frederic Watts's *Study with the Peacock's Feathers*, Solomon's *'Habet!'*, Leighton's *Mother and Child (Cherries)*, Albert Moore's *The Marble Seat*, and Whistler's *Little White Girl* (with Swinburne's poem 'Before the Mirror' to accompany it). On 6 November 1865 Gerard Manley Hopkins noted in his journal that, 'On this day by God's grace I resolved to give up all beauty until I had His leave for it'.[33] As if to confirm the wisdom of that pious decision, Swinburne published his *Poems and Ballads* just eight months later, in July 1866, and was promptly condemned as 'the libidinous laureate of a pack of satyrs'.[34]

By the mid-1860s, in other words, the aesthetic movement was a vigorous and versatile phenomenon, conspicuously active in poetry, painting, and criticism, as well as the decorative arts. Pater would begin to support it (at first anonymously) in 1867 and only be widely associated with it after the publication of *Studies in the History of the Renaissance* in 1873. What contribution to this flourishing mode of art and thought did his work make? One possible answer is suggested by David DeLaura's claim that 'Aestheticism ... found an adequate rhetoric only in Pater'.[35] Pater's style, that is, made the concept comprehensible and arresting in ways which previous writers had not. This is possible, though hard to demonstrate. One might, perhaps, at least allow that Pater's manner comes closer to 'prose style for prose style's sake' than anything to be found in the writing of his predecessors. As such, it could be said to enact its topic, where they had merely stated it.

More tangibly, it can be argued that Pater gave philosophical depth and seriousness to aestheticism, turning what had previously been a scattered body of critical and artistic opinion into a coherent doctrine. Pater was, of course, a professional philosopher. Kate Hext has called him 'the philosophical centre of aestheticism'[36] and the title page of *Studies in the History of the Renaissance* stressed his academic credentials: 'Fellow of Brasenose College, Oxford'. The problem here is that Pater's theoretical contributions to the aesthetic movement, though real, were necessarily partial. Other philosophers had been there before him. The idea had developed in the work of Baumgarten, Lessing, Schiller, and Schelling. Victor Cousin had disseminated it while teaching philosophy at the Sorbonne. Coleridge and Carlyle may not have been academics but were, like Gautier and Baudelaire in France, closely engaged with the new thought of their era. Swinburne went down from Oxford without a degree. In *Poems and Ballads*, however, he demonstrated that beautiful texts could be written about ugly or wicked topics and, in *William Blake. A Critical Essay* (1868), provided a lucid account of the theory behind such practice:

> Art is not like fire or water, a good servant and a bad master; rather the reverse ... Handmaid of religion, exponent of duty, servant of fact, pioneer of morality, she cannot in any way become ... Her business is not to do good on other grounds, but to be good on her own ... Art for art's sake first of all ... The one fact for her which is worth taking account of is simply mere excellence of verse or colour ...[37]

Swinburne returned to the subject in 1872 to distinguish his view from the negative sense of art for art's sake. A work of art does not have to have a morally good topic in order to be a good work of art and is not made better by a better one: 'the praise of a Caesar as sung by Virgil, of a Stuart as sung by Dryden, is preferable to the most magnanimous invective against tyranny which love of country and of liberty could wring from a Bavius or a Shadwell.' This does not, however, mean that good works of art *cannot* have good topics. The point is simply that the merits, or otherwise, of the topic are irrelevant to the judgement of a work of art:

> In a word, the doctrine of art for art is true in the positive sense, false in the negative ... the only absolute duty of art is the duty she owes to herself ... But while we refuse to any artist ... the licence to infringe in the least article the letter of this law ... we do not refuse to him the liberty of bringing within the range of it any subject that ... may be ... included within his proper scope of work.[38]

What could Pater add to this? Germain D'Hangest, in 1974, argued that '*Pater ne puisse avoir dans ce movement aucune originalité propre*' ['Pater could not have, in this movement, any true originality'].[39] Pater was certainly a philosopher. But many of his most interesting ideas were only incidentally or indirectly linked to art for art's sake: his subtle defence of Epicurean ethics in his philosophical novel *Marius the Epicurean*, for example. It might, in practice, be easier to be an aesthete if you are an Epicurean. It is not, however, obligatory.

Where, then, did Pater directly contribute to the conceptual schema of the aesthetic movement? D'Hangest suggested that, despite his lack of '*originalité propre*', he gave 'definite outline to a philosophy which was examining itself without yet arriving at an understanding'.[40] Like DeLaura's claim that Pater gave the Movement its first adequate 'rhetoric', I think that this, though not untrue, is, nonetheless, an overstatement. Rather than defining Aestheticism, Pater augmented it – filled gaps, supplied contexts, provided clarifications – in order to create his own, deeply considered but in some respects rather idiosyncratic, version of it. The key texts are, of course, the Preface and Conclusion of *Studies in the History of the Renaissance*. In the Preface he argues that beauty should be defined 'not in the most abstract, but in the most concrete terms possible' and suggests that 'the first step' towards Matthew Arnold's criterion of seeing 'the object as in itself it really is' would be 'to know one's own impression as it really is'.[41] This is Pater, the philosopher, first insisting on the necessary limits of philosophy, and then applying a version of Hume's argument that beauty is not a 'quality in things themselves' but an experience 'in the mind which contemplates them'.[42] It is reassuring for an aesthete to know that it is not necessary to have an abstract definition of beauty. It might also be comforting to have an understanding of it which would not fall foul of Humeian scepticism. But many aesthetes, both before and after 1873, functioned without such views and neither proposition is indispensable to the creed. These are sophisticated embellishments of aestheticism, rather than its core doctrine.

Pater addresses art for art's sake more directly in the Conclusion, reminding us that life is short and that 'the wisest' seek to get 'as many pulsations as possible into the given time'. Of that wisdom, he insists, 'the desire of beauty, the love of art for art's sake has most'. Though it is possible to rephrase this in more elaborately theoretical terms (for Dianne Sachko Macleod, 'It was Walter Pater who developed aestheticism into a reception theory based on individual gratification'[43]), the proposition is not, in itself, an original one. Swinburne told Dante Gabriel Rossetti, in October 1869, that, 'art ... is to me the highest, deepest, most precious and serious pleasure to be got out of life'[44] and Friedrich Schlegel had identified the person who 'lives only for the beautiful, unheeding of the good and true' as early as 1794. What is new about Pater's formulation is the way in which he justifies this choice. Ingeniously combining ancient philosophy (Heraclitus and Aristippus of Cyrene) with modern science (Thomas Huxley and Herbert Spencer), he presents human experience as a series of ephemeral 'impressions ... in perpetual flight'. In these circumstances, 'While all melts under our feet', we might indeed turn to 'the love of art for art's sake' to give significance to our momentary sensations.[45] This is a striking context for, or recommendation of, aestheticism. It is not a fresh account of the theory as such.

Pater's most celebrated contribution to the conceptual apparatus of the aesthetic movement, his assertion in 'The School of Giorgione' (1877) that *'All art constantly aspires towards the condition of music'*,[46] is, once again, a matter of emphasis rather than invention. Though Kenneth Clark called this 'a revolutionary doctrine',[47] a privileging of form over content had always been implicit in the idea of art for art's sake. When Swinburne advocated 'mere excellence of verse or colour' and insisted that the admirable political views of Bavius and Shadwell did not make their poetry good, he had been saying something very similar. But Swinburne's focus was, characteristically, on the topic of content – on the fact that art for art's sake legitimises ugly or immoral material, thus releasing art from a 'scope of sight ... bounded by the nursery walls'.[48] Pater's stress is on the other half of the equation – on the form which, in art, makes issues of content thus unimportant. He knows, of course, that for literature and figurative painting pure form is merely an aspiration and meticulously says so ('aspires'). The contentless, form-for-form's-sake quality of music remains, nonetheless, the ideal of art in an Aesthetic understanding. If not an entirely new idea, it was at least one which Pater made very much his own.

Pater's neighbour Mary Arnold said that he had Morris wallpaper in his Oxford house and he would be caricatured as the aesthete Mr Rose in W. H. Mallock's *The New Republic* (1876). Despite this, he seems to have had rather limited contact with his aesthetic contemporaries and wrote very little about them. The review of William Morris's poems was reused, partly in *The Renaissance* and partly as the essay 'Aesthetic Poetry' in the first edition (only) of *Appreciations* (1889), at which point the description of *The Defence of Guenevere* as 'the first typical specimen of aesthetic poetry' was (briefly) inserted. He contributed an essay on Dante Gabriel Rossetti's poetry to the second edition of T. H. Ward's anthology *The English Poets* in 1883. He referred to a Rossetti sonnet in 'The School of Giorgione' and suggested that his 'painted work often comes to mind as one ponders over these precious things', though the footnote identifying Rossetti would not be added until the essay reappeared in the third edition of *The Renaissance*

(1888). He praised Burne-Jones's painting *Day* in 'The Myth of Demeter and Persephone' and Solomon's *Bacchus* in 'A Study of Dionysius', in both cases without naming the painter. In 'The School of Giorgione' the etching used to show how 'the mere matter of a picture' is 'nothing without the form'[49] was by Alphonse Legros, an artist personally close to Whistler and Rossetti but, in practice, a realist of the school of Courbet. In 1891 he would review Wilde's *The Picture of Dorian Gray* in *The Bookman*. By 1891, however, he was writing in the era of decadence, rather than aestheticism, and had himself had retreated from his art-for-art's-sake stance in his 'Style' essay (1888), where 'great art' is distinguished from merely 'good art' by the superior moral dignity of its 'matter' or 'interests'.[50]

Why then did Pater come to be seen as so significant a representative of the aesthetic movement? One answer is a simple matter of timing. *Studies in the History of the Renaissance* was published in February 1873 in the later stages of the 'Fleshly School' controversy. Robert Buchanan's review of Rossetti's *Poems* (1870), 'The Fleshly School of Poetry; Mr D. G. Rossetti', appeared in *The Contemporary Review* in October 1871. It provoked the print equivalent of a Twitterstorm, including Rossetti's 'The Stealthy School of Criticism' (December 1871), Buchanan's enlargement of his insulting review into a book (May 1872), Swinburne's savage pamphlet *Under the Microscope* (1872), and the review (almost certainly by Buchanan himself) of Buchanan's book in *The Echo* in which Swinburne and Rossetti were mocked as 'aestheticised simulacra of humanity'.[51] In this tempestuous atmosphere, the appearance of a serene and serious restatement of the principles of the aesthetic movement would have seemed particularly valuable.

As well as restating the principles of aestheticism, Pater demonstrated its practice. While avoiding, for the most part, contemporary material, he wrote distinctively aesthetic criticism of writers and painters of previous eras. In the 'On Wordsworth' essay of 1874, for example, he acutely distinguished 'the real aesthetic value' of the work 'hidden away in part under those weaker elements in Wordsworth's poetry', which made him 'at times a declaimer on moral and social topics'.[52] In *Plato and Platonism*, more radically if less convincingly, he would split Plato from Socrates, attributing the logical and moral rigour of the texts to the latter, and presenting (or constructing) Plato as an aesthete who 'anticipates the modern notion that art as such has no end but its own perfection, – "art for art's sake"'.[53]

More fundamentally, Pater provided a philosophical basis for some key assumptions of the aesthetic movement, spontaneously practised but not previously explained. To a greater extent than most artistic movements, aestheticism prompted a distinctive choice of personal and domestic décor. Pater provided a rationale for this belief that furniture and fashion could be more than a matter of utility or a display of wealth and social status by linking it, in 'The School of Giorgione', to Kant's concept of an end in itself (rather than a means to an end) from the *Groundwork of the Metaphysics of Morals* of 1785:

> [...] the ideal types of poetry are those in which this distinction [between matter and form] is reduced to its minimum ... And this principle holds good of all things that partake in any degree of artistic qualities, of the furniture of our houses and of dress, for instance ... these also, for the wise, being susceptible of a suavity and charm caught from the way in which they are done, which gives them a value in themselves ... which elevates the trivialities of speech, and manner, and dress, into an end in themselves.[54]

George du Maurier's Mrs Cimabue Brown, with her house full of blue and white china, peacock feathers, and Art Furniture, is, in fact, a Kantian.

Still more significantly, Pater provided a theoretical model for the eclecticism which was so marked a characteristic of aesthetic movement art and design. In the 1850s Gothic Revival and Neo-Classical architecture had been stark alternatives, a disagreement conspicuously demonstrated by the 'Battle of the Styles' over the design of the new Foreign Office. Aesthetic movement architects and designers broke this pattern of irreconcilable extremes by blending the Gothic and the Classical into an eclectic mixture. Aesthetic movement writers produced a literary equivalent of this irenical conjunction and Pater the critic was quick to spot it. William Morris, in *The Life and Death of Jason*, was, he noted in 1868, practising 'the Hellenism of Chaucer'.[55] Five years later, Pater himself performed this act of cultural amalgamation in the argument and design of *Studies in the History of the Renaissance*. Ruskin had seen the Renaissance as a malign force which, in the years after 1420, had destroyed a vital medieval culture. Pater could simply have turned the tables and celebrated 'the revival of classical antiquity in the fifteenth century'[56] as a good thing. He didn't. Instead, he dissolved or deconstructed the customary distinction between the Middle Ages and the Renaissance, suggesting instead a new conception of the latter as a state of heart and mind which can be found as readily in French prose fiction of the early thirteenth century as in the work of Leonardo da Vinci. Not appreciating the significance of this shift, critics attacked the book as 'unhistorical' – so much so that Pater changed the title in 1877 to remove the reference to history. It remained, nonetheless, in successive editions, an embodiment of aesthetic eclecticism as the movement passed, from it peak in the 1870s, to popularisation, ridicule, and eventual decline in the so-called 'Aesthetic 80s'. By the time of the third edition in 1888, when the Conclusion was restored and 'The School of Giorgione' added, the book was perhaps best seen as an epilogue to, or apologia for, the aesthetic movement. It is, as such, a significant part of that movement's achievement.

Notes

1. John Ruskin, *The Stones of Venice*, 3 vols (London: Smith, Elder, 1851–3), 1: 225.
2. Walter Pater, *Studies in the History of the Renaissance*, ed. Matthew Beaumont (Oxford: Oxford World's Classics, 2010), 3–5.
3. [John Morley], 'Mr Pater's Essays', *Fortnightly Review*, 19 (April 1873): 475.
4. Samuel Wright, *A Bibliography of the Writings of Walter H. Pater* (New York: Garland, 1975), 168.
5. [Walter Pater], 'Winckelmann', *Westminster Review*, 31, no. 1 (January 1867): 85.
6. [Walter Pater], 'Poems by William Morris', *Westminster Review*, 34, no. 2 (October 1868): 312.
7. [Walter Pater], 'Notes on Leonardo da Vinci', *Fortnightly Review*, 6, no. 35 (November 1869): 503.
8. Dante Gabriel Rossetti, letter to C. E. Norton, 9 January 1862, *Letters of Dante Gabriel Rossetti*, Oswald Doughty and John Robert Wahl, eds. (Oxford: Oxford University Press, 1965), 2. 435.
9. Dante Gabriel Rossetti letter to Mrs Gabriele Rossetti, 12 November 1864, *Letters of Dante Gabriel Rossetti*, 2: 527.
10. Simeon Solomon letter to Algernon Charles Swinburne, [date unknown] 1863, *The Swinburne Letters*, ed. Cecil Y. Lang, 6 vols (Oxford: Oxford University Press, 1959), 2.33 (where conjecturally dated 1869; re-dated to 1863 by Gayle Marie Seymour).
11. J. M. Brydon, 'William Eden Nesfield', *The Architectural Review* (1 April 1897): 238.
12. Charles Locke Eastlake, 'The Fashion of Furniture', *The Cornhill Magazine* 9 (March 1864): 340, 349.
13. 'The Cestus of Aglaia', *The Art-Journal* 28 (February 1866): 34.
14. Matthew Beaumont, 'Introduction', in *Studies in the History of the Renaissance*, Matthew Beaumont, ed. (Oxford: Oxford World's Classics, 2010), p. x.
15. [Unsigned], *Saturday Review*, 36 (26 July 1873), 123.
16. Gotthold Ephraim Lessing, *Laocoön*, transl. Robert Phillimore (1874) (London: Routledge, n.d), 107–108.
17. Frederick von Schlegel, *The Aesthetic & Miscellaneous Works of Frederick von Schlegel*, transl. E. J. Millington (London: Henry G. Bohn, 1849), 415.
18. Benjamin Constant, *Journal Intime de Benjamin Constant*, ed. D. Melegari (Paris: Ollendorff, 1895), 7.
19. Baroness Staël Holstein, *Germany*, translator unknown, 3 vols. (London: John Murray, 1814) 3. 138.
20. Leigh Hunt, *The Examiner*, 497 (6 July 1817), 428; Samuel Taylor Coleridge, *Biographia Literaria*, ed. Adam Roberts (Edinburgh: Edinburgh University Press, 2014), 211.

21. Walter Pater, 'The Character of the Humourist. Charles Lamb', *Fortnightly Review*, 24 (October 1878): 468.

22. Thomas Carlyle, 'State of German Literature', *Edinburgh Review*, 46 (October 1827): 327–328.

23. G.H. Lewes, 'Balzac and George Sand', *Foreign Quarterly Review*, 32 (July 1844): 160.

24. Published 1841, preface added 1845, here quoted from Sir Edward Bulwer Lytton, *Night and Morning* (London: Chapman & Hall, 1851), vii.

25. John Ruskin, *Modern Painters* (London: Smith, Elder, 1846) 2: 9.

26. Algernon Charles Swinburne, letter to John Nichol, 11 February [1857], *The Swinburne Letters*, ed. Cecil Y. Lang 6 vols (Oxford: Oxford University Press, 1959), 1.10.

27. *Academy Notes*, here quoted from *The Works of John Ruskin*, ed. Edward Tyas Cook and Alexander Wedderburn (London: Allen Lane, 1903–12), 14.26 and 22–23.

28. Walter Pater, 'Aesthetic Poetry', in *Appreciations* (London: Macmillan, 1889), 215.

29. 'The Fine Art of 1858 – Oil Pictures', *Saturday Review*, 5 (15 May 1858), 500.

30. 'Charles Baudelaire: Les Fleurs du mal', *The Spectator* (6 September 1862), 998.

31. Alexander Gilchrist, *Life of William Blake* 2 vols (London: Macmillan, 1863), 1: 281.

32. W. M. Rossetti, 'The Royal Academy Exhibition', *Fraser's Magazine*, 67 (June 1863): 790; Sidney Colvin, 'English Painters and Painting in 1867', *Fortnightly Review*, 2 (October 1867): 473, 465.

33. Gerard Manley Hopkins, *Diaries, Journals, and Notebooks* in *Collected Works of Gerard Manley Hopkins*, Lesley Higgins, ed. 7 vols (Oxford: Oxford University Press, 2015), 3: 335.

34. [Unsigned] 'Mr Swinburne's New Poems', *Saturday Review*, 22 (4 August 1866): 147.

35. David J. DeLaura, *Hebrew and Hellene in Victorian England* (Austin, TX: University of Texas Press, 1969), 230.

36. Kate Hext, *Walter Pater: Individualism and Aesthetic Philosophy* (Edinburgh: Edinburgh University Press, 2013), 1.

37. Algernon Charles Swinburne, *William Blake. A Critical Essay* (London: Hotten, 1868), 90–92.

38. Algernon Charles Swinburne, 'Victor Hugo: L'Année terrible', *Fortnightly Review* 69 (September 1872): 258; 'Settle' was substituted for 'Shadwell' in *Essays and Studies* (1875).

39. G. D'Hangest, 'La Place de Walter Pater dans le movement esthétique', *Études anglaises*, 27 (1974): 160.

40. D'Hangest, 'La Place', 160: ' … donné un corps et un contour définis à une philosophie qui se chercait sans parvenir encore à s'appréhender elle-même'.

41. Pater, *The Renaissance*, (ed. Beaumont, 2010) 3.

42. 'Beauty is no quality in things themselves: it exists merely in the mind which contemplates them', David Hume, 'Of the Standard of Taste', in *Four Dissertations* (London: A. Millar, 1757), 208–209.

43. Dianne Sachko Macleod, *Art and the Victorian Middle Class: Money and the Making of Cultural Identity* (Cambridge: Cambridge University Press, 1996), 272.
44. Swinburne, letter to D. G. Rossetti, October 28 [1869], *Swinburne Letters*, 2.47.
45. Pater, *The Renaissance* (ed. Beaumont, 2010), 119–120.
46. Walter Pater, 'The School of Giorgione', *Fortnightly Review*, 22 (October 1877): 528.
47. Kenneth Clark, *The Renaissance*, ed. Kenneth Clark (London: Collins, 1961), 22.
48. Swinburne, letter in defence of Meredith's *Modern Love*, *Spectator* (7 June 1862), *Swinburne Letters*, 1.52.
49. Pater, 'The School of Giorgione', *Fortnightly Review* 22 (October 1877): 528.
50. Water Pater, 'Style', *Fortnightly Review*, 44 (December 1888): 743.
51. 'Fleshing the Fleshly', *The Echo*, London, 18 May 1872, here quoted from Christopher D. Murray, 'The Fleshly School Revisited', *Bulletin of the John Rylands Library*, 65 (Spring 1983): 205.
52. Walter Pater, 'On Wordsworth', *Fortnightly Review*, 15 (April 1874): 455.
53. Walter Pater, *Plato and Platonism* (London: Macmillan, 1922), 268.
54. Pater, 'The School of Giorgione', *Fortnightly Review* 22 (October 1877): 529–530.
55. Pater, 'Poems by William Morris', 5.
56. Pater, *The Renaissance* ed. (Beaumont, 2010): 5.

12

KATE HEXT

Pater among the Decadents

Walter Pater's relationship with the so-called 'decadent movement' is vexed. It always has been. There is no doubt that he is a lynch pin between French and British decadent writers in the late nineteenth century. Without him, the decadent movement in England would look very different: he was its chief theorist; one of its great, albeit reluctant, poster children; and the thinker who proposed 'decadence' as a response to or a symptom of modernity. Decadence – or, more precisely, the notion or possibility of decadent writing – defined Pater's thinking and through him it shaped this vibrant alternative current in British culture.

Can we say that Pater was a decadent writer? No, or not in any straightforward sense. He influenced decadent writers including Arthur Symons, Lionel Johnson, and Oscar Wilde, and in the early 1890s he was celebrated by them and others as the epitome of decadence. He resisted though the decadence label and all that it connoted, ever careful of the misunderstandings that come with such totalising terms. Such resistance was futile and in modern criticism disassociating Pater from self-avowed decadent writers in England 'has been the crux of serious attention to his writings'. For, reading across from decadence to selected moments of Pater's writings is frequently to blame for what Lional Johnson described as a 'certain misconstruction of [Pater's] "philosophy"'.[1]

Yet, Pater cannot be fully understood without an account of the decadent writers he influenced and the spirit of decadence that he himself entertained. Understood properly, decadence is not a thing or a collection of writers and artists: it is a perilous possibility and conceived thus Pater is its most careful thinker. Addressing his ambivalent, dynamic place in (and outside) the decadent movement we see that he was a reluctant decadent writer, one whose alleged decadence leaves him with an unresolvable moral dilemma.

The Origins of Decadence

When we think about Pater and the decadents, the first problem is 'decadence' and the second is the 'decadents'. Decadence was a serious aesthetic position but a notoriously slippery term and one prone to pastiche. At its zenith – or nadir, depending on one's perspective – in 1890s' London, decadence was less a movement than a motley crew of adherents with notable guest appearances from others who vaguely illustrated its fashionable styles and motifs.

It is this reputation rather than anything inherent in the concept of decadence *per se* that caused Pater and his sympathetic critics to shy away. He often thought of himself, as Nicholas Shrimpton writes in this volume's previous chapter, as 'the key spokesman of the aesthetic movement' and he is much more at home himself among the artists and writers of this earlier English movement, which put 'art for art's sake' at the centre of artistic, literary, decorative, and critical practices. It is the way Pater brings 'art for art's sake' together with a radical ethical position on what it is to be human under the conditions of modernity that brings us – and him – to decadence.

At the outset we have to draw three distinctions: between decadence as a social and cultural phenomenon, decadent writing, and the decadent movement. These are subtly but significantly different categories. When they are bundled in with each other, as they invariably are, the result is reductive and causes confusion. Various critics, since the mid-nineteenth century, have tried to pin decadence down to a single defining feature. All told, though, decadence is a multifaceted zeitgeist that comprises a nexus of features, given different emphasis depending on the author, cultural and period being termed *decadent*. The following features, identified by nineteenth-century writers and subsequent critics, are essential: an acute awareness of the body's decay, and that of ephemeral nature of all around us, set within the view that civilisation is in a state of moral and spiritual decline. Such moral decline is illustrated by the culture's preoccupation with sensual indulgences and excesses, which take the place of constructive action or moral considerations.

The first example of a decadent period is the final decades of the Roman Empire. Following the reign of Marcus Aurelius, around 180AD, a series of despotic emperors presided over the empire's waning military strength, political ineffectiveness, increasingly poor physical health among its subjects, precipitating its fall. When the French and British Empires seemed to be in a state of inexorable entropy in the late nineteenth century, writers and artists looked to Rome as the model by which to understand the decline of once-great empires. For example, Thomas Couture's painting *The Romans in their*

Decadence (1847) depicts a torpid, luxuriant, and debauched assortment of intoxicated people in a drunken orgy, beneath heroic statuary from Rome's earlier glories. Exhibited at the Paris Salon of 1847, the painting was a damning comment on the liberal monarchy in France, which was to be overthrown in the 1848 Revolution.

Writers in France also looked back to ancient Rome to find a precedent for their own end-of-days sensibility. Unlike Couture's painting though, their depictions of its decadence were amoral and politically disinterested: they embraced the precarious personal freedoms afforded by a degenerate empire, writing of intoxication and sexual pleasures in the shadows of decline. French decadent poetry and fiction self-consciously articulated decadence as a cultural experience, a moral position, and a personal feeling. Its writers were punks and misfits – including Théophile Gautier, Stéphane Mallarmé, Joris-Karl Huysmans, and Paul Verlaine – who sought to create self-consciously modern styles of writing that could capture this new, or renewed, sensibility. Charles Baudelaire's *The Flowers of Evil* (*Les fleurs du mal*, 1857; 1861) may be the ultimate example as a collection of poetry that evoked the perverse pleasures of desire, degeneration, and intoxication, as they mingle in the body and imagination. Its opening address 'To the Reader' set the tone for the 1861 edition: 'Stupidity, error, sin, and meanness possess our minds and work upon our bodies, and we nourish our fond remorses as beggars suckle their own lice. Our sins are obstinate, our repentance cowardly.'[2] It was defiantly immoral. Moreover, as Baudelaire explained elsewhere, the poetic language of decadence sought to express 'emotional intensity', 'mysticism', 'compulsive carelessness of passion', by which 'words are adapted to new senses'.[3]

As an amorphous, diverse range of 'decadent' writers emerged in France, Great Britain and, later, in America and beyond, attempts to define this literary phenomenon burgeoned. It has a few definitive thematic and stylistic characteristics: multifaceted decay or decline set in dynamic relation to the pursuit of pleasure, in a style and address that is half-nostalgic for an innocent past and half-determined to – borrowing from Ezra Pound for a moment – 'make it new'. Decadent fiction often came together around an antinomian central protagonist, who is defined by a sense of belatedness, as well as decline and a taste for pleasure, as in Huysmans' *Against Nature* (*À rebours*, 1884). The emphasis of these decadent features shifted between different authors, between national traditions, and across time. The moral force of these decadent characteristics was though what occupied its contemporary critics. For Desiré Nisard, Paul Bourget, and Havelock Ellis, the decadent preoccupation with fine writing was emblematic of social degeneration in society, in which 'the individuation of parts led to the disintegration of the whole'.[4] The conservative critic Max Nordau stormed that the decadent coterie of writers were a 'rabble, which claims for itself a top place at the scale of the intellectual rank, and freedom from the constraint of all moral laws as its most noble privilege, is certainly baser than the lowest scavenger'.[5] In very different mode, the journalist Anatole Baju wrote of French decadence in 1887, that 'What it wants is life; it is thirsty for the intensity of life shaped by progress, it needs to get drunk on it [...] and to set itself aquiver'.[6]

As decadence migrated to Great Britain, this endeavour to set things 'aquiver' began to take precedence over vivid evocations of physical and moral decay. At its root decadent literature in Great Britain was a response to new and pressing questions that ran down deep into the spiritual foundations of Western society – and this is where Pater comes in. Drawing on the styles and ideas of French decadence, and fusing them with the aestheticist ethos established by Dante Gabriel Rossetti, William Morris, and others, Pater positions himself at the centre of a new way to think about writing and ethics. His interest in decadence emerged, in part, as a response to an assortment of philosophical issues raised for how people in the West thought about themselves and metaphysics. William Thomson's theory of entropy (1850), Charles Darwin's *Origin of Species* (1859) and *The Descent of Man* (1871) raised innumerable questions for scientific thought and religious faith, as did *Essays and Reviews* (1860), in which seven prominent churchmen challenged the orthodoxy of the Anglican Church. *Mind*, founded by Alexander Bain in 1876, created a forum for the emerging discipline of psychology, and the revolution in thinking about self-identity that it would create. For Pater, these seemingly disparate changes in thinking about self and world came together in an existential problem: if, in the deep time of evolutionary history, the individual is but an ephemeral speck as evolution and entropy imply; if urban migration has unfastened the social and familial ties that define how people live; if doubt in the verities of Church of England doctrine opens larger, unanswerable metaphysical questions; if we are strangers even to ourselves with unconscious drives we cannot understand as the emerging field of psychology theorised, then how do we make life meaningful?

Pater's 'Decadent' Thought

In his Conclusion to *Studies in the History of the Renaissance* (1873) – a book that is neither a history nor about the Italian Renaissance – Pater takes up this question. The Conclusion inaugurated Pater's troubled relationship with decadence in three ways: most obviously, its vivid, sensual evocation of decay and death seems to position it alongside French decadent writing. At the same time – herein lies the tension – Pater's approach is singular and tentative especially when understood in the context of his larger ethos and, crucially, it was taken up in a reductive way as the manifesto of the British decadent movement.

With French decadence very much in the air of the late 1860s and early 1870s in London and Oxford, it is not difficult to see how Pater's Conclusion was read as an English version of this already-established current. There are parallels with Baudelaire's decadent poetry, for the Conclusion begins by focusing on the inexorable processes of life by which 'our physical life' becomes 'waste', 'death', in which the individual life 'is but the concurrence, renewed from moment to moment, of forces parting sooner or later on their ways'.[7] The short, tightly written Conclusion dramatises the very basis of decadence: the inevitable decay of the material world and us, as individuals, within it, hesitating and fragmenting as if assailed by the ever-changing conditions of the external world. Inevitable death, conceived without an afterlife, lowers over the Conclusion. Even as Pater turns in his final paragraph to Jean Jacques Rousseau, he is framed with the description of how 'An undefinable taint of death had clung always about him, and now in early manhood he believed himself smitten by mortal disease'.[8]

In contrast with Baudelaire's *Fleurs du mal*, though, Pater's narrative does not luxuriate in descriptions of decay or illness. Reeling in the wreckage of Christian faith, Pater's Conclusion answers that the 'awful brevity' of life and its ever-changing conditions can yield a vibrant new consciousness in which each moment is worthwhile for its own sake. 'To burn always with this hard, gem-like flame, to maintain this ecstasy is success in life', Pater proposes. 'For art comes to you proposing frankly to give nothing but the highest quality to your moments as they pass, and simply for those moments' sake.'[9] This is Pater all aquiver. His delicious suggestion is that life could be reevaluated independently of reason, virtue, duty, hard work, or kindness. These values based in faith and a social contract are obsolete in the secular, shifting world that the Conclusion has vividly depicted. Instead, life would be valued around 'moments' of intense sensation; 'ecstasy' salvaged from the reality of our ultimate fate for as long as possible. With this, Pater replaces Rene Descartes' *cogito ergo sum* ('I think therefore I am') with *sentio ergo sum* ('I sense therefore I am'). As he writes, his overwrought and sensual prose style put sensual pleasure not realism at its core. Such moments depict the subject's perverse pleasure in experiences of decay, disease, and moral turpitude. However, the basis of this pleasure is very different from that depicted by Baudelaire or Huysmans. Later, Andre Gide, an admirer of Pater, pointed towards the nature of Paterian pleasure when he asked, 'Don't you understand that the moment would not take on such incomparable vividness, if it were not thrown up, so to speak, on the dark background of death?'[10] For Gide and Pater, the knowledge that life is finite endows each moment with vivid beauty and intensity. If it is decadent, it has none of the world-weary cynicism or ennui of Baudelaire or Huysmans; it is a renewed enthusiasm for a life and sensations for their own sake, salvaged from the ultimate reality of death eternal.

Pater's Conclusion expressed this philosophy as a statement on how to live in the secular, perpetually changing world as it had been described by Darwin and others. In each stuttering sentence – fragmented by commas, dashes, frequent pivots in focus – we hear a mind in turmoil but gathering resolution near the end. It was not the turmoil, that people first noticed about the Conclusion, but the resolution of the glimmering possibility that life might be lived on new terms: 'the hard, gem-like flame' and its promise of ecstasy and art for its own sake, as quoted above. The conflicted ethics of this position became clear quite quickly, for the concept of the moment had the potential to be dangerous. When the pursuit of pleasure becomes the imperative of life, is excessive indulgence the inevitable end? If man is the measure of all things, but with a sensation not reason at his core, anything is possible. It was exciting, terrifying, unthinkable, yet increasingly incontrovertible. Pater's prose style in the Conclusion mirrors the motions of the mind as it comes to terms – or tries to – with the idea of life lived for intense sensations

Pater didn't want a scandal so in 1877 he withdrew the Conclusion from his second edition of *The Renaissance*. However, it was already beginning to take on a life of its own. Pater was most immediately associated with French decadence on one side and with English aestheticism and the so-called 'Fleshly School' on the other. His name mingled in the public imagination with that of Algernon Charles Swinburne, another young Oxford radical, whose *Poems and Ballads* (1866) conjured up a sensual pleasure. It was the way in which Pater's work was read selectively and interpreted loudly and stylishly by avowed decadents that defined him as *decadent*.

From early in his career, Oscar Wilde was an ambivalent force in Pater's reception. As an undergraduate, he sought out Pater at Oxford, and when lecturing in America in 1882, he found Pater's ideas to be a rich source for material.[11] Wilde referred to *The Renaissance* as his 'golden book', elaborating that 'it is the very flower of decadence: the last trumpet should have been sounded when it was written'.[12] Whether or not Pater agreed with this assessment, Wilde's only novel, *The Picture of Dorian Gray* (1890, 1891), presented it as such. Dorian's story is Wilde's version of what might follow the philosophy of the Conclusion. Let's take for example the scene in which

Lord Henry first meets the beautiful young Dorian and incites him to live hedonistically:

> Live! Live the wonderful life that is in you! Let nothing be lost upon you. Be always searching for new sensations. Be afraid of nothing … A new Hedonism – that is what our century wants … [W]e never get back our youth. The pulse of joy that beats in us at twenty, becomes sluggish. Our limbs fails, our senses rot. We degenerate into hideous puppet, haunted by the memory of the passions of which we were too much afraid, and the exquisite temptations that we had not the courage to yield to. Youth! Youth! There is absolutely nothing in the world but youth![13]

Henry's speech pastiches and distorts Pater's Conclusion. It uses the same terms (*sensations*, *pulses*) and imperatives as Pater as it sets the decay of the body and the natural world in dialogue with a question about how one should revalue life under such circumstances. References to hedonism here are reflected in classical allusions elsewhere in the scene, and framed by the way in which Dorian figures Henry's words as music, to recall Pater's celebrated statement that '*All art aspires towards the condition of music*'.[14] Henry's effect on Dorian is immediate and profound: he is left 'wide-eyed and wondering' at this revelation of his youth and its inevitable fate.[15] In the Faustian pact and unravelling life that follow, Dorian loses all sight of morality and restraint: he lives for hedonism, as Lord Henry counselled. Henry was not Pater, nor did Wilde mean him to be. However, Wilde's novel trades on the association and it's not difficult to see how rumours of Pater's unsavoury influence on Oxford undergraduates could be sharpened by Henry into soundbites so catchy that they, not Pater, were what lived in the popular imagination.

In the 1890s, Arthur Symons, another of Pater's acolytes, wrote an essay titled 'The Decadent Movement in Literature' (1893) – and he put Pater at its centre. As Symons set out to identify and define decadence as a literary phenomenon in his essay, he explained that it was defined by

> an intense self-consciousness, a restless curiosity in research, an over-subtilizing refinement upon refinement, a spiritual and moral perversity, if what we call the classic is indeed the supreme art – those qualities of perfect simplicity, perfect sanity, perfect proportion, the supreme qualities – then this representative literature of to-day, interesting, beautiful as it is, is really a new and beautiful and interesting disease.[16]

Symons brings together characteristics already familiar from French decadent writing and Roman decadence: degeneration, immorality, and beauty, conceived as a modern phenomenon, and one that requires new modes of expression. The essay goes on to explore French decadent writers including the Goncourts and Huysmans, but it ends in a flourish with the today-almost-forgotten poet W. E. Henley and Pater, as the English exemplars of his 'movement'. Regarding *The Renaissance, Marius the Epicurean,* and *Imaginary Portraits,* Symons asks, 'have they not that morbid subtlety of analysis, that morbid curiosity of form, that we have found in the works of the French Decadents?'[17]

Symons is an astute reader of Pater. His essay briefly analyses how Pater's prose departs 'from classical ideals of style'. It is instead defined by its 'strangeness', an effect produced by its 'morbid subtlety of analysis, that morbid curiosity of form', his 'fastidiousness equal to that of Flaubert'; 'there is not a page that is not perfectly finished, with a conscious art of perfection. In its minute elaboration it can be compared only with goldsmith's work – so fine, so delicate is the handling of so delicate, so precious a material.'[18] In this way, Symons defines Pater's place in the decadent movement on different terms to those of Wilde, with style not hedonism as the focus. They are, however, closely related, with the elaboration and perfection of style providing a stylistic motif of the hedonistic imperative. Symons's essay slips between its discussion of writing style and categories of moral action. The decadent styles identified by Symons are emblematic of a broader shift, as he saw it, in ethics, one in which the individual or single unit is prioritised over society or the whole. It is a common criticism of decadent writing that it is stylistically superficial. 'In periods of decadence', Nisard writes for instance, 'beauty appears in the form of the flourish', continuing with the view that its style is 'too beautified' to the point where stylish expression becomes an end in itself.[19] Paul Bourget referred to 'purple prose' and it was a phrase that readily stuck to Pater to describe that strange self-conscious style – but it only makes sense to those who aren't really taking enough notice.

Pater's association with the decadent movement gave him a *caché* unparalleled by any quiet Oxford don in history. It was a case of appearance over reality, underlined with guilt by association. The damage to his intellectual reputation was significant. The way in which Pater's central maxims and style were bundled into the decadent movement flattened the nuances of his thinking, ensuring that both he and those who took him seriously would, forever after, seek to distance him from this movement. As Lesley Higgins argues,

> Wilde's unstinting praise for Pater, his efforts to canonize the writings in the discourse of decadence helped to ensure that, in the afterwards of masculinist highmodernist culture, in the 'after-words' of T. S. Eliot, T. E. Hulme, and Wyndham Lewis, there was never any time for positive assessments of beauty or beauty's most radical champion.[20]

In large part this was due to homophobia: association with Wilde highlighted the effeminacy and eroticism in Pater's own work. At the same time, Wilde edited out Pater's careful nuances so that his ideas became soundbites and epigrams. It is true that he pitches a kind of hedonism as an answer to the modern condition; true that his writing is beautiful and modern in its construction. However, these crude facts do not mean that his own aesthetic and ethical position is what Wilde's Lord Henry summarises or that it can be scooped up into the movement Symons tried to give some shape to.

Pater's Decadent Problem

It's easy to see how awkward and frustrating it must have been for so careful a thinker to be bundled into a movement. He wouldn't want to belong to any club that would define anything so crude as a manifesto for its members. The fact that Pater did not consider himself to be in the decadent movement, whatever that meant in practice, does not mean that he was not a decadent writer. Indeed, he is, in so far as such a thing exists at all. His work evinces the defining features of decadent literature: a preoccupation with personal and cultural decline and a commitment to intense pleasurable experiences that ease the knowledge of that ultimate fate, rendered in a form and style that responds to this state of being.

Pater keeps coming back to decadence as an ethical problem, contemplating the possibility and danger of submitting to sensation at length. Only, he wanted – to borrow a technical term first used by the Duke of Norfolk to Thomas Cromwell in the sixteenth century – to have his cake and eat it. How? As we know, Pater's ongoing endeavour is to delineate both how to live a full life 'under sentence of death' and how to create new modes with which to articulate the condition of the individual faced with such a fate. Having set out the ephemeral, instable state of the empirical world, Pater reflects on two main points: first, that this life is all we have and there is no afterlife in which virtuous deeds might be accounted; second, that we should live as intensely as possible during the time we have on earth. He believes contemporary civilisation, including faith in God, to be in a state of decadence, but, in response to this, his characters are not laggards and drunks. They are sensitive figures, morally unspoilt, with no unsavoury physical signs of degeneration or over-indulgence. They are not, in short, decadent; rather, they must find a way to face the inexorable decay of everything around them.

Moral decadence – by which I mean letting oneself go, losing control, indulgence beyond what is reasonable – is clearly a possibility. The notion of unreflective sensual experiences teeters on the brink of moral decadence, like that depicted in Thomas Couture's painting. Pater consistently resists this fate. His position assumes that burning 'always with this hard, gem-like flame, to maintain this ecstasy' can be practiced proportionately and so without moral harm. It's true that Pater briefly considers the possibility of 'listlessness' as a response to human finitude. That state defines the decadence of Dorian Gray or De Esseintes, the ultimate decadent antiheroes, who sequester themselves inside their houses to live for sensations and pleasure. But Pater's final response to the 'brief interval' is Victorian in its purposiveness. If, Pater suggests, there is no afterlife, pleasures will be industriously satisfied by 'getting as many pulsations as possible into the given time'.[21]

It is difficult to believe that Pater had no idea where this might lead: in truth, the possibility that the Conclusion would mislead its readers is integral to it. After all, as the Conclusions' narrative runs away, it offers a glimpse of the possibility – never fulfilled – of pure sensation. 'With this sense of the splendour of our experience and of its awful brevity', it suggests, 'gathering all we are into one desperate effort to see and touch, we shall hardly have time to make theories about the things we see and touch'.[22] Pater's narrative trembles with trepidation but also with excitement at the thought. When sensation and passion become the measure of value, is it really possible to moderate behaviour? Where does this leave society? Another of Pater's paradoxes ends the famous sentence quoted above, and it is telling: 'to maintain that ecstasy'. Ecstasy cannot, by definition, be maintained. It is an exceptional state that can only be recognised in relation to its contraries. When Pater's narratives and characters seek ecstasy, they want an impossible state of being in which ecstasy can be kept under control and extended forever. But ecstasy, by definition, annihilates reasoned reflection. If maintained at all, ecstasy degenerates into ennui as the senses become dulled by over-stimulation. So this is where Pater wants to have and eat the cake: his sensation will be unreflective but somehow held in check; ecstasy will be maintained without ennui. Would that it were possible.

When Pater reinstated the Conclusion to *The Renaissance* for its third edition in 1888, he added a note of explanation on the alterations: having 'conceived it might possibly mislead some of those young men into whose hands it might fall', he had removed it, but now, 'I have dealt more fully in *Marius the Epicurean* with the thoughts suggested by it.'[23] *Marius* returns to explore the relationship between secular life, inevitable decay, and death through the experience of the title protagonist. Like all of Pater's young male protagonists, Marius's young life is ringed around with death and grief. The sense of 'decadence' – of inevitable decline – rendered in the circumstances of his life is reflected in Rome, which is figured as 'city of tombs, layer upon layer of dead things and people'.[24] With no comfort to be found in metaphysics, a version of hedonism provides a way for Marius to make life meaningful. When Marius comes to study the philosophy of Cyrenaicism, an ancient Greek school of hedonism, his reflections evoke the Conclusion to reposition its hedonistic suggestions. For example, contemplating the ephemerality of the present, Marius thinks, 'he would at least fill up the measure of that present with vivid sensations, and such intellectual apprehensions, as, in strength and directness and their immediately realised values at the bar of actual experience, are most like sensations.'[25] Pater stresses that the hedonism he has in mind is intellectual, not merely sensual. It was to be 'a wide, a complete, education' which was 'directed especially to the expansion and refinement of the power of reception'.[26] This is sensualism conceived as an aesthetic and moral education.

Still, the questions that got Pater into trouble with the Conclusion, and which he sought to answer with *Marius*, could not be put to rest. His second essay collection, 'Dionysus and Other Studies', was contracted to Macmillan but withdrawn by the author in 1878. *Gaston de Latour* was withdrawn during its serial publication and never finished, while a suggested third planned novel never appeared. Pater's career is haunted by these ghost works following *The Renaissance*'s Conclusion. In them, the title characters live by the imperative of intense and acutely felt sensation, like Marius and as in Pater's Conclusion. However, the endeavour ends in chaos.

Pater is defined by decadence and the decadent movement. All told, though, Pater is in a tussle with decadence, one that was never resolved. In his uncertain condition, he agonises in print over how to truly live a meaningful life in a decadent world. Often the questions we most need to ask have no final answers and, for Pater, decadence was a spectre, a hope, and a curse. His nuanced contemplation of what this means for our ethics is lost when we think of him as part of the decadent movement, but it can be put into relief when we consider that he was a decadent writer.

Notes

1. Stephen Cheeke, *Walter Pater and Persons* (Oxford: Oxford University Press, 2024), 152–153.
2. Charles Baudelaire, 'To the Reader' ['Au Lecteur]', *The Complete Verse*, translated by Francis Scarfe, 2 vols (London: Anvil Press, 1991), 1: 53.
3. Charles Baudelaire, Note to *Franciscae meae laudes* (1857), translated by Chris Baldick, *Decadence: An Annotated Anthology*, edited by Jane Desmarais and Chris Baldick (Manchester: Manchester University Press, 2012), 80–81.
4. Regenia Gagnier, 'The Decadence of the West in Huysmans and Houellebecq: Decadence in the Longue Durée', *ELT* 60.4 (2017): 419–430, 419. https://muse.jhu.edu/pub/74/article/657889/pdf
5. Max Nordau, *Degeneration*, translator unknown (London: Heinemann, 1920), 337.

6. Anatole Baju, 'The School of Decadence', translated by Jane Desmarais, in *Decadence: An Annotated Anthology*, edited by Jane Desmarais and Chris Baldick (Manchester: Manchester University Press, 2012), 29.

7. Walter Pater, *The Renaissance: Studies in Art and Poetry*, ed. Hilary Fraser (Oxford: Oxford University Press, 2025), 197.

8. Pater, *Renaissance*, 199.

9. Pater, *Renaissance*, 200.

10. André Gide, *Fruits of the Earth* (London: Vintage, 2002), 25.

11. For further discussion see Kate Hext, 'Wilde in America', in *Oxford Handbook of Oscar Wilde*, Kate Hext and Alex Murray eds. (Oxford: Oxford University Press, 2025).

12. Qtd. in William Butler Yeats, *The Trembling of the Veil* (London: T. Werner Laurie, 1922), 20.

13. Oscar Wilde, *The Picture of Dorian Gray* (Oxford: Oxford University Press, 1998), 22.

14. Pater, *Renaissance*, 145 (italics in original).

15. Wilde, *Dorian Gray*, 22–24.

16. Arthur Symons, 'The Decadent Movement in Literature', *Harper's Magazine* 87 (November 1893): 859.

17. Symons, 'Decadent Movement', 867.

18. Symons, *Decadent Movement*, 867.

19. Désiré Nisard, 'Lucan, or the Decadence' [1834], translated by Jane Desmarais and Chris Baldick in *Decadence: An Annotated Anthology*, 75–6.

20. Lesley Higgins, 'No Time for Pater: The Silenced Other of Masculinist Modernism', in *Walter Pater: Transparencies of Desire* Laurel Brake, Lesley Higgins, and Carolyn Williams eds. (Greensboro, NC: ELT Press, 2002), 37. Project MUSE. https://muse.jhu.edu/book/11053.

21. Pater, *The Renaissance*, 199–200.

22. Pater, *The Renaissance*, 199.

23. Pater, *The Renaissance*, 197.

24. Walter Pater, *Marius the Epicurean*, 2 vols (London: Soho Book, 1985), 1: 200.

25. Pater, *Marius*, 1: 144.

26. Pater, *Marius*, 1: 147.

13

LESLEY HIGGINS

Pater among the Modernists

In *The Cambridge Companion to Modernism* (1999), Pater is mentioned a grand total of – twice. But only in the essay on modern drama, and only because the author believes art constantly aspires to the condition of music.[1] Overall, the notion of Pater's work being significant for one's understanding of Modernism is never entertained by the other contributors. And yet, when W. B. Yeats assembled the *Oxford Book of Modern Verse* (1936), he recast Pater's description of Leonardo's *Mona Lisa* into a free verse poem and launched the collection with that wholly suggestive ekphrastic textual experience. It was a brilliant gesture and challenge. One of Pater's great themes was the renaissance of the ancient spirit in subsequent centuries; Yeats staged the revival of Pater's appreciative method after decades of some peers' antipathy. During his lifetime and posthumously, Pater was a polarising figure: for every Oscar Wilde embracing *Studies in the History of the Renaissance* (1873) as his 'golden book' there was a Samuel Wilberforce, bishop of Oxford, offering to burn the volume publicly (as a response to the incendiary Conclusion). For every Yeats who wanted to celebrate Pater's writings, there was a Wyndham Lewis or T. S. Eliot who not only decried their significance but wanted to 'place' them in the dustbin of Victoriana. Exploring both *how* 'we realise the under-texture'[2] of Pater's concepts and 'phrases' in diverse Modernist texts and *why* denying or denigrating Pater was so important to certain men provides the warp and weft of this analysis.

Three caveats must be acknowledged. First, the Anglo-Irish-American Modernists who responded to Pater constituted an important segment of their cultural domain, but they were not the only avant-garde writers of their day. Thus Henry James, James Joyce, Virginia Woolf, and H.D. (Hilda Doolittle) play a role in this study, but Mina Loy, Langston Hughes, and David Jones do not. (Just as Pater studies have burgeoned in the last three decades, approaches to the Modernisms that flourished have multiplied, encouraged by feminists, critics of the Harlem Renaissance, and students of

World Literature. The predominance of the 'men of 1914' historical narrative, in Lewis's pithy and misogynistic phrase,[3] is finally waning.) Second,
exposure to Pater's works happened variously. Henry James was enjoined by
his brother, William, to read 'exquisite' Pater carefully.[4] Eliot's mother
Charlotte gave him his first volume, *The Renaissance* (bought second-
hand);[5] Virginia Woolf borrowed the book given by Pater to her father,
Leslie Stephen, then purchased her own deluxe edition.[6] For others, exposure
to Pater's ideas and phrases was distilled and distorted by the writings of
Oscar Wilde and Arthur Symons. Third, surveying and summarising 'Pater
among the Modernists' is possible now because the work of recuperating
Pater's 'widely diffused' contributions to early twentieth-century poetry,
prose, and aesthetic discourse began sporadically in the 1960s and was
thriving by the 1980s thanks to Sharon Bassett, Harold Bloom, Linda
Dowling, F. C. McGrath, and Wolfgang Iser.[7] Pater's 'stature', as Geoffrey
Sadock observes, 'then and now, acts as a kind of lightning rod for larger
cultural issues, such as tolerance, literary history, diversity, epistemology,
and the struggle for religious affirmation'.[8] Given that diversity of impact,
and Pater's crucial transitional role because he held 'simultaneously late
romantic, late Victorian, and early modern positions',[9] it is impossible to
be exhaustive, but one can be both inclusive and indicative by tracing
reinscriptions, modifications, and the Paterian textual networks that
developed.

Subtle, Suggestive Provocations

In his essay on Shakespeare's *Measure for Measure* (1874), Pater praises 'that
sort of writing which is sometimes described as *suggestive*, and ... brings into
distinct shape the reader's own half-developed imaginings'.[10] Studying
Literae Humaniores at Oxford encouraged his proficiency as a 'great intellectual synthesizer' (McGrath 1); the cultivation of contemporary writers,
including Théophile Gautier, Charles Baudelaire, and Gustave Flaubert,
stimulated his cosmopolitanism and his commitment to provocative originality. Pater's writings proved memorable not simply because of his lapidary
style but because of his compelling interdisciplinarity. He challenged dominant theories of time, subjectivity, and experience, one consequence of which
was a new mode of narrative representation: literary impressionism. He
developed a distinctively different type of 'appreciative' aesthetic criticism;
established a new genre, the 'imaginary portrait', the potential of which
resonated equally with prose writers such as James, Joyce, Woolf, Gertrude
Stein, and Edith Sitwell, and poets (Pound and Eliot). He demonstrated how
a study of 'The Child in the House'[11] could animate fiction (a lesson repeated

in James's *What Maisie Knew* (1897), Joyce's *A Portrait of the Artist as a Young Man* (1916), and Woolf's *To the Lighthouse* (1927)). He argued for the cultural significance of religious practices rather than defended orthodoxies, and insisted that ancient religions be discussed substantially, not dismissed as pagan myths. He demonstrated how classical studies and archaeology are vital to the present, and contributed to the emergence of a queer aesthetic and canon. Furthermore, he did so by stressing the burdens of modernity, repeatedly asking, 'And what does the spirit need in the face of modern life?'[12] and situating himself and his readers as 'us of the modern world, with its conflicting claims, its entangled interests, distracted by so many sorrows, with many preoccupations' and 'ready to be lost in the perplexed currents of modern thought' (*TR* 194). In Pater's writings there emerged the 'inward' turn, the close regard for interiority and 'the world within' that characterises literary experiments in 'the self-pondering, perfectly educated, modern world'.[13] Nonetheless, he insisted that 'modern art', working in the 'service of culture', can contribute to the 'sense of freedom' necessary to ameliorate 'modern life' (*TR* 196).

Forty years before Einstein, Pater startled people by espousing a special theory of relativity. Of course he was referring to philosophical discourse, not physics, when he championed the 'relative spirit' in 'Coleridge's Writings' (1866) – less 'a review of Coleridge's prose than a manifesto of his own', one of 'the opening salvos of the Modernist movement in literature and the arts' (McGrath 24). Pater's particular anti-Hegelian, anti-positivistic fusion of Heraclitus, David Hume, and Charles Darwin produced shockwaves that reverberated for more than six decades (and inspired counterarguments ranging from Gerard Manley Hopkins's 'That Nature Is a Heraclitean Fire and of the comfort of the Resurrection', 1888, to Eliot's 'Burnt Norton', 1936). Arguing against absolutism but reaffirming a commitment to an ethics of self-fashioning, Pater launched his essay with the assertion that, 'To the modern spirit nothing can be rightly known, except relatively and under conditions', and concluded by insisting, 'The relative spirit, by dwelling constantly on the more fugitive conditions or circumstances of things, ... and giving elasticity to inflexible principles, begets an intellectual finesse, of which the ethical result is a delicate and tender justness in the criticism of human life'.[14]

In response to such 'fugitive conditions' of existence, Pater grounded his approach to perception and epistemology in the 'primary data' of impressions. 'Our education becomes complete', the Preface to *The Renaissance* states, 'in proportion as our susceptibility to these impressions increases in depth and variety' (*TR* 74). The 'aesthetic critic' is enjoined to respond to the 'special impression of beauty or pleasure' (*TR* 74) produced by art and cultural artefacts. As several commentators have explored, it was more than a coincidence that Pater was theorising an impressionist method at exactly the same time that painters including Claude Monet and Camille Pissarro were developing techniques that challenged irrevocably the realist mode of visual representation.[15] Provisionality *and* scientific acumen were co-determinants in literary and painterly impressionism: one presented the object of contemplation *and* one's subjective experience of it, and at the same time suggested the evanescence of such an ephemeral experience. What Pater tried to accomplish in *Marius the Epicurean* (1885), 'A Prince of Court Painters' (1885), and 'Emerald Uthwart' (1892), Henry James refined in 'The Art of Fiction' (1881), *What Maisie Knew* (1897), and *The Golden Bowl* (1904), and Joseph Conrad and Ford Madox Ford polished in texts such as *Heart of Darkness* (1899) and *The Good Soldier* (1915), and codified in 'On Impressionism' (1914).[16] Virginia Woolf absorbed lessons from all of these models, but did not find her own sure method until she understood the literary impressionism of Katherine Mansfield, whose experimental short stories including 'Prelude' (published by the Woolfs' Hogarth Press, 1918) provided inspiration for the experiments of 'The Mark on the Wall' (1917), 'Kew Gardens' (1919), and *Jacob's Room* (1922).

Impressionism is necessarily temporal: 'A sudden light transfigures some trivial thing, a weather-vane, a windmill, a winnowing-fan. . . . A moment – and the thing has vanished, because it is pure effect' (*TR* 168). Fittingly, *The Renaissance* concludes by restating this radical notion in aesthetic terms: 'For art comes to you proposing frankly to give nothing but the highest quality to your moments as they pass, and simply for those moments' sake' (*TR* 200). Among the many Modernists who endorse the epistemological possibilities of this moment of heightened awareness are the following: Thomas Hardy, whose poem 'Moments of Vision' (a phrase borrowed from *Plato and Platonism*[17]) provides the title and governing theme for his 1917 volume; and Woolf, who repeats the phrase to compliment Conrad in 1923: his 'books are full of moments of vision'.[18] Yeats's 'The Second Coming' (1920) also hinges on a revelatory moment, a temporary stasis in the inexorable flux of time, but one that is personally and historically ominous. Eliot's *The Waste Land* (1922), which included a satirical, misogynistic scene involving a Pater enthusiast until Ezra Pound excised it,[19] is animated by vignettes and fragments in which 'the awful daring of a moment's surrender' is never realized.[20] *Four Quartets* theorises 'the moment' differently from the Conclusion to *The Renaissance* in order to rescue it from Paterian relativism and restore its transcendent possibilities at the interstices of aesthetic and religious discourse. But the speaker of

'East Coker' cannot imagine otherwise without invoking the very words being refuted:

> As we grow older
> The world becomes stranger, the pattern more complicated
> Of dead and living. Not the intense moment
> Isolated, with no before and after,
> But a lifetime burning in every moment
> And not the lifetime of one man only
> But of old stones that cannot be deciphered.   (CPP 182)

The speaker has answered Pater's claim that our life is "flame-like ... that it is but the concurrence, renewed from moment to moment, of forces parting sooner or later on their ways' (TR 197), but can only do so in images and assertions hopelessly 'complicated' by their intertextuality. In 'The School of Giorgione' (1877), Pater praises dramatic poetry because 'it presents us with a kind of profoundly significant and animated instance ... some brief and wholly concrete moment ... which seem[s] to absorb past and future in an intense consciousness of the present' (TR 153). For Eliot, the intersection of 'Time present and time past / ... both perhaps present in the time future' is 'renewed, transfigured, in another pattern': 'Quick now, here, now, always – / A condition of complete simplicity / (Costing not less than everything) (CPP 171, 195, 198), a glimpse of redemption that is nonetheless indebted to Pater's imaginative articulations.

James Joyce, whom Eliot described to Woolf as a writer 'founded upon Walter Pater with a dash of Newman',[21] not only owned The Renaissance but copied into his notebooks 'long passages from Marius and Imaginary Portraits' (McGrath 231). Joyce famously narrativised and recast the Paterian 'moment' as the 'epiphany', a scene of heightened awareness used to vivid effect in 'The Dead' (the culminating story of Dubliners) and the climax of Chapter 4 in A Portrait of the Artist as a Young Man (1916), in which Stephen Dedalus rejects religious orthodoxies and dedicates himself instead to aesthetic pleasure.[22] Like Woolf and Eliot, however, Joyce is very aware of Pater's unsettling proximities: not only 'exquisite pauses in time' that are the 'quintessence of life' (TR 153) but the 'sense of death and the desire of beauty: the desire of beauty quickened by the sense of death' (Ap 227).

Commitments to flux and relativity had a major impact on Pater's approach to subjectivity, consciousness, and 'the self's labile existence in time'.[23] Again, Modernists' reactions varied acutely. James's first major attempt to develop a narrative mode that registers the mind's myriad fluctuations comes in chapter 42 of The Portrait of a Lady (1881), in which Isabel Archer Osmond realises that 'her soul was haunted with terrors' as she considers her marital state and the 'strange impression[s]' generated by her husband and Mme Merle (his lover).[24] To the suggestion that the self was neither fixed, wholly knowable, nor autonomous (yet God-related), that the 'strange, perpetual, weaving and unweaving of ourselves' could yield the 'fruit of a quickened, multiplied consciousness' (*TR* 198, 200), Joyce had his Dedalus respond with tongue in cheek, in the 'Scylla and Charybdis' episode of *Ulysses* (1922):

> As we, or mother Dana, weave and unweave our bodies ... from day to day, their molecules shuttled to and fro, so does the artist weave and unweave his image. And as the mole on my right breast is where it was when I was born, though all my body has been woven of new stuff time after time, so through the ghost of the unquiet father the image of the unliving son looks forth.[25]

Woolf, one of the first to grasp congruencies between Pater's work with self and mind and the explorations of William James and Henri Bergson,[26] developed a feminist approach to 'becoming' that also positioned the self as 'a dynamic process of continual creativity'.[27] In her novel *Orlando* (1928), a *jeu d'esprit* in which a person thrives from the 1590s until the late 1920s, changing sex in the 1730s, the title figure feels, as a woman, 'haunted':

> for though one may say, as Orlando said ... Orlando? still the Orlando she needs may not come; these selves of which we are built up, one on top of another ... have attachments elsewhere, sympathies, ... for everybody can multiply from his own experience the different terms which his different selves have made with him ...[28]

Subjectivity is enacted as a series of overlaying selves in a text that questions the meaning and limits of gender. Yet, as in all Woolf novels, the number of 'selves' that are allowed to come out always depends upon historically constructed conventions and normalising pressures. Of Pater's many Modernist readers, Woolf most fruitfully complicates the concept of the moment by stressing its ontological implications. In 'Moments of Being: Slater's Pins Have No Points' (1927), a story that fictionalises Pater's sister Clara, Woolf's first Greek tutor, same-sex desire is the catalyst for realising 'in its bareness and intensity the effluence of her spirit'.[29] In *To the Lighthouse* (1927), Mrs Ramsay experiences – by wedging down into the core of darkness in a rare moment of solitude, and while reading a Shakespeare sonnet – what Woolf formally explicates in 'A Sketch of the Past' (1939–40) as 'moments of being' and 'non-being' (the 'nondescript cotton wool' of quotidian existence).[30] These moments not only 'constitute the structural principle[s]' of her fiction,[31] they permeate her experience of life. As she notes in her diary for 31 December 1932, 'If one does not lie back

& sum up & say to the moment, this very moment, stay you are so fair, what will be one's gain, dying? No: stay, this moment. No one ever says that enough' (Woolf *D* 4: 135).

Eliot, typically, dwelt on the negative inferences of Pater's 'experiencing subject',[32] especially the idea that when the 'narrow chamber of the individual mind' is probed, one learns that experience, 'already reduced to a group of impressions, is ringed round for each one of us by that thick wall of personality through which no real voice has ever pierced on its way to us. ... each mind keeping as a solitary prisoner its own dream of a world' (*TR* 198). Marius's 'philosophical reading' of the human condition confirms this view: 'We are never to get beyond the walls of the closely shut cell of one's own personality' (*ME* 1: 146). Pater's 'solitary prisoner' is reduced to fragmented artefacts in Eliot's poetry: the 'key' of memory that threatens in 'Rhapsody on a Windy Night' resurfaces in the 'memories' haunting the penultimate movement of *The Waste Land*: '*Dayadhvam*: I have heard the key / Turn in the door once and turn once only / We think of the key, each in his prison / Thinking of the key, each confirms a prison' (*CPP* 74). The apocalyptic ambience of *The Waste Land* is very different from the claustrophobic, *fin-de-siècle* salon world of 'The Love Song of J. Alfred Prufrock' (1915), but the Paterian spectre of someone 'imprisoned now in the narrow cell of [his] own subjective experience' remains constant (*MS* 12). Furthermore, Eliot was obviously struck by the way in which Pater imagines an external world parallel to this inner state: it is variously the 'hollow ring of fundamental nothingness under the apparent surface of things' (*MS* 14) detected by Prosper Mérimée or 'the vast unseen hollow places of nature, of humanity, just beneath one's feet or at one's side' apprehended by Blaise Pascal (*MS* 82). 'Between the conception / And the creation' of 'The Hollow Men' falls the shadow of Pater's prose (1925; *CPP* 85).

In Joyce's *Ulysses*, Dedalus declares that history is 'a nightmare from which I am trying to awake' (*U* 47). Pater would have reproved the young instructor for being so defeatist, because thinking historically, according to the Oxford don, is an opportunity to reawaken the past and to reimagine the categories and conditions of each age. Chronological boundaries are actually porous and provisional, according to Pater, who redefined Attic studies by alternately stressing the significance of 'early' works of Greek sculpture and 'run[ning] together several strata of time'[33] and who redefined the Renaissance 'spirit' by extending its purview both antecedently (two 'early' medieval French stories) and subsequently (to include the ultimate Renaissance man and scholar Johann Winkelmann, 1717–68). Perhaps the most delightful response to such historiographic shenanigans is Woolf's *Orlando*, in which the main character enjoys the prime of life from the 'great frost' of 1606–07 until the 1920s, surviving a sex change, war, and marriage. (Pater is among those 'thanked' in the Acknowledgements.) Unlike Yeats's monumental treatment of the *Gioconda* passage, or Freud's serious analysis of Pater's biographical speculations in 'Leonardo da Vinci',[34] Woolf stages a full-scale parody of the figure whom '[a]ll the thoughts and experience of the world have etched and moulded' (*TR* 140). Orlando is definitely 'the embodiment of the old fancy, the symbol of the modern idea' (*TR* 140), but served up as a satire of patriarchal privilege, Victorian gender discrimination, and a writer's desire for fame.

Orlando's unending story updates and upends, wittily, the fate of Pater's 'Denys L'Auxerrois' (1886) and 'Apollo in Picardy' (1893), two tortured figures who embody Heinrich Heine's argument about the 'gods in exile'.[35] Several modernists developed their 'mythic methods' from Pater's example, including Yeats, Eliot, Joyce, Pound (who preferred to mock Pater; see below), and H.D. Yeats learned from Pater how myth makes 'sensible' and concrete ancient beliefs, and their 'strange' relevance to the present. But more than any one poem, such as 'When You Are Old',[36] 'No Second Troy', or 'Leda and the Swan', Yeats's theory of mythologised personality types, in *A Vision* (1925), provides a sustained Paterian exercise in 'aesthetic historicism' (Bloom 21).[37] Before Joyce's epic attempts at Hellenizing the mundane plentitude of Dublin life in *Ulysses*, he focused on the particular possibilities of mythic metamorphosis. In 'The Beginnings of Greek Sculpture', Pater praises Hephaestus, the 'uncomely god', who 'becomes the patron of smiths, bent with his labour at the forge', the 'god of all art' and 'the most perfectly developed of all the Daedali'.[38] Joyce's Stephen Dedalus finally triumphs over the 'nets' of family, sexual desire, Church, and country by dedicating himself to art – to 'Old father, old artificer' – both to celebrate his own imagination and 'to forge in the smithy of my soul the uncreated conscience of my race'.[39]

H.D., as Cassandra Laity and Eileen Gregory have amply demonstrated, responded to Pater in five ways: savouring, as so many poems in *Sea Garden* (1918) do, the 'conjunction of beauty and violence' (Nicholls 198) and death in the mythic portraits; borrowing descriptions of classical landscapes from *Plato and Platonism* (1893) for her 1927 novel *Her*; demonstrating the feminist potential of Demeter (compare Pater's 'The Myth of Demeter and Persephone' and H.D.'s dramatic monologue, 'Demeter'); recasting Euripides' play *Hippolytus* (Pater's prose portrait 'Hippolytus Veiled' and H.D.'s verse drama *Hippolytus Temporizes*, 1927); and, more generally, using ancient sculptures to express contemporary transgressive desire. She 'openly acknowledged her own "sense of continuity" with' Pater and other late Victorian authors in *Asphodel* (the novel in manuscript, 1920s) and

'H.D. By Delia Alton' (1940s).[40] Another major under-texture for H.D. is the 'crystalline' figure of unusual character celebrated in 'Diaphaneitè'.[41] It is very likely that H.D.'s Paterian investigations in the mid-1940s inspired the critical work of her ex-husband, Richard Aldington, once a minor Imagist poet and Eliot protégé, who produced a substantial anthology of Pater's *Selected Works* in 1948.

One of the academics who responded most thoroughly and vividly to the 'exhilaration' of Pater's mythic studies (especially those focusing on Dionysus and the Eleusinian mysteries) was Jane Harrison, Cambridge classicist and author of *The Mythology and Monuments of Ancient Athens* (1890) and *Prolegomena to the Study of Greek Religion* (1903).[42] As Yopie Prins states, Harrison's 'sense of style – in her classical scholarship, and in her life as a classical scholar – can be understood as a reworking of Pater's late-Victorian legacy from a feminine and increasingly feminist perspective'.[43] Harrison's studies in relation to Pater's are best defined by an observation from 'The Myth of Demeter and Persephone': they 'extrac[t] by a kind of subtle alchemy, a beauty, not without the elements of tranquility, of dignity and order, out of a matter, at first sight painful and strange' (*CS* 197). And what Harrison realised in her own work greatly influenced other Cambridge Ritualists, including Gilbert Murray and Francis M. Cornford, 'a community of scholars pushing the disciplinary boundaries of the Classics as they created new fields in anthropology and archaeology'.[44] Harrison also provides a personal portrait of Pater: 'Pater and his sisters were good, and opened their house to me; I always think of him as a soft, kind cat; he purred so persuasively that I lost the sense of what he was saying.'[45]

Forces of Exclusion

There is a profound irony to the fact that, at every turn in Eliot's quest to communicate, Pater's voice is 'heard, half-heard, in the stillness / Between two waves' of new verse (*CPP* 198) – not a welcome guest, certainly, 'accepted and accepting', but one cannot 'resolv[e] the enigma' of *Four Quartets* or *The Waste Land* or 'Prufrock' without admitting Pater to the dance of words. The narrator of *Gaston de Latour* (1888) cites the 'very presence of the past' in books 'which had already found tongues to speak of a still living humanity – somewhere, in the world! – waiting for him in the distance'.[46] Pater makes a similar comment, in a religious context, in the introduction to C. L. Shadwell's translation of the *Purgatorio*, noting 'the belief in a constant, helpful, beneficent interaction between the souls of the living and the dead'.[47] Eliot concludes the first part of 'Little Gidding' by defining the grace that is prayer and faith:

> And what the dead had no speech for, when living,
> They can tell you, being dead: the communication
> Of the dead is tongued with fire beyond the language of the living.
> Here, the intersection of the timeless moment
> Is England and nowhere. Never and always.   (*CPP* 192)

The compelling presence of Pater in Eliot's writings could not be better summarised: never and always.

Although many modernists struggled with the idea of 'art for its own sake' (*TR* 200), the intermedial assertion that '*All art constantly aspires towards the condition of music*' (*TR* 145) was readily embraced by Yeats, Joyce, and Pound, among others, for its nondiscursive potential and its affective and expressive appeal. To achieve a fusion of form and content, however temporarily, meant the grace of harmonious equipoise – viewer and artwork, dancer and dance, reader and text. Yet Eliot continued to argue against this paradigm, contained in 'The School of Giorgione', for decades. In 'Poetry and Drama' (1951), regarding those feelings 'beyond the nameable, classifiable emotions and motives of our conscious life', Eliot states that in 'moments of greatest intensity. ... we touch the border of those feelings which only music can express. We can never emulate music, because to arrive at the condition of music would be the annihilation of poetry, and especially dramatic poetry'.[48]

Critics antagonistic to Pater can easily make the notion of burning 'with a hard, gem-like flame' seem risible (*TR* 199).[49] When first published, however, Pater's injunctions to experience everything intensely – art, life, desire – were deemed subversive, even dangerous. How dangerous? The textual attacks began almost immediately, as several essays in this volume demonstrate. But motives other than malice were involved, and long-sustained. In the case of Henry James, the need to disavow Pater's transgressive insights was partly fuelled by homosexual panic (in Eve Kosofsky Sedgwick's trenchant phrase). Hence the portraits of distempered aesthetes or artist manqués such as the eponymous Roderick Hudson, Gilbert Osmond in *Portrait of a Lady* (1881), Graham Nash in *The Tragic Muse* (1890), and Adam Verver in *The Golden Bowl* (for whom 'the aesthetic principle [is] planted where it could burn with a cold still flame',[50] 1904). So familiar did tropes of disparagement become that Arthur Conan Doyle presents Cecil Brown in *The Tragedy of the Korosko* (1898) as a diplomat 'slightly tainted with the Oxford manner', who 'chose Walter Pater for his travelling author'.[51] Wilde's professed enthusiasm for Pater, coupled with his personal misfortunates, guaranteed that, in the early twentieth century, Pater could not be easily separated from Wilde, or, more accurately, from the scandal that dared to speak its name. In masculinist high modernist culture, in the homophobic 'blasts' of Eliot, Pound, Lewis, and T. E. Hulme, contempt for Pater is often disguised as moral and aesthetic umbrage countering the dangers of 'effete modern civilization'.[52] Lewis, typically, is the most outspoken and direct in disparaging the 'homo' [sic] (BLAST, 1914; The Art of Being Ruled, 1926) and damning Pater (Men without Art, 1934). On Eliot's part, taking pains to denigrate Pater's writings – Marius has not 'influenced a single first-rate mind of a later generation'[53] – was not only furthering the cause of the 'men of 1914' but following in the discursive footsteps of mentors Paul Elmer More and Irving Babbitt, Harvard-trained intellectuals who decried Romanticism and held Pater responsible for setting readers 'afloat on a boundless sea of relativity'.[54] For them, Pater was the vampiric figure who, in the early twentieth century, ruled from 'the grave' (TR 92); theirs would be the silver bullets of criticism that would silence him forever. Edmund Wilson, at least, disagreed. In his Modernist canon-making exercise Axel's Castle (1931), Pater is cited as a foundational figure of 'much intellectual originality'.[55]

It is the work of another essay to consider Pater's place among modern art critics. Without question, however, he is a key interlocutor for Bernard Bosanquet's A History of Aesthetic (1892; 2nd ed., 1904), especially the Winckelmann chapter; for Bernard Berenson's work; and that of Roger Fry and his major synthesiser, Clive Bell.[56] When Bell summarises Fry's admiration for Post-Impressionist painters such as Paul Cézanne and Henri Matisse, he coins the phrase 'significant form' – an adaptation from Plato and Platonism, which states: 'the form is new. But then, in the creation of philosophical literature, as in all other products of art, form, in the full signification of that word, is everything, and the mere matter is nothing' (PP 8).

Conclusion

'We are sharply cut off from our predecessors', Woolf asserts in 'How It Strikes a Contemporary': 'No age can have been more rich than ours in writers determined to give expression to the differences which separate them from the past and not to the resemblances which connect them with it' (Woolf E 3: 357). Pater had made a similar point in 'Coleridge's Writings': 'Then comes the spectacle of the reserve of the elder generation exquisitely refined by the antagonism of the new' ('CW' 106). In the first four decades of the twentieth century, whether motivated by homophobia or typical 'youngergenerationconsciousness' [sic],[57] writers determined to separate their work from Pater's certainly overshadowed those who acknowledged unforgettable 'undercurrents' (MS 252). And yet, their texts suggested otherwise, enacted a different story of engagement. Pater had predicted as much in *The Renaissance*: artists 'do not live in isolation'; they 'catch light and heat from each other's thoughts' (*TR* 76).

Notes

1. Christopher Innes, 'Modernism in Drama', in *The Cambridge Companion to Modernism*, Michael Levenson, ed. (Cambridge: Cambridge University Press, 1999), 137, 154.
2. 'Pascal's thoughts we shall never understand unless we realise the under-texture in them of Montaigne's very phrases.' Pater, *Miscellaneous Studies* (London: Macmillan, 1920), 84. Hereafter cited parenthetically as *MS*.
3. Wyndham Lewis, *Blasting and Bombardiering* (London: Eyre & Spottiswoode – 1937), 252.
4. Richard Ellmann, *A Long the Riverrun: Selected Essays* (New York: Vintage, 1990), 132–133. For William James's Paterian under-textures, see 'The Stream of Thought', *The Principles of Psychology*, 1890 (New York: Dover Publications, 1950), 1: 233 ff.
5. Lesley Higgins, *The Modernist Cult of Ugliness: Aesthetic and Gender Politics* (New York: Palgrave Macmillan, 2002), 95.
6. Perry Meisel, *The Absent Father: Virginia Woolf and Walter Pater* (New Haven, CT: Yale University Press, 1980), 16–17.
7. Harold Bloom, Introduction to *Walter Pater: Modern Critical Views*, ed. Harold Bloom (New York: Chelsea House, 1985), 3; Sharon Bassett, 'The Uncanny Critic of Brasenose: Walter Pater and Modernism', *The Victorian Newsletter* 58 (Fall 1980), 10–14; Linda Dowling, *Language and Decadence in the Victorian Fin de Siècle* (Princeton, NJ: Princeton University Press, 1986); Francis Charles McGrath, *The Sensible Spirit: Walter Pater and the Modernist Paradigm* (Tampa, FL: University Presses of Florida, 1986); Wolfgang Iser, *Walter Pater: The Aesthetic Moment*, trans. David Henry Wilson (Cambridge: Cambridge University Press, 1987). See also Denis Donoghue, *Walter Pater: Lover of Strange Souls* (New York: Alfred A. Knopf, 1995). McGrath is cited parenthetically hereafter.
8. Geoffrey Sadock, 'The Contemporary Critical Reception of Walter Pater: Retrospective and Proleptical Views', *Cahiers victoriens et édouardiens* 68 (automne 2008): 2.
9. Carolyn Williams, *Transfigured World: Walter Pater's Aesthetic Historicism* (Ithaca, NY: Cornell University Press, 1989), 24.
10. Walter Pater, 'Measure for Measure', in *Appreciations, with an Essay on Style* (London: Macmillan, 1897), 179. Hereafter, *Ap*.
11. Pater published his first 'imaginary portrait' in August 1878: 'Imaginary Portraits. I. The Child in the House'; it was revised for the Daniel Press in

1894. See Lene Østermark-Johansen, 'Critical Introduction' for Walter Pater, *Imaginary Portraits* (Oxford: Oxford University Press, 2018), 1–48.

12. Walter Pater, *The Renaissance: Studies in Art and Poetry*, ed. Hilary Fraser (Oxford: Oxford University Press, 2025), 195. Hereafter, cited parenthetically as *TR*.

13. Walter Pater, 'Browning', in *Essays from 'The Guardian'*, ed. Edmund Gosse (London: Macmillan, 1920), 43.

14. Walter Pater, 'Coleridge's Writings', *Westminster Review*, 29, no. 1 (January 1866): 107, 131–132. Hereafter, 'CW'.

15. Paul Zietlow, 'Pater's Impressionism Reconsidered', *ELH* 44 (1977): 150–170; Jesse Matz, *Literary Impressionism and Modernist Aesthetics* (Cambridge: Cambridge University Press, 2001).

16. See also Ford Madox Ford, 'On Impressionism', in *Critical Writings of Ford Madox Ford*, Frank MacShane, ed. (Lincoln, NE: University of Nebraska Press, 1964), 33–55; and *Joseph Conrad: A Personal Remembrance* (1924).

17. Walter Pater, *Plato and Platonism, 1893* (London: Macmillan, 1905), 156. Hereafter, *PP*.

18. Virginia Woolf, *The Essays of Virginia Woolf*, ed. Andrew McNeillie (New York: Harcourt Brace Jovanovich, 1988), 3: 378. Hereafter, Woof *E*.

19. For the 'Fresca' scene ('baptised in a soapy sea of / Of Symonds – Walter Pater – Vernon Lee'), see T. S. Eliot, *'The Waste Land': A Facsimile and Transcripts*, Valerie Eliot, ed (London: Faber, 1971), 41.

20. Thomas Stearns Eliot, *The Complete Poems and Plays of T. S. Eliot* (London: Faber, 1969), 74. Hereafter, referenced parenthetically as *CPP*.

21. Virginia Woolf, *The Diary of Virginia Woolf*, vol. 2, ed. Anne Olivier Bell and Andrew McNeillie (New York: Harcourt Brace Jovanovich, 1978), 202. Hereafter, Woolf *D*.

22. See Morris Beja, *Epiphany in the Modern Novel* (London: Owen, 1971); Robert M. Scotto, '"Visions" and "Epiphanies": Fictional technique in Pater's *Marius* and Joyce's *Portrait*', *James Joyce Quarterly*, 11, no. 1 (Fall 1973): 41–50; Ashton Nichols, *The Poetics of Epiphanies: Nineteenth-Century Origins of the Modern Literary Moment* (Tuscaloosa, AL: University of Alabama Press, 1987).

23. Peter Nicholls, *Modernisms: A Literary Guide* (London: Macmillan, 1995), 254.

24. Henry James, *The Portrait of a Lady* (1881), www.gutenberg.org/files/2834/2834-h/2834-h.htm#link2HCH0015.

25. James Joyce, *Ulysses*, ed. Hans Walter Gabler (New York: Vintage, 1984), 159. Hereafter, *U*. Pater is also parodied in the 'Oxen of the Sun' episode.

26. Gerald Monsman, 'Pater and His Younger Contemporaries', *Victorian Newsletter* 48 (Fall 1975): 1–9 at 5.

27. Max Saunders, 'Life Writing: Biography, Portraits and Self-Portraits, Masked Authorship, and Autobiografictions', in *Late Victorian into Modern*, Laura Marcus, Michèle Mendelssohn, and Kirsten E. Shepherd-Barr, eds. (Oxford: Oxford University Press, 2016), 518.

28. Virginia Woolf, *Orlando: A Biography* (London: Panther Books, 1977), 192.

29. Virginia Woolf, *The Complete Shorter Fiction*, ed. Susan Dick (New York: Harcourt Brace Jovanovich, 1985), 214.

30. Virginia Woolf, *Moments of Being*, 2nd ed., ed. Jeanne Schulkind (New York: Harcourt, 1985), 70.

31. Naomi Toth, 'Re-membering "moments of being": Perception, language and memory in Virginia Woolf's "A Sketch of the Past"', *Cycnos*, 33, no. 1 (2017): 203.

32. Brad Bucknell, *Literary Modernism and Musical Aesthetics: Pater, Pound, Joyce and Stein* (Cambridge: Cambridge University Press, 2001), 40.

33. Lene Østermark-Johansen, *Walter Pater and the Language of Sculpture* (London: Routledge, 2016), 31.

34. Sigmund Freud, *Leonardo da Vinci: A memory of his childhood* [Eine Kindheitserinnerung des Leonardo da Vinci], trans. Alan Tyson (London: Routledge, 2001), 65–72.

35. In his 1854 essay '*Die Götter im Exil*' [Gods in Exile], German poet Heinrich Heine imagines the ancient Greek gods reincarnated, living among humans and creating havoc.

36. When Yeats's speaker declares that 'one man loved the pilgrim soul in you', he is echoing the 'clothing of the pilgrim soul' from Pater's *Marius the Epicurean*, 2 vols., 1885 (London: Macmillan, 1892), 1: 254.

37. Unlike his 'Tragic 90s' peers, Yeats was often clearest when disagreeing with Pater. See for example the Preface to *Poems* (1920), rpt in Peter Allt and Russell K. Alspach, *The Variorum Edition of the Poems of W. B. Yeats* (New York: Macmillan, 1977), 849. For Pater's significance, see Yeats, *Autobiographies* (London: Macmillan, 1966), 130 and 138 (regarding Wilde), 302, 303, 321, 437, 477.

38. Pater, *Classical Studies* (Oxford: Oxford University Press, 2020), 129. Hereafter, *CS*.

39. James Joyce, *A Portrait of the Artist as a Young Man* (London: The Egoist, 1916), 299. The declaration begins with a salute to Pater's Conclusion ('Not the fruit of experience, but experience itself, is the end' [*TR* 188]): 'I go to encounter for the millionth time the reality of experience.'

40. Cassandra Laity, *H.D. and the Victorian Fin De Siècle: Gender, Modernism, Decadence* (Cambridge: Cambridge University Press, 1996), 43, 30; Eileen Gregory, *H.D. and Hellenism: Classic Lines* (Cambridge: Cambridge University Press, 1997).

41. See 'H.D. by Delia Alton', *Iowa Review*, 16, no. 3 (Fall 1986): 180–221 at 221. 'Diaphaneitè' (1864), written by Pater for Oxford's Old Mortality essay society, was first published in 1895.

42. Jane Harrison, *Prolegomena to the Study of Greek Religion* (Cambridge: Cambridge University Press, 1903), 452.

43. Yopie Prins, *Ladies' Greek: Victorian Translations of Tragedy* (Princeton, NJ: Princeton University Press, 2017), 211.

44. Jean Mills, *Virginia Woolf, Jane Ellen Harrison, and the Spirit of Modernist Classicism* (Columbus, OH: Ohio State University Press, 2014), 7, 23.

45. Jane Ellen Harrison, *Reminiscences of a Student's Life* (London: Hogarth Press, 1925), 46.

46. Walter Pater, *Gaston de Latour*, ed. Gerald Monsman (Oxford: Oxford University Press, 2019), 47.

47. Walter Pater, Introduction to Charles Shadwell, ed. and trans., *The Purgatory of Dante Alighieri* (London: Macmillan, 1892), xxi.

48. T. S. Eliot, *On Poetry and Poets* (London: Faber, 1957), 87.

49. See, however, Virginia Woolf, 'Reading' (1919): Woolf *E* 3: 153.
50. Henry James, *The Golden Bowl* (New York: Scribner's, 1904), 1: 197. See Adeline R. Tintner, 'Pater in *The Portrait of a Lady* and *The Golden Bowl*, Including Some Unpublished Henry James Letters', *The Henry James Review*, 3, no. 2 (Winter 1982): 80–95. Pound scorns 'the Paterine art of appreciation' in his essay on James, 'A Shake Down' (1918); *Instigations of Ezra Pound* (New York: Boni and Liveright, 1920); www.gutenberg.org/files/40852/40852-h/40852-h.htm.
51. Arthur Conan Doyle, *The Tragedy of the Korosko* (1898): www.gutenberg.org/files/12555/12555-0.txt.
52. Ezra Pound, 'Redondillas, or Something of that sort', in *Collected Early Poems*, Michael John King, ed. (New York: New Directions, 1976), 281.
53. Thomas Stearns Eliot, *Selected Essays* (New York: Harcourt, Brace & World, 1950), 443.
54. Irving Babbitt, *The Masters of Modern French Criticism* (Boston, MA: Houghton Mifflin, 1912), 174.
55. Edmund Wilson, *Axel's Castle: A Study in the Imaginative Literature of 1870–1930* (New York: Charles Scribner's Sons, 1931), 32.
56. For a comparison of Fry's prose and Pater's, see Woolf, *Roger Fry: A Biography* (1940).
57. Wyndham Lewis, *The Doom of Youth* (London: Chatto & Windus, 1932), 5.

14

JULIANNA K. WILL

Pater and Gender

The way in which gender appears in Pater's work is integral to the articulation of his aesthetic philosophy. This articulation begins with his conception of the renaissance, which is largely characterised by examples of artistic transmissions, made possible through cycles of decay and reincarnation. His habitual emphasis on 'fresh sources' for aesthetic 'new experiences' is balanced by a sustained insistence that novelty in art represents 'a Renaissance, a revival'.[1] Renewal and rebirth were strongly gendered concepts in the Victorian period; thus, Pater's understanding and interrogations of sex and gender form a vital basis for the aesthetic philosophy he constructs across his literary *oeuvre*, a basis which revolves around metaphors of pregnancy and childbirth.

In *Studies in the History of the Renaissance*, Pater defines his ideal of aesthetic experience as a highly subjective moment that is nevertheless shared across a community. Throughout the series of essays that comprise this volume, and most starkly in its Conclusion, he grapples with the impossibility, but nevertheless necessity, of combining the individual/mind and the collective/body, which he (and the popular Victorian imagination) routinely identifies, respectively, with the masculine and feminine. These gendered associations are defined in such texts as Coventry Patmore's *The Angel in the House* (1854, 1862) and John Ruskin's *Sesame and Lilies* (1865). Ruskin summarises the basic stereotypes of Victorian gender categories: 'the man's power is active', and his 'intellect is for speculation and invention'; 'the woman's power' is passive, 'her intellect' for neither 'invention [n]or creation'.[2] Pater does not challenge these frameworks, but rather applies the implications of segregate, gendered traits to both his aesthetic philosophy and his notions of what Michel Foucault would call care of the self.[3]

Pater's representations of gender have been investigated in relation to sexual difference and queer desire, an avenue of study for which the foundations were laid in the 1990s. Herbert Sussman (1995), for example, explores Pater's appropriation of the 'male fantasies and masculine poetics of his time' in relation to 'his own homoeroticism and the emerging homoerotic discourse of 1860s Oxford', through which he constructs his ideas of 'masculinity' and the 'masculine poetic', and within which he grounds 'fantasies of the male body and the male psyche'.[4] Linda Dowling's *Hellenism and Homosexuality in Victorian Oxford* (1992) provides the groundwork for the analysis of this Oxfordian homoerotic discourse, especially in relation to Benjamin Jowett's revival of Plato within the university's classics curriculum. On this basis, scholars have continued to explore how homoerotic sexual interest inflects Pater's work and informs his conceptions of Victorian masculinities. Stefano Evangelista (2004), for example, persuasively outlines a Foucauldian understanding of Pater's critical approaches to literature and art as 'an encoded confession' of desire, 'a relationship between critic and object (or critic and artist) in which intellectual and erotic passions are collapsed'.[5] Both Sussman and Evangelista conclude that if the middle-class Victorian 'definition of manhood' and its 'masculine poetics' emphasise the 'ability to control male energy' through productive outward expression,[6] then Pater 'deviates' from these norms by channelling energy inward, 'freeing it from societal and moral imperatives'.[7]

Less research has been done on Pater in relation to women and femininity. Through her engagement with Pater's 'refreshing sensitivity to gender and its cultural implications', Lesley Higgins's 'But who is "she"?: Forms of Subjectivity in Walter Pater's Writings' (1997) has laid meticulous and compelling foundations on Pater's deployment of 'dominant Victorian discourses on femininity'.[8] Billie Andrew Inman has commented in several places on Pater's depictions of maternity and motherhood, especially in his representations of the Virgin Mary. More recent scholarship has assessed the impact of Pater's works on female writers at the *fin de siècle*, such as in Joseph Bristow's *Extraordinary Aesthetes: Decadents, New Women, and Fin-de-Siècle Culture* (2023). Yopie Prins's *Ladies Greek: Victorian Translations of Tragedy* (2017) explores Paterian inflections in the writings of such women as Vernon Lee, Michael Field, Jane Harrison, Gertrude Stein, and H. D. (Hilda Doolittle). Prins is especially interested in how Pater sublimates femininity in his expressions of same-sex desire through his analysis of the Greek god Dionysus.

In my approach to Pater and gender, I move away from interrogating the relationships between sexuality and gender expression, to examine instead how Pater applies traditional Victorian gender norms as categories broader than sexual difference and desire to his ideas of renaissance and aestheticism. I do not entirely separate gender and sexuality, nor do I think it possible or desirable to enact a complete distinction. My approach, however, considers gender in its less tangible permeations, as a series of social conventions and assumptions that humans routinely apply to objects and concepts that are inherently sexless. For Pater, art and artistic creation are masculine, but the great and cyclical cultural moments that produce them are feminine. In several essays, for example, 'he stresses the crucial importance of Venus as an epiphanic figure signaling the rebirth of culture and aesthetic values . . . the transcultural figure of a "second birth," and a third, and so on'.[9] The pursuit of cultural and aesthetic values is, of course, immediately masculine-coded by Victorian gender stereotypes, and often these 'second birth[s]' are beautiful young men – but they die without the promise of renewal, without the possibility of being reborn. Instead, these youths conceive, inspire the conception of, or indeed represent lasting art and literature: 'the divination of fresh sources' within each feminine-birthed epoch (*TR* 77). Because aesthetic experience requires one to accept art's (masculine-coded) subjectivity, its 'design in the web', while nevertheless maintaining an awareness of the entirety of the (feminine) web itself, Pater's true aesthete must 'hea[l] that rupture' of gender and embody the wholeness of human experience, masculine and feminine (*TR* 78; *TS* 2).

In this chapter, I establish how Pater conceives renaissance metaphorically as a perpetual series of matrilineal transmissions (of mothers giving birth to daughters). Within these feminine-coded, repetitive cycles, Pater imagines the male artist as one who, working in isolation, produces creations that give cultural epochs their significance, but also as one who is denied the endless feminine potential for renewal. While Pater plays with these ideas in his writings on modern art and literature, it is ultimately through the anthropomorphism of classical myth and literature that he is able to articulate and explore his conceptions of gender, aestheticism, and renaissance. Through the ambiguously gendered god Dionysus and his equally ambiguous birth, Pater finds a way to combine feminine and masculine functions into a 'single, imaginable form' that is able to achieve a complete aesthetic moment.[10] Ultimately, then, I reveal what I call the originality of Pater's conventional thinking: rather than challenge or subvert Victorian gender stereotypes, he instead works within and deploys these norms to articulate a state of aesthetic awareness that surpasses gender.

Maternal Cultural Cycles: Demeter, Persephone, and the *Mona Lisa*

Pater's concept of renaissance is defined by a consistent metaphor of female reproductive biology, made through his motif of the mother and daughter as a chain (or 'thread') of connectivity and 'perpetual motion' across human history (*TR* 197). The most famous example of this motif is part of Pater's description of *La Gioconda* (the *Mona Lisa*) in his essay on 'Leonardo da Vinci':

> [A]s Leda, [she] was the mother of Helen of Troy, and, as Saint Anne, the mother of Mary ... The fancy of a perpetual life, sweeping together ten thousand experiences, is an old one; and modern philosophy has conceived the idea of humanity as wrought upon by, and summing up in itself, all modes of thought and life. (*TR* 140)

The woman in the portrait becomes, for Pater, a 'single, imaginable form' in whom 'all modes of thought and life' are contained, in whom 'the old fancy' and the 'modern ideal' exist simultaneously (*CS* 92; *TR* 140). She is, as Pater later says of the goddess Persephone, a 'strange, dual being' (*CS* 66), a self-renewing 'vampire' (*TR* 140), in whom resides the possibilities of both the beginning and end of every cultural and artistic epoch.

Pater's fantasy of da Vinci's 'masterpiece' lingers on 'Lady Lisa', not as one of those 'languid women' of Italian painting – nor as the more traditional Helen or Mary – but as an eternal mother, through whom are 'conceived' and birthed female figures at the centre of significant cultural and artistic moments (TR 139–40). In one sense, the possibilities anticipated by the births of these daughters, as Higgins argues, revolve around 'male endeavor and pain'.[11] In Pater's description of the *Mona Lisa*, those 'male endeavors' are the Trojan War (foreboded by his mention of Leda) and the Passion of Christ (St Anne). Pater's fascination with this particular painting, however, remains fixed upon the mother/daughter transference. The rich mytho-history of the Trojan War, the epicentre of ancient Greek and Roman art and literature, depends upon the catalyst of Leda's exceptional parturition, on the birth of Helen. The successor of this cultural focal point, the Judeo-Christian tradition, is likewise a birth for Pater, but not, fascinatingly, the divine birth of Christ.[12] Instead, Pater envisions this next renaissance, this next cultural reincarnation, as St Anne to Mary – as mother and daughter, components of his 'perpetual motion' of death and rebirth, 'that strange, perpetual, weaving and unweaving of ourselves' (*TR* 198).

Pater's emphasis on the mother and daughter in his famous description of da Vinci's painting latterly becomes a more definite, more expansive vector in his aesthetic philosophy through the vehicle of classical myth and religions, which he explores in 'The Myth of Demeter and Persephone' (1876). Just as *La Gioconda* embodies the 'modern ideal' through her transmigration from the classical (Leda) and Christian (St Anne) tradition, so too does Demeter inhabit Christian and early modern subject positions. Higgins has identified an 'uncanny formal resemblance' between Pater's description of the *Mona Lisa* and his description of the statue of *Demeter Knidos* (*c*.350 BCE).[13] This statue, unearthed by Sir Charles Newton in 1857 and housed at the British Museum, becomes a visual focal point for Pater's essay: she is another 'seated figure', 'another non-smiling, mature, mysteriously impassive female figure whose surface placidity belies a turbulent personal and cultural history'.[14] The two figures are not necessarily interchangeable for Pater but rather are different iterations of the same being. The smiling woman of the *Mona Lisa* has been 'dead many times' and 'learned the secrets of the grave', just as Demeter, the Greek goddess of agriculture, has seen 'the seed fall into the ground and die, many times' (*TR* 140; *CS* 88). Inman has similarly chronicled how Pater carefully selects and omits sections of his source materials in order to transform the goddess into the older incarnation of another famous mother: the Virgin Mary.[15] Pater makes this connection, Inman argues, through his selective translations of Demeter's garments in the *Homeric Hymn*.[16] Although Pater's 'blue hood' and 'blue robe' are accurate translations for *kyaneos kalymma* and *kyanos peplos/kyanopeplos* (*CS* 61; 62),[17] Inman demonstrates that Pater's rendering nevertheless departs from earlier and contemporary translations of *kyanos* in this context as 'dark'. Pater's unqualified usage of 'blue' suggests a Demeter 'appareled as the Virgin Mary was[,] in innumerable paintings of the late Medieval period and the Renaissance'.[18] Through this blue cloth, Pater 'weaves' and 're-weaves' his perpetual, maternal 'threads' into Demeter and Mary.

This myth of the mother and daughter is expanded into an allegory for Pater's imagined epochal cycles. 'Following [the myth's] changes', he explains, 'we come across various phases of Greek culture, which are not without their likenesses in the modern mind' (*CS* 59). These 'various phases of Greek culture,' coupled with Pater's persistent application of cycles of death and rebirth, suggest an uniquely Paterian approach to prevalent Victorian ideas concerning the so-called evolution of human progress, popularised by Roman historians Edward Gibbon and Thomas Arnold. Both were proponents of a Viconian cyclical view of history, from which Auguste Comte draws to establish his Positivist philosophy in the 1830s. Comte argues that human development can be described through 'the law of three stages': theological, metaphysical, and positive. Humans first attribute the phenomena of the universe to the divine or supernatural, then attempt to understand its workings through a metaphysical inquiry into abstract concepts, and lastly turn to scientific method as the ultimate means of understanding the world. Both Ludwig Preller and John Ruskin adapt these 'three stages of development' into their analysis of myth, arguing for a positivist evolution or Hegelian progress, maintaining that myth and religion begin in 'physical existence' or in 'the natural world'; the natural world is then personified into anthropomorphic deities, who are in turn extrapolated into the exploration of universal truths for human existence.

Unlike his Italian, German, and British precursors, however, Pater refuses a Hegelian or Comtian approach (a 'facile orthodoxy' [*TR* 189]) to understanding ancient religions, approaches which would characterise these three phases as a linear form of improvement or development. His outline, which he introduces in 'Demeter and Persephone', as Matthew Potolsky describes, does not 'pertai[n] to the relative sophistication of mythic expression ... but to its changing function in the larger culture'.[19] Pater clarifies that his three phases of myth, instinctive/mystical, poetical/literary, and ethical, 'are fixed very plainly in the story of Demeter' (*CS* 65). Just as Demeter, St Anne, Mary, and *La Gioconda* are all variously iterations of the same, communal feminine experience, 'age to age always the same',[20] each of Pater's 'phases' are also different riffs on the same theme: what Pater defines in *Plato and Platonism* (1893) as Plato's 'process of becoming' or 'law of change,' the earth and its potentials of 'birth and death and decay'.[21] Demeter, Pater explains, 'is first the earth ... in all the accident and decay of its children' (*CS* 64). She and her daughter Persephone are joined together 'in a sort of confused union', in which 'together they had represented the earth and its changes' (*CS* 64). In Pater's second phase, the mother and daughter become more distinctly and individually defined by their 'special functions' (*CS* 65): Demeter is now the earth, from whom grow the flowers of spring and into whom the flowers dissolve in winter. Persephone is now the changing flowers, the spring and the winter, who begins, ends, and renews within her mother's realm. Finally, in Pater's final phase, Demeter becomes more firmly the embodiment of 'all-encompassing maternity', from whom is formed the potentialities for death and renewal – personified as her daughter, Persephone, 'a goddess of death, yet with the promise of life to come' (*CS* 65).[22]

Pater anthropomorphises his conception of death and rebirth through the motif of these two Greek goddesses. By identifying Demeter as the original *mater dolorosa*, Pater once again connects ancient Greek and Christian cultural traditions through a matrilineal transmission: the eternal earth is rewoven into Demeter, into Leda, into St Anne, into Mary, into 'Lady Lisa'. Just as in his description of the *Mona Lisa*, which prioritises the birth of Mary over the birth of Christ, Pater relocates the significant moment of the Judaeo-Christian tradition from Mary's birth of a divine son (Christ) to the Hellenic birth of a divine daughter (Persephone) – eschewing Christ's *mythos* of death and resurrection in favour of Persephone's eternal renaissance. (Pater makes a point of including that Demeter's surrogate son, Demophoon, is denied a chance at immortality [*CS* 62–63]). Persephone, as Pater describes, is the 'goddess of summer and the goddess of death', the 'strange dual being' who dies and is reborn within the cycle of every annual season. She is always Kore, 'fresh and blithe' daughter of the earth, and she always *becomes* Persephone, 'the wholly terrible goddess of death'. It is through Demeter, the eternal mother, that 'these two contrasted images have been brought into intimate relationship' (*CS* 66). The myth of Persephone's abduction becomes a focal point for Pater's reflections on aesthetic transmissions and renewal: Demeter is the all-encompassing earth, who gives birth to a daughter of death and rebirth, of 'summer and winter' (*CS* 64).

Thus Demeter and Persephone, mother and daughter, become physical incarnations of Pater's conception of cultural life cycles.[23] Ultimately both figures are 'rewoven' versions of an anthropomorphised and all-encompassing earth, which gives birth to daughters that embody the possibilities of birth and death simultaneously. They are sharers in the 'uncouth energy of the older and more primitive "Mighty Mother"' (*TR* 100). Pater argues that it is through Demeter that the Greeks 'nam[e] together in her all their fluctuating thoughts, impressions, suspicions of the earth and its appearances, their whole complex divination of a mysterious life, a perpetual working, a continuous act of conception' (*CS* 67). These 'perpetual workings' associated with the goddess become communal, feminine sensations that are shared across generations of mothers; through her 'continuous act of conception', she 'continuously' gives birth to daughters who perpetuate the necessary cycles of death and renewal – of renaissance.

Male Parthenogenesis as Artistic Creation: *Plato and Platonism* and *Imaginary Portraits*

Despite Pater's perennial focus on female rebirth, his male artist is nevertheless the one who creates aesthetic meaning for these matrilineal cycles. It is after all da Vinci who gives *La Gioconda* her special significance. As his 'masterpiece', the woman on the canvas is transformed from 'a living Florentine' into a 'creature of his thought', defined 'on the fabric of his dreams' (*TR* 139). The connective moments of Pater's feminine cultural phases are afforded their 'highest quality' by the individual – *pace* male – artist and his work (*TR* 200). This male artist and his critics are all aware of an entirely subjective and personal experience produced in the creation and contemplation of art, which differs strongly from the repetitive epochal cycles in which they labour – although they are nevertheless a part of these feminine epochs. It is because these cycles are felt by 'men of genius,' as Pater explains in 'Diaphaneitè', that the next cultural epoch can be 'renerved, modified, by the ideas of [the artist]'.[24] Pater's declaration in *Gaston de*

Latour, that the feminine soul is 'age to age always the same' (*GL* 150), is thus an echo of William Blake's maxim, quoted in the preface of *The Renaissance*, that the 'ages are all equal ... but genius is always above its age'.[25] In this sexist, yet pervasive gender paradigm, the masculine-coded genius of the artist transcends, rather than repeats, history.

Like Thomas Carlyle, Robert Browning, Alfred Tennyson, and many other male Victorian writers, Pater envisages artistic creation as an extension of masculine virility and seminal reproduction. The very term *genius* is etymologically linked to procreation and birth through the Greek root γεν-/*gen*. The analogy of the creative act as a heteronormative 'fathering' of children on a fecund and passive (*pace* feminine) canvas or page – as 'God father[ing] the world' – has been, as Sandra Gilbert and Susan Gubar established in the 1970s, 'pervasive in Western literary civilization'.[26] It is also one, however, that is analogous to specific perceptions of artistic and intellectual production as a form of male pregnancy (and not impregnation), engendered through homoerotic desire.

Plato has a particular interest in creativity as masculine pregnancy in his interrogations of *eros* (sexual desire). His *Symposium*, a key text on this topic, comprises a series of speeches devoted to the praise of *eros* and the benefits of its controlled, proper comportment. The speeches culminate with one delivered by the character Socrates, who relates (through the conceit the priestess Diotima) his theory of *to orthôs paiderastei*, or 'correct *paederastia*',[27] in an attempt to give, as Foucault argues, Athenian male homoeroticism 'an ethical form different from the one that was required when it came to loving a woman'.[28] *Paederastia* relates to an Athenian social custom, in which a male citizen who has reached his majority (the *erastes*) provides mentorship to a youth who has not yet reached his (the *eromenos*). The practice often, but not always, involves an exchange of sexual favours. In this particular speech, Diotima outlines Plato's infamous 'ladder of love' analogy, through which she argues that measured *eros* directed at beautiful, youthful male bodies begins the essential process of desire for beautiful ideas, and then eventually desire for the 'beautiful itself' – all facilitated by the homosocial/homoerotic relationship between man and youth.[29] David Halperin summarises how 'Diotima introduces and develops the unprecedented imagery of male pregnancy' in this *paederastic* philosophy, in which 'men become pregnant (*kyein*), suffer birth pangs (*ôdis*), bear (*gennan*) and bring forth (*tiktein*) offspring, and nourish their young (*trephein*)' in service of the 'ultimate aim of erotic desire'.[30] The purpose of homoerotic *eros*, Diotima reveals, is not to possess what is beautiful but for male 'procreation and parturition in the beautiful', because procreation is the only means to attain 'immortality in mortal life'.[31] 'All men are pregnant, Socrates', Diotima reveals, 'both in body and soul'.[32]

In *Plato and Platonism* (1893), Pater frequently engages with Plato's metaphor of masculine pregnancy in his descriptions of intellectual endeavour. The verses of earlier poets are what 'had given birth' to Platonic philosophy (*PP* 3); 'the knowledge of man ... may be brought to birth in every man's soul'; through Athenian homosocial relationships, 'the power of words to convey thoughts' can be 'brought to birth' in the youthful disciple of the philosopher (*PP* 73; 78). The 'shining' Greek examples of fraternal love, Castor and Polydeuces, are 'two stars ... at their original birth in men's minds' (*PP* 209). Throughout the essays in this collection, Pater applies the procreative homoerotic philosophy of the *Symposium* to 'the essence of all artistic beauty' and, like Plato, expresses the results of intellectual creativity as masculine-birthed offspring (*PP* 107). Fascinatingly, however, Pater uses this metaphorical, *paederastic* language of engendering, pregnancy, and birth almost exclusively in *Plato and Platonism*. One of the few instances in which this imagery appears outside *Plato and Platonism* is in Pater's unfinished novel *Gaston de Latour* – a novel in which the titular protagonist mirrors the *paederastic* model by interacting with various older writers who contribute to his understanding of Platonism. Pater's narrator thus explains how Giordano Bruno reveals to the youthful Gaston that 'To excite, to surprise, to move men's minds ... and, according to the Socratic fancy, to bring them to the birth, was after all the proper function of the teacher' (*GL* 119). For Plato, as Pater describes, the 'children' that pederastic relationships ultimately 'birth in beauty' are essential truths, 'real things ... that [are] "in an end themselves"' ('Sophists' 110–11). They are decidedly *not* art or literature, which Plato considers misleading representations of reality: 'The Shadows of Ideas: *De Umbris Idearum*' (*GL* 120). To Pater, however, 'the offspring of these more noble begetters are works of art', because for Pater, to study art is to 'define beauty' (*TR* 73).[33]

When he describes the creation and appreciation of art in *The Renaissance*, Pater does not use the language of childbirth but instead suggests that artistic creations are physical manifestations of the artist's intellect – are pieces of the artist himself. (There are, of course, possible exceptions, such as in 'An English Poet', when the narrator describes 'fancies ... germinating rapidly' in the boy [*IP* 155]). *La Gioconda* is not a child of da Vinci but instead '[p]resent from the first incorporeally in Leonardo's brain' and then later 'found present at last in *Il Giocondo*'s house' (*TR* 140).[34] Thus, Pater wonders whether she was produced physically by 'renewed labour' and 'never really finished', or successfully 'projected' from the artist's mind 'as by stroke of magic' (*TR* 140). In 'Sebastian Van Storck', the germination is likewise parthenogenic. The youth, 'looking backward for the generative source of that creative power of thought in him' finds that it is a reflection, an 'enlarged pattern of himself' (*IP* 108–9). The creative 'juices' of Pater's chosen artists are channelled inward, and their artistic creations are creatures of ideas, not bodies. Sussman suggests that this suppression of sexual desire is, for Pater, a necessary process in the conception of beautiful things, which constitutes a departure from the outwardly expressed *eros* of Platonic homosocial philosophy and the 'masculine poetics' of the early nineteenth century, from which Pater draws.[35] 'Sealing the valves of desire' in order to direct seminal energy inward as a method of artistic invention is paradoxically both procreative and sterile.[36] It is seminal energy uniquely trapped 'in the narrow chamber of the individual mind' (*TR* 198). It is, I suggest, a masculine adaptation of parthenogenesis – in which the male reproductive component transforms into an artistic embryo.

Unlike Plato's homosocial paradigm, Pater's artistic parthenogenic model relies on 'the individual in his isolation' and is therefore ultimately and paradoxically sterile, ephemeral, and doomed (*TS* 187–88). 'There is a violence, an impossibility about men who have ideas', he describes in 'Diaphaneitè', 'which makes one suspect that they could never be the type of any widespread life'.[37] Indeed, unlike the mothers and daughters of Pater's imagination, the beautiful boys in his *Imaginary Portraits* (1887) are strangely remote. They rarely participate in the 'fathering' of child or art, and often the possibility of their sexual relations with women are equated with death – such as in 'Duke Carl of Rosenmold' and *Marius the Epicurean* (1885).[38] In 'Hippolytus Veiled: A Study from Euripides', the advances of the youth's stepmother, Phaedra, ignite the chain of events that ultimately leads to Hippolytus's demise. But these boys are also often isolated from the homosocial, or homoerotic, interactions which would impregnate them with Platonic intellectual children, and instead they 'wast[e] away in . . . self-imposed isolation from the social world'.[39] Hippolytus himself spends most of his days in a pastoral idyll, accompanied by the maternal figures of Antiope and Artemis.

During the 1880s, Pater describes his semi-autobiographical imaginary portrait, 'The Child in the House', as 'the germinating, / original, source, specimen, / of all my *imaginative* work'.[40] He also attempts to define the portrait as 'imaginary: because – / and portraits, because they present, / not an action, a story, revealed / especially, in outward / detail'.[41] The 'source' of Pater's imaginary portraits is, therefore, a child, who 'germinates' within the author, which is suggestive of Plato's male pregnancy, but without the external expressions of *eros* that allow Plato's homoerotic couples to 'give birth in beauty' and thereby achieve immortality. These children are not 'birthed' but 'revealed' in the observer's fancy of a life invented for the artwork. The narrators of these stories uncover (un-veil?) the protagonist youths in the ekphrastic process of the genre, the stories of which are often 'germinated' from a work of art. As Østermark-Johansen explains, the youths at the centres of the imaginary portraits are of the type Pater describes in 'Diaphaneité': 'transparent characters' with a 'delicate, and heightened sense of sensitivity, which leads them into morbid isolation'.[42] Just as Demeter and Kore become personifications of Pater's renaissance, these boys, through their remote 'ghostly transparency', are personifications of art and artistic experience.[43]

Doomed and beautiful boys populate Pater's imaginary portraits. Gerald Monsman has suggested that Pater's boys are celibate because 'they have ritually consecrated their virility to their Great Mother' (the endlessly 'rewoven' Demeter) in a 'consummation of marriage' to her that results in their deaths.[44] In 'Hippolytus Veiled', Pater explores the implications of that which is only briefly noted in 'Demeter and Persephone': Demophoon, the infant mortal boy whom Demeter tries and fails to adopt into immortality, is inevitably doomed '[to] share the common destiny of all men' and die without hope of rebirth (CS 62). Demeter reappears in 'Hippolytus Veiled' again as a mother of death and renaissance, but this time her daughter is Artemis, portrayed as the potential for birth and death through her dual *numen* of parturition and maternal mortality. 'Here was that secret', Pater's narrator muses, 'at once of that genial, all-embracing maternity, and ... of sudden death. For the late birth of this shadowy daughter was identified dimly with the sudden passing into Hades of Persephone, her first-born' (IP 165). Again, Pater characterises his *kore* ('daughter' and alternative name for Persephone) not only as the daughter of Demeter, as the daughter of all mothers, but as the daughter of St Anne, evoking Mary in his description of her as the 'virgin mother' of the 'immaculate' Hippolytus (IP 165).

The chaste boy, however, is not part of the matrilineal cycle of death and rebirth, nor is he immortalised by 'giving birth in beauty', as the homosocial philosopher is. Pater 'toys with the resurrection of Hippolytus as the Roman deity Virius in Aricia outside Rome', but concludes that such a renaissance is impossible.[45] These Greek boys, 'Adonis, and Icarus, and Hyacinth, and other doomed creatures of immature radiance' (IP 173), must instead lie 'in heroic graves', eternal only in their remembrance as 'something that could never be brought to life again' (IP 161). As subjective, ephemeral, fleeting moments, these boys can neither reproduce nor be reborn – they instead give meaning to moments and are remembered only in death, never to be reincarnated, but always to be connected across time through their presence in repetitive maternal cycles – through renaissance.

The Transubstantiation of Gender: 'A Study of Dionysus'

In 'Hippolytus Veiled', Hippolytus cannot be reborn. This fate sets him apart from the other two subjects of Pater's Greek-themed imaginary portraits, 'Apollo in Picardy' and 'Denys L'Auxerrois'. In these latter stories, Pater imagines the Greek gods, Apollo and Dionysus, reincarnated and transplanted into a new society, ever ready to be born again, allowing his narrator to imagine 'to have actually seen the tortured figure [of Denys] ... to have met [him] in the streets' (*IP* 95). Dionysus is the most elusive member of the Greek pantheon, due to his inherently contradictory nature: a fertile god of creation, who ruptures boundaries, both literal and figurative. Victorian interpretations of this enigmatic figure and his mystery cult shifted from its being a precursor to Christianity to a decadent, sometimes dangerous, figure of gender and sexual dissidence. Pater places him at the pinnacle of the 'hierarchy of the creatures of water and sunlight' (*CS* 93). The seer Teiresias, in Euripides's *Bacchae*, calls him the god of the 'wet' principle, as opposed to Demeter's 'dry'. This distinction is a significant indicator of Dionysus's lack of gender fixity; women, in classical Greek ideology, were routinely associated with (a sometimes overabundance of) moisture.[46] For Pater especially, Dionysus occupies a space of indeterminate, or perhaps more aptly, mixed, gender: he is a 'woman-like god' (*CS* 157). His primary function as 'the principle that destroys differences' causes him to play a crucial role in Pater's aesthetic philosophy (Segal 234).

In his essay 'A Study of Dionysus', Pater's interest in maternity shifts from the mother/daughter dynamic and instead turns to the ways in which childbirth merges – blurs together – seemingly binary events into a single moment. While pregnant with the son of Zeus, mortal Semele is tricked by 'immortal Hera' into exposing herself to 'her lover' in his 'glory' (as lightning), which destroys the woman and, as Pater imagines it, causes her to give 'premature birth' to the infant Dionysus (*CS* 98). Semele perishes, but Zeus sews the premature foetus into his thigh and carries the infant to term, becoming, in a sense, his sole, parthenogenic parent: a circumstance which allows the child to be divine. In Greek myth, children born from the sexual union of a mortal and an immortal are not normally gods themselves, merely human heroes, such as Helen, Perseus, Sarpedon, and Heracles (who is born mortal but attains godhood as an adult). Dionysus is therefore only able to be a god because he is eventually born from Zeus alone, emphasising that his second birth is parthenogenic.

The event of Dionysus's first birth, as described by Pater, is a moment of dissolved differences – a moment during which life and death exist concomitantly:

> The mother faints, and is parched up by the heat, which brings the child to the birth; and it pierces through, a wonder of freshness, drawing its everlasting

green and typical coolness out of the midst of the ashes; its own stem becoming
at last like a tangled mass of tortured metal.   (CS 99)

The natural pains of childbirth are ambiguously combined with the divine
agony of Zeus's thunderbolt – itself an oblique reference to intercourse. The
boundaries between the natural and the supernatural, between life and
death, are suspended at the moment of Dionysus's birth; it is unclear which
phenomenon brings the baby to term and which causes the mortal mother's
death – or whether both phenomena are equally responsible. Each image
Pater creates combines beauty with pain: 'smitten volcanic soil' produces
'virtues'; the 'parched' (a word with 'barren' connotations) and fainting
mother results in the birth of the child; 'a wonder of freshness' rises from
ashes and 'tortured metal'. (This strange 'congruence' between beauty and
death is something Pater first explores in his review essay 'Poems by William
Morris' [1868], which he eventually edits into the Conclusion to *The
Renaissance*.) The instant of Dionysus's birth is a moment of simultaneous
opposites – in which the immortal god experiences human mortality through
his mother's death.

The focus Pater places upon Semele's actual act of delivery is, in and of
itself, striking in a nineteenth-century context, the literature of which often
shrinks from describing the physicality and danger of childbirth. In Pater's
imagination, Semele in her labour personifies the 'travail of nature', a link
solidified by her etymology: 'Semele, an old Greek word, as it seems, for the
surface of the earth' (CS 98). Through the act of giving birth she joins the
feminine collectivity, enduring a physical agony that is shared by women
across time and space. 'The anguish of the human mother', Pater explains, is
felt by the communal, feminine, 'mystical body of the earth' (CS 99). Semele
becomes another perpetual link in Pater's ideas of renaissance and death,
another personification of earth – of Gaia, of Demeter, of St Anne, of *La
Gioconda*.

Yet Semele is also uniquely cut off from the matrilineal cycle, for that same
'mystical body of the earth' is '*forgotten* in the human anguish of the mother
of Dionysus' (CS 99; my emphasis). In Semele's labour, specific gendered
associations are confused: mortal Semele becomes the dead youth in place of
her divine son, lying eternally in her smoking grave (CS 99). Divine Dionysus
takes on the maternal 'travail of nature' in his embodiment of the earthy 'fire
and dew' (CS 99). Yet, he is also – through his gestation in, and delivery from,
Zeus's thigh – the offspring of the parthenogenic, male parturition of Zeus
alone: 'born once and again' (CS 99). The ephemeral, subjective, and masculine moments Pater details as necessary for aesthetic experience thereby
combine into the immortal, shared, feminine experience of renaissance

within this ambiguously gendered figure of Greek mythology. He is thus the embodiment of 'Renaissance, the name of a many-sided but yet united movement' in which one finds 'new experiences, new subjects of poetry, new forms of art' connected by (or to) the endless rebirth of cultural cycles (*TR* 77).

Conclusion

Pater therefore imagines true aesthetic experience as a series of heavily gendered roles, but also as the internal combination of those genders within the self. Although Pater maintains the stereotype that immortalising art is gendered masculine, his 'fancy of perpetual life', is a feminine one – a fancy of matrilineal transmissions, within which artists labour and to which their art provides meaning. It is unsurprising that he relies on the literature and philosophy of ancient Greece – a tradition to which he regularly recurs – in order to articulate these associations, especially given the necessity of anthropomorphising the intangible in order to gender it. His applications of both male and female gender paradigms to his aesthetic philosophy place a surprising emphasis on the processes of birth: the eternally fecund rebirths of feminine epochal cycles, and the parthenogenic, isolated act of artistic creation/appreciation. One must, however, inhabit both subject positions, masculine and feminine, simultaneously and become, like Dionysus, transubstantial in the moment of the aesthetic experience. Each of these subjective moments constitutes a personal rebirth – a renaissance.

Notes

1. Walter Pater, *The Renaissance: Studies in Art and Poetry*, ed. Hilary Fraser (Oxford: Oxford University Press, 2025), 78. Hereafter, cited parenthetically as *TR*.
2. John Ruskin, *Sesame and Lilies* (New York: John Wiley and Sons, 1979), 90.
3. See Michel Foucault, *Ethics: Subjectivity and Truth*, volume I, trans. Robert Hurley, ed. Paul Rabinow (London: Penguin Classics, 2020), 283–301.
4. Herbert Sussman, *Victorian Masculinities: Manhood and Masculine Poetics in Early Victorian Literature and Art* (Cambridge: Cambridge University Press, 1995), 174.
5. Stefano Evangelista, 'Walter Pater Unmasked: Impressionistic Criticism and the Gender of Aesthetic Writing', *Literature Compass*, 1, no. 1 (2004): 3.
6. Sussman, *Victorian Masculinities*, 11, 178.
7. Evangelista, 'Unmasked,' 3.
8. Lesley Higgins, 'But who is "she"?: Forms of Subjectivity in Walter Pater's Writings', *Nineteenth Century Prose*, 24, no. 3 (1997): 37–38.
9. Higgins, 'But who is "she"?,' 44.

10. Walter Pater, *Classical Studies*, Matthew Potolsky, ed. (Oxford: Oxford University Press, 2020), 92. Hereafter, cited parenthetically in the text as *CS*.
11. Higgins, 'But who is "she"?', 45. Higgins's argument is made in connection with Botticelli's *Birth of Venus* and the Madonna.
12. Pater repeatedly suggests that the Greco-Roman tradition and Judaeo-Christian are cyclical reincarnations of each other: 'But it was inevitable that from time to time minds should arise … to ask themselves whether the religion of Greece was indeed a revival of the religion of Christ' (*TR* 91).
13. Higgins, 'But who is "she"?', 47.
14. Higgins, 'But who is "she"?', 47.
15. Billie Andrew Inman, *Walter Pater and His Reading, 1874–1877, With a Bibliography of His Library Borrowings, 1878–1894* (New York: Garland Publishing, 1990), 175.
16. Inman, *Pater*, 175.
17. Callimachus, *Hymn to Demeter*, ll. 42, 183–184, 319, 360, 374, 442.
18. Inman, *Pater 1874–1877*, 174–175.
19. Matthew Potolsky, 'Critical Introduction', in *Classical Studies*, Walter Pater, ed. (Oxford: Oxford University Press, 2020), 20.
20. Walter Pater, *Gaston de Latour: An Unfinished Romance*, Gerald Monsman, ed. (Oxford: Oxford University Press, 2019), 150. Hereafter, cited parenthetically in the text as *GL*.
21. Pater, *Plato and Platonism* (London: Macmillan, 1893), 150. Hereafter, cited parenthetically in the text as *PP*.
22. Pater, *Imaginary Portraits*, Lene Østermark-Johansen, ed. (Oxford: Oxford University Press, 2018), 65. Hereafter, cited parenthetically in the text as *IP*.
23. A striking exception to this pattern (of framing death and rebirth as feminine) appears in Pater's description of Castor and Polydeuces in *Plato and Platonism* ('Lacedaemon', *PP* 230–231). A comparison of Pater's Dioscuri and his Demeter and Persephone would comprise a fruitful avenue for further study on this topic.
24. Pater, 'Diaphaneitè', in *Miscellaneous Studies: A Series of Essays*, Charles L. Shadwell, ed. (London: Macmillan, 1895), 254.
25. Qtd. *TR* 74. Hill identifies the source as William Blake's annotations to *The Works of Sir Joshua Reynolds*, vol. 1, ed. 2 (London, 1798), 17 (located in the British Museum).
26. Sandra Gilbert and Susan Gubar, *Madwoman in the Attic: The Woman Writer and the Nineteenth-Century Literary Imagination, 1979* (New York: Yale University Press, 2020), 4.
27. Plato, *Symposium*, 211b5–6; cf. 210a4–5, 211b7–c1.
28. Michel Foucault, *History of Sexuality Volume 2: The Use of Pleasure*, trans. Robert Hurley (New York: Random House, 1985), 192.
29. Plato, *Symposium*, 210a ff.
30. *kyein* (*Symposium* 2026c1, 7, d4, 7–8; 208e2; 209a1–2, b1, 5, c3); *ôdis* (*Symposium* 206e1); *gennan* (*Symposium* 206c –d1, 3, 5, 7, e5, 7–8; 207a8–9, b2, d3, 7, e4; 208a1; 209a4, b2–4, c3–4, 8, d7, e2–3, 21007; 211a1, b3); *tiktein* (*Symposium* 206b7, c3–4, 6, d5, e5; 209a3, b2, c3; 210c1, d5, 212a3, 5); 'offspring' (*Symposium, apoblastema*: 208b5; *paides, ekgona*: 209c–e4). See David M. Halperin's discussion of 'Why is Diotima a Woman?' in his study, *One Hundred Years of Homosexuality and Other Essays on Greek Love* (New York: Routledge, 1990), 117.

31. Plato, *Symposium*, 206e.
32. Plato, *Symposium*, 206c.
33. Lee, *The Platonism of Walter Pater: Embodied Equity* (Oxford: Oxford University Press, 2020), 169.
34. Pater's description of the creation of *La Gioconda* bears striking resemblances to the parthenogenic birth of Athena in Greek mythology.
35. Sussman, *Victorian Masculinities*, 178.
36. Sussman, *Victorian Masculinities*, 178.
37. Pater, 'Diaphaneitè', 254.
38. 'Sebastian Van Storck' provides an interesting complication to the general sterility of Pater's young men: he does not beget children, but his death is suggestive of a maternal death in childbirth. 'It was in the saving of [a] child', the narrator recounts, 'that Sebastian lost his life' (*IP* 113).
39. Østermark-Johansen, 'Critical Introduction', 12.
40. Pater Collection, Houghton Library, bMS Eng. 1150, 1, 23ᵛ.
41. Brasenose College Archives Oxford, PP I B2/I. Both descriptions were written on small slips of paper, which Pater carried with him to jot down notes. ('Walter Pater: A Portrait' *Contemporary Review*, 66, (December 1894), 795–810, p. 806.) The transcriptions come from Østermark-Johansen's 'Critical Introduction', 3–4.
42. Østermark-Johansen, 'Critical Introduction', 16.
43. Østermark-Johansen, 'Critical Introduction', 16.
44. Gerald Monsman, *Pater's Portraits: Mythic Pattern in the Fiction of Walter Pater*, 1967 (Baltimore, MD: Johns Hopkins University Press, 2019), 253.
45. Lene Østermark-Johansen, 'Pater's "Hippolytus Veiled": A Study from Euripides?', in *Pater the Classicist*, Charles Martindale, ed. (Oxford: Oxford University Press, 2017), 188.
46. Euripides, *Bacchae*, 2. 275–280. See also Anne Carson, 'Putting Her in Her Place: Women, Dirt, and Desire', in *Before Sexuality: The Construction of Erotic Experience in the Ancient World*, David M. Halperin et al., ed. (Princeton: Princeton University Press, 1990), 135–170.

15

DUSTIN FRIEDMAN

Pater and Race

For many readers 'Walter Pater' and 'race' – the categorising of humans into distinct groups based on presumed inherited biological differences – may appear to be an unpromising conjunction. After all, Pater's famously indirect and understated prose contains few explicit references to racial identities. His writings are often associated with 'art for art's sake' Victorian aestheticism, which ostensibly promoted the idea that art and aesthetic experiences are (or at least should be) separate from any moral, social, or political concerns. Consequently, it would appear that race is simply immaterial to Pater's more obvious interests in beauty, pleasure, and the history of Western art and literature.

However, in recent decades critics have revealed that many Victorian aesthetes, including Pater, were not as indifferent to worldly matters as superficial readings of their works might suggest. Much has been written about his and other aesthetes' engagement with the non-normative gender and sexual identities that began to emerge in the closing decades of the nineteenth-century.[1] Recent research has also shown that decadence, a transnational literary and artistic movement whose English-language manifestation was heavily influenced by Pater, had a much broader impact that previously believed, extending to the works of racialised authors in colonial and postcolonial settings.[2] Despite these insights, however, there has been limited discussion of the significance of race in Pater's own writings.

In this chapter, I turn to two critical methods developed by cultural theorists – Sylvia Wynter's 'decipherment' and Kandice Chuh's 'aesthetic inquiry' – to gain insight into the role race plays in Pater's thinking, despite it not being an overt topic in his writings. First, I discuss how this inattention to race is the result of certain methodological limitations in the field of Victorian studies, which in turn reflect a larger, culture-wide misapprehension of the relationship between aesthetics and politics. I then seek to remedy this false impression by contextualising Pater's writings within racial politics of eighteenth- and nineteenth-century Western aesthetic discourse, especially in the work of two of Pater's major intellectual influences, the art historian Johann Joachim Winckelmann and the philosopher Immanuel Kant, who profoundly shaped the cultural context of discussions of art and beauty in the West. Winckelmann was most famous for his breathlessly homoerotic celebration of the statue known as the *Apollo Belvedere*, a depiction of the ancient Greek god of sunlight and reason that, for him, stood as the superlative artistic expression of the human ideals of rationality and love of freedom. Kant, inspired by Winckelmann, explicitly associated these ideals with white Europeans due to their physiognomy and, above all, their skin colour, presenting whiteness as the equivalent of neutrality itself.

Next I analyse how Pater's writings on classical Greek sculptures and the ancient Greek god Apollo responded to this earlier cultural history, focusing on his early essay 'Winckelmann' (1873) and his later short story 'Apollo in Picardy' (1893). I argue that the former conveys how Pater's impressions of Greek statues were shaped by the racialised aesthetic standards promoted in the eighteenth and nineteenth centuries, and how the latter demonstrates his awareness of and resentment towards this influence that developed over the course of his literary career. In the intervening years between these two works, Pater had redirected his attention towards Dionysus, the god of wine and spiritual ecstasy who stood as Apollo's dialectical counterpart in the Greek pantheon. Accordingly, in the final section of this chapter I examine Pater's 'A Study of Dionysus: The Spiritual Form of Fire and Dew' (1876) and 'Denys l'Auxerrois' (1886), works where Pater portrays the wine-god, traditionally depicted as the embodiment of Oriental excess, violence, and irrationality, in a manner that affirms marginalised forms knowledge and ways of perceiving the world associated with 'Orientalised' racial groups. I conclude by suggesting that Pater's writings allow the reader to both decipher the racist logic of Western aesthetics and inquire into how racialised, marginalised, and denigrated creative practices can undermine that logic. Even though Pater was not, I believe, primarily driven by an antiracist ethic or politics in his literary career, his interest in 'curiously testing new opinions and courting new impressions, never acquiescing in a facile orthodoxy' led him to question the limits placed upon this project by racial thinking and generate insights into the intimate relationship between aesthetics and the politics of race.[3]

Race and Aesthetics

In the influential essay 'Undisciplining Victorian Studies', Ronjaunee Chatterjee, Alicia Mireles Christoff, and Amy Wong assert that the field has been hindered by an inclination 'to treat politics as an adjunct to aesthetic analysis,' effectively aligning itself with the notion of aesthetic autonomy associated with aesthetes like Pater.[4] In most scholarship of Victorian literature (as well as in literary criticism generally), 'aesthetics' typically refers to humanity's capacity to render disinterested judgements upon creative works, our ability to look at a painting, read a poem, listen to music, et cetera and deem it to be beautiful or sublime, giving us pleasure apart from any practical use or mere sensual gratification it might otherwise provide us.

This understanding of aesthetics that Chatterjee, Christoff, and Wong identify as plaguing literary criticism can be traced back to Kant's *Critique of Judgment* (1790), which presents art as 'an object of pure contemplation or, when it does reflect on social concerns, it reflects on them in their unresolved complexity rather than insisting on the justice of a particular point of view', in the words of David Lloyd. By contrast, politics encompasses 'the conflicting interests and partiality' inherent to ongoing human struggles for power.[5] In this view, politics represents the ephemeral, contingent, and ideological aspects of humanity, while aesthetics refers to experiences that speak to what is eternal, universal, and disinterested in us, which address to the whole self and all of humanity beyond narrow interests and partisan concerns. Art, in other words, creates conditions that allow us to access the core of selfhood shared by every human being. By learning to discern art's beauty and sublimity, we paradoxically become both more truly ourselves and more in touch with the universal spirit of humankind. There are no political implications to aesthetics because, during those moments when we truly appreciate art or nature's beauty, there is no conflict between the self and others.

This is the story we have been told, at least. Chatterjee, Christoff, and Wong, however, contend that there is actually a 'firm link between aesthetics and politics', particularly concerning race.[6] Their claim builds upon the work of many cultural and critical race theorists who have reinterpreted aesthetic discourse as presenting the qualities and cultural practices specific to bourgeois white European men as if they existed beyond the realm of political struggle, equating them with a universal human subjectivity that is definitionally beyond sectarian conflict. Essentially, judging a work of art's beauty 'disinterestedly' implies judging it from the perspective of the white Euro-American middle class, without knowing that one is doing so. When one supposedly rises above factionalism in the contemplation of beauty and sublimity, one actually yet unconsciously internalises the prerogatives of that culture as one's own under the guise of having achieved an 'objective' point of view.

Consequently, Wynter has identified the role played by the aesthetic in what she terms 'the overrepresentation of Man', the historical process by which Western culture transformed whiteness and white culture (what she calls 'Man' to distinguish it from the more inclusive term 'human') into the universal norm of all humanity, 'the measuring stick through which all other forms of being are measured' and always found lacking.[7] Specifically, for Wynter the aesthetic plays a role in the process she calls, after Frantz Fanon, 'sociogeny': the intimate shaping of one's subjectivity and perceptions such that the overrepresentation of Man and the deficiencies of all other ways of being in the world seem normal, natural, and commonsensical.[8]

Chuh builds upon Wynter's insight to observe that '[g]iven this history, it is no wonder that aesthetics has been met with wariness if not complete dismissal' by those seeking to dismantle racial oppression.[9] However, she reminds us that critics should be cautious not to reproduce the same division between aesthetics and politics by solely emphasising the latter at the expense of the former. Wynter suggests that these two realms should be brought together through a critical practice she terms 'decipherment'. This practice involves examining a work of art to uncover 'systems of meaning ... instituted by our cultural imaginaries (outside the conscious awareness of their bearer-subjects)'.[10] In other words, the goal of criticism is to scrutinise a work of art and uncover the concealed sociogenic processes by which it, and similar works, indoctrinates its audience into seeing the racial logic of white Western culture as normal and natural. Such processes have to be hidden in order to do their work, convincing us that the racial hierarchies they create are incontrovertibly true rather than a cultural construction.

Building upon Wynter's ideas, Chuh proposes the concept of 'aesthetic inquiry'. This critical approach aims to resist and actively undo such indoctrination by restoring particularity to universalised whiteness. It achieves this by affirming 'subjugated ways of life and knowing'.[11] Aesthetic inquiry involves retraining our senses to recognise that Western culture's aesthetic categories are constructs rooted in white supremacy rather than universal humanity. It enables us to derive positive emotions from racialised creative works and practices that we have been taught to disregard or scorn due to their supposed aesthetic inferiority, their inability to rise above their cultural particularity and elicit 'disinterested' and 'universal' (i.e., white) beauty or sublimity. Together, Wynter and Chuh convey that although the aesthetic has played a role in creating and perpetuating our existing racial hierarchy, it also provides a space from which we can begin to dismantle that hierarchy.

Neutralising Whiteness: Winckelmann and Kant

One consequence of critics' inability or unwillingness to acknowledge the connection between aesthetics and politics is their failure to recognise when whiteness – both the race and the colour with which it is indelibly associated – is presented as the universal human norm. According to Chatterjee, Christoff, and Wong, Victorian studies has 'historically framed our objects of study as either "about" race or as race-neutral', rather than recognising that 'race-neutral' works actually contribute to the rendering of whiteness as invisible, the default position, and thereby contributing to Man's overrepresentation.[12] This is why Rei Terada argues that we need to 'expand the methodology of the study of race' not only 'beyond attention to instances that already assume that the reader can recognise what counts as race and racism (and therefore what counts as a reference to it), or attention that limits itself to what a period text thinks race is'.[13] If one of the goals of decipherment is to uncover the rules of the cultural imagination that equate whiteness with normativity and universality, then we must contextualise Pater's seemingly race-neutral celebration of the whiteness of Greek sculpture in the broader cultural history of Western aesthetic discourse, which has depoliticised and deracialised whiteness by presenting it as equivalent to neutrality itself.

This history can be traced back to the late eighteenth-century writings of the German art historian and archaeologist Johann Joachim Winckelmann. He would eventually become the subject of the longest and most intellectually substantial essay in Pater's *Studies in the History of the Renaissance* (1873), discussed in the next section of this chapter. Although 'Winckelmann did not contribute directly to theories of race', as Nell Irvin Painter explains, his highly influential writings on ancient Greek sculpture, particularly his *History of the Art of Antiquity* (1764–67), propagated 'assumptions on the ideal form and color of human beauty that inspired much eighteenth-and-nineteenth-century racial theorizing' not just in art history but also in philosophy and the burgeoning biological sciences.[14]

According to Winckelmann, the epitome of perfect human beauty could be found in the ancient statue of the *Apollo Belvedere*, then as now part of the Vatican's art collection. His appreciation of this work carried distinctly homoerotic overtones which would later appeal to the similarly inclined Pater, who would approvingly quote Winckelmann's claim that 'those who are observant of beauty only in women, and are moved little or not at all by the beauty of men, seldom have an impartial, vital, inborn instinct for beauty in art' (*Renaissance*, 176). In Winckelmann's perspective, ancient Greek men's physical form was the material embodiment of the concept of '[l]iberty' which in turn 'inspired thinking that was grand, noble, and eloquent by contrast with slave nations, whose enslavement was as much mental as physical'.[15] This is why for him the whiteness of classical sculpture indicated that '[w]hite skin ... makes bodily appearance more beautiful'.[16] The supposedly innate pleasure we derive from gazing at the statue's white marble – and, by extension, the white skin it supposedly represents – speaks to its possessor's inherent purity, virtue, and instinct for freedom. Whiteness is like 'the purest water taken from the source of a spring', he says; 'the less taste it has, the more healthy it is seen to be, because it is cleansed of all foreign elements.'[17] Conversely, Winckelmann and his followers associated colour with 'barbarism' and 'primitivism'.[18]

Although Winckelmann had intended to contrast the perfection of ancient Greece with what he viewed as the degradation of modern Europeans, later scientists and philosophers ignored this aspect of his thinking. Instead, they embraced the 'assumption that the Greek ideal represented the generic typology of "civilized" Europeans'.[19] This was especially true in the writings of Kant, of which Pater was an avid reader throughout the 1860s. Kant drew on Winckelmann's writings and particularly his description of the *Apollo Belvedere* to provide theoretical justification for this white ideal. In his essay 'On National Characteristics So Far as They Depend on the Distinct Feeling of the Beautiful and Sublime' (1764) he claims that, unlike white Europeans, the African 'has no feeling beyond the trifling' due to the 'ugliness of appearance' and 'stupidity' of the 'Negro'.[20] While his racism is less overt in his later landmark work of aesthetic theory, the *Critique of Judgment*, he discusses beautiful bodies that 'please universally' due to their 'bodily manifestation' of internal moral qualities such as a 'noble' profile and 'goodness of soul, or purity, or strength, or repose', which he associates with white, European humanity.[21]

In contrast, Kant cites the 'Iroquois' and 'Carib' as examples of people who have not achieved the 'universal communicability' of the *sensus communis* because they remain subject to the 'charm of sense', engrossed in uncommunicable physical sensations and merely personal sensual gratifications rather than the disinterested 'universality' evoked by properly aesthetic forms.[22] This is why, in Kant's words, 'when civilization has reached its height ... the entire value of sensations is placed in the degree to which they permit of universal communication'.[23] By contrast, subjection to the 'charm of sense' signifies the 'heteronomy' of the savage, their lack of self-control and susceptibility to external influence, in contrast to the 'autonomy' that characterises the universal (i.e., bourgeois white male European) citizen-subject's capacity for self-direction and self-governance through his ability to commune with and communicate via the *sensus communis*.[24] Emmanuel

Chukwudi Eze explains that 'Kant's position manifests an inarticulate sub-scription to a system of thought which assumes that what is different, especially that which is "black," is bad, evil, inferior, or a moral negation of "white," light, and goodness'. This position, derived from Winckelmann's art historical writings, leads Kant to assume 'that the particularity of European existence is *the* empirical as well as ideal model of humanity, of *universal* humanity, so that others are more or less human or civilized ("educable" or "educated") as they approximate this European ideal'.[25]

In essence, Kant asserts that white people and white culture are the actually existing embodiment of the ideals of universality and impartiality that can be achieved through the development of proper aesthetic judgement. As J. Kameron Carter says of Kant's writings on race, whiteness 'is a present reality, and yet it is also moving toward and awaiting its perfection'. While

> the consummation of all things within the economic, political and aesthetic . . . reality called 'whiteness,' is on the one hand made present and available now in white people and in white culture. And on the other hand, it is through these white people and culture that the fully reality of whiteness will globally expand to 'eschatologically' encompass all things and so bring the world to perfect.[26]

It is thus that Kant's celebration of whiteness in his aesthetic philosophy anticipated and preemptively justified the late-Victorian imperial civilising mission by nearly a century, contributing to the sociogenic endeavour of 'Man's overrepresentation' by reinforcing the equation between whiteness and humanity *qua* humanity seem like mere common sense.

Apollonian Decipherment

I present this historical background to provide context for 'deciphering' the racial implications of Pater's apparently race-neutral remarks on ancient Greek sculpture and Apollo. While much has been written about Pater's affinity with Winckelmann's homoeroticism in the context of Victorian sexuality, few have explored Pater's place within the racial aesthetics that also forms part of Winckelmann's and Kant's legacies. In the essay, 'Winckelmann', Pater might resist heteronormativity, but he also contributes to the deracination of whiteness inaugurated by the two German thinkers.

When Pater characterises the 'white light' of ancient Greek sculpture as 'purged from the angry, bloodlike stains of action and passion', such that it 'reveals, not what is accidental in man, but the tranquil godship in his, as opposed to the restless accidents of life', the racial implications of his statement may go unnoticed without an understanding of the cultural logic that has, since Winckelmann's time, rendered whiteness invisible *as* whiteness by idealising it (*Renaissance*, 186–7). For Pater, the beauty of whiteness indicates the possession of a character fit for omniscient judgement and impartial rule. Being white is akin to being godlike – a serene entity transcending social and political conflict, purged of all incidentals, and embodying universality itself.

In a later passage, he describes how Greek statues represent the 'colourless, unclassified purity of life' that is 'the highest expression of the indifference which lies beyond all that is relative and partial' (*Renaissance*, 189). He treats whiteness not as a colour but as the lack of colour, 'unclassified' just as whiteness is considered not a racial class but the lack of race, the neutral, 'colourless' standard that highlights the lack of 'purity' in every other race. He does go on to say that this 'white light' takes 'no colour from any one-sided experience'. It 'is characterless, so far as *character* involves subjection to the accidental influences of life' (*Renaissance*, 189). Whiteness and those who possess it embody indifference beyond relativity and sectarianism, the very embodiment of cool rationality itself. Conversely, possessing colour is associated with anger, blood, partiality, fanaticism, agitation, and an excessive preoccupation with trivialities at the expense of a comprehensive view.

By treating these associations as natural and repeating them in his own essay, Pater contributes to an aesthetic discourse that reinforces the perceptions of racial difference that subtend the imperial civilising mission, the belief that the skin colour of colonised subjects are inherently inferior in character and possess backward cultural practices such that they require paternalistic guidance from rational, reasonable, all-knowing white individuals capable of ruling and judging impartially, is presented as common sense – an indisputable fact of life that tolerates no dissent. Such comments indicate a subjectivity shaped by the sociogenic influences of Western aesthetics and late-Victorian imperial culture.

What makes the sociogenic process so insidious is that it operates in a covert manner, allowing individuals to perpetuate it unconsciously. When aesthetic judgements are shaped by sociogenesis, they are experienced as deeply authentic to the self and inherent to the world, rather than being recognised as socially constructed and imposed through cultural and institutional pedagogies. However, I contend that Pater, over the course of his career, developed a nascent awareness of this process and actively endeavoured to subvert its influence. As Kate Flint notes in her contribution to the present volume, Pater's lifelong 'fondness for white' shifted in his later writings, as indicated by the desire expressed in an essay like 'The Beginnings of Greek Sculpture' (1880) that 'the original colouring' be restored 'to Greek sculpture – or at least reminding us that these statues were not always monochromatic'. In what she calls 'one of the most notable realignments in Pater's aesthetic approaches', his preoccupation with 'light and whiteness' transforms into a critique of 'the white heat of violence'.[27] In this context, a compelling comparison can be drawn between the 'Winckelmann' essay, originally published in *The Westminster Review* in 1867 before he revised it for publication in *Studies in the History of the Renaissance* in 1873, and his short story 'Apollo in Picardy', released shortly before his death. 'Apollo in Picardy', like his earlier short story 'Denys l'Auxerrois' (discussed in detail in the next section of this chapter), was inspired by the German author Heinrich Heine's 'The Gods in Exile' (1853), which fancifully describes the Greek gods hiding in disguise throughout medieval Europe, dethroned in the wake of Christianity's triumph. In 'Winckelmann', Pater describes Apollo as 'rational, chastened, debonair, with his unbroken daylight' (*Renaissance*, 182). However, in 'Apollo in Picardy' he portrays the god as 'a devil' whose 'devil's work' includes the 'inversion . . . of his old beneficent and properly solar doings' with 'a touch of malign magic' that 'makes men pay sometimes a terrible price'.[28] Unlike the 'white light' of the earlier depiction, this later version emits a 'violent beam, a blaze of new light' that is a 'curse . . . to its receiver' (*IP*, 272).

Pater's story tells of the god's reappearance in a medieval French monastery under the guise of a labourer whose name, Apollyon, is 'a malignant one in Scripture', synonymous with the Devil in the Book of Revelation (*IP*, 272). The story unfolds with the protagonist, the Prior Saint-Jean, being initially captivated by Apollyon's beauty until the disguised god kills Hyacinth, the Prior's young acolyte, by decapitating him with a discus (recalling another famous Greek depiction of the male form, the *Discobolus*, which Pater would discuss in his essay 'The Age of Athletic Prizemen' [1894]). Pater's narrator vividly describes Apollyon in the moments before the fatal act as 'shining from within with a light of his own, like that of the glow-worm in the thicket, or the dead and rotten roots of the old trees' (*IP*, 288). Afterward, the physical presence of Apollyon drives Saint-Jean to madness and his eventual demise. In a nearly complete inversion from 'Winckelmann', which had focused on Greek sculptures of beautiful men as the material expression of godlike knowledge, neutrality, and reason, 'Apollo in Picardy' transforms the god into the embodiment of violence, destruction, decay, and malevolence.

Pater's change of perspective was not, I believe, primarily driven by the development of an antiracist ethos. Instead, he recognised the limitations imposed upon one's aesthetic impressions when beauty is exclusively associated with white European culture, a viewpoint espoused by Kant as well as other Victorian art writers, such as John Ruskin.[29] Pater's renowned and influential expression of aesthetic impressionism in the Preface and Conclusion to *Studies in the History of the Renaissance* rejects the imposition of any regulative concepts in aesthetics. We must not seek, he says, '[t]o define beauty' by finding 'a universal formula for it', because '[t]he theory or idea or system which requires of us the sacrifice of any part of this experience, in consideration of some interest into which we cannot enter, or some abstract theory we have not identified with ourselves, or of what is only conventional, has no real claim upon us' (*Renaissance*, 73; 199). Accordingly, Pater's writings on Dionysus challenge the regulatory role assigned to white, European, Apollonian beauty as the sole of aesthetic expression with universal communicability. By contrasting the Dionysian with the Apollonian, he begins to question the role of race as regulatory principle that imposes restrictive and 'only conventional' limits on our visual impressions of human bodies. Pater critiques the disregard for sensory experiences that fall outside these conventional limits, often associated with racialised bodies that, as Kant argued, remain heteronomously enthralled to the mere 'charm of sense'.

Dionysian Analysis

The most well-known exploration of the Apollonian and the Dionysian as contrasting aesthetic principles is in Friedrich Nietzsche's *The Birth of Tragedy* (1872). There is no conclusive evidence to suggest that Pater read *The Birth of Tragedy*, though it is plausible that he kept abreast of its reception in the Victorian periodical press. What is evident, though, is that in the 1870s both Pater and Nietzsche began to develop an interest in affirming the primal forces symbolised by Dionysus, which had traditionally been denigrated by the Apollonian ideal of classical serenity offered by Winckelmann and his nineteenth-century followers. Between 1875 and 1878, Pater delved deeply into the study of Greek mythology and produced several essays on the topic including two pieces centred on the wine-god, 'A Study of Dionysus: The Spiritual Form of Fire and Dew' and 'The Bacchanals of Euripides' (1889; likely composed in 1878). This culminated in Pater's short story 'Denys l'Auxerrois', which tells of Dionysus's appearance in a medieval French village as a young man named Denys.

For Pater, a Dionysian aesthetic illuminates the universality of the embodied experiences of a group that was often perceived to be ineluctably partial, fanatical, and sectarian: Jews, who were commonly regarded as an 'oriental' people during this period. While Jewish people had long been considered 'other' within European Christian culture, it was in the nineteenth-century that this distinction took on biologised and racialised connotations. According to Edward Said, Dionysus serves as the quintessential figure of Western Orientalism, depicted as the 'Eastern god' who travels from Asia to Greece in Euripides's play *The Bacchae* – also the subject of an essay by Pater.[30] Said asserts that the play employs the god to show how Western '[r]ationality is undermined by Eastern excesses', which the ancient playwright presents as 'mysteriously attractive opposites to what seem to be normal values'.[31] Said further observes that the nineteenth-century witnessed the biologisation of this long-standing trope, as the burgeoning field of racial sciences sought to establish biocentric justification for the perceived differences between the 'Orient' and the West.[32]

In 'A Study of Dionysus', Pater refers to a painting titled '*Bacchus*' (the Roman name for Dionysus) by 'a young Hebrew painter'.[33] The painter in question is Simeon Solomon, a Jewish Pre-Raphaelite artist who, a year before the publication of Pater's essay, was arrested and charged with attempting to commit sodomy in a public urinal. While Solomon's homosexuality was known among his social circles prior to his arrest, the ensuing public scandal resulted in him being abandoned by nearly all his acquaintance, including the poet A. C. Swinburne. It is conceivable that Pater turned to Dionysus as a means of exploring a less constrained homoerotic ideal than Winckelmann's emphasis on Apollonianism.

Pater's mention of Solomon shortly after his arrest was bold, and his comments allude to previous criticisms of Solomon's work voiced by Swinburne even prior to the scandal. In an 1871 article in the literary magazine *The Dark Blue*, Swinburne wrote that the Solomon's classical artworks, such as *Bacchus*, display 'an expression ... which is not pure Greek, a shade or tone of thought or feeling beyond Hellenic contemplation; whether it be Oriental or modern in its origin, and derive from national or personal sources'.[34] Swinburne stated that these works imperfectly combine 'the fervent violence of feeling or faith which is peculiar to the Hebrews with the sensitive acuteness of desire, the sublime reserve and balance of passion, which is peculiar to the Greeks'.[35]

Stefano Evangelista notes that in this article 'Swinburne attributes Solomon's impure Greekness to his Jewishness', implying that Solomon's artworks are marred by his racial particularity, with these 'national or personal' qualities preventing him from achieving the proper Hellenic balance.[36] Swinburne's language here reflects the racist rhetoric of Winckelmann and his followers, emphasising the biological and cultural superiority of the 'pure Greek'. Solomon, instead of recognising the classical universality of Apollonian 'sublime reserve and balance of passion', is accused by Swinburne of exhibiting a 'fervent violence' that is 'peculiar to the Hebrews' (echoing Pater's reference to 'angry, bloodlike stains of action and passion' in 'Winckelmann'). Solomon's Hellenism is considered aesthetically inferior because it is irrevocably marked by racial specificity, characterised by primitively unrestrained emotions ('feeling') and irrational beliefs ('faith') that cannot be sublimated into Greek (i.e., effectively, white) universality, impartiality, and calm indifference.

Pater's description of Solomon's *Bacchus* resonates with Swinburne's review, focusing on the painter's race. However, unlike Swinburne, Pater identifies Dionysus's 'Eastern' origins with Solomon's 'Hebrew' background in order to challenge the dichotomy between Oriental irrationality and Western reason. Pater rhetorically questions, 'whether anything similar in feeling [to Solomon's melancholy modern Bacchus] is to be actually found in the range of Greek ideas', and he emphatically answers 'yes ... something corresponding to this deeper, more refined idea, really existed' in the earlier figure of Dionysus Zagreus, the Dionysus who was literally 'torn apart' by the *mainades* in an alternative version of the myth (*GS*, 37). In doing so, he affirms the genuine universality expressed by Solomon's distinctively 'Oriental' and Jewish vision, which he considers not 'a late after-thought' but 'a tradition really primitive, and harmonious with the original motive of the idea of Dionysus': primitive not in the sense of backward or undeveloped but first and primary (*GS*, 38).

Pater implicitly challenges Swinburne's version of Hellenism by asserting that Solomon's painting unveils the melancholy inherent to the myth even if it has often gone unnoticed by modern viewers, characterising *Bacchus* as a kind of aesthetic 'decipherment', in Wynter's sense, of the ancient Greek cultural imagination. 'You have no sooner caught a glimpse of this image', he says, 'than a certain perceptible shadow comes creeping over the whole story; for, in effect, we have seen glimpses of the sorrowing Dionysus, all along' (*GS*, 39). Pater suggests that Solomon's Hebrew and Oriental perspective allows us to perceive the myth's history through new eyes, revealing a more emotionally inclusive version of universality that has been obscured by modern Europe's white, Apollonian biases. Pater demonstrates that what Swinburne's Apollonian Hellenism sees as a constraining racial particularity can instead be seen as universal, 'complete and very fascinating' in its own right (*GS*, 37). Pater's universalisation of the Dionysian aesthetic expresses a new, more capacious conceptualisations of the human, a challenge to Wynter's description of 'Man's overrepresentation' in the wake of European colonisation, the way aesthetic discourse has universalised a specifically white, Western definition of humanity as the single standard against which all other peoples and cultures should be judged and inevitably found wanting.

As Flint argues in her contribution to this volume, Pater's attempts to understand the nature of the subjective aesthetic impression paradoxically led him to remain 'focused on what was outside of himself, not within – how mediated this exterior world might be by personal experience'.[37] I argue that this included not just an interest in how the scientific processes typically associated with the non-human world affect one's impressions but also a concern with how social processes, such as racialisation, shape one's aesthetic perceptions of reality. This is why Pater's short story 'Denys l'Auxerrois' anticipates the insights of Fanon and Wynter by depicting the role played by sociogeny – that is, the shaping of one's subjectivity and intimately felt perceptions of the world by external social forces – plays in sustaining and justifying racial violence. Like the later 'Apollo in Picardy', Pater's tale makes use of the 'Gods in Exile' trope to recount Dionysus's arrival in the medieval French village of Auxerre as Denys, a sensitive and artistic young man of Eastern origins. At first, he inspires transformative artistic and political change among the villagers, but they eventually destroy him violently [in] in a reenactment of the ancient pagan ritual of the *sparagmos*, where Dionysus is torn apart by his followers in a fit of irrational spiritual transport.

Initially, Denys' racial differences captivate the residents of Auxerre, who find them exotic and alluring. Upon his first appearance, he evokes 'a delightful glee that became contagious' among them, a sense of communal solidarity that Pater describes as akin to the 'sympathies of mere numbers' he associates with the ancient Dionysian cult in his essay 'The Bacchanals of Euripides' (*IP*, 175; *GS*, 53). The villagers are fascinated by Denys' cosmopolitan background, the fact that 'he had trafficked with sailors from all parts of the world, from Arabia and India' (*IP*, 179). In his performance as 'the God of Wine' in a 'stage-play' for the delighted villagers, Denys subtly hints at his true identity and portrays his own return 'in triumph from the East'. He accentuates his Asian origins through the use of stereotypically Orientalist elements, including a 'headdress' of 'a strange elephant-scalp with gilded tusks' (*IP*, 178).

This infusion of new and non-native energy ushers in a 'golden age' in the town. 'Just then', the narrator says, 'Auxerre had its turn in that political movement which broke out sympathetically, first in one, then in another of the towns in France, turning their narrow, feudal institutions into a free, communistic life'. This cultural shift also gives rise to a 'new, free, generous manner in art' with the village embodying the essence of this proto-Renaissance spirit (*IP*, 173). However, the townspeople's initial fascination with Denys transforms into 'a deep suspicion and hatred' as the town's material circumstances begin to deteriorate (*IP*, 180). The narrator informs us that

> [t]hose fat years were over. It was a time of scarcity. The working people might not eat and drink of the good things they had helped store away. Tears rose in the eyes of needy children, of old and weak people like children, as they woke up again to frost-bound, ruinous mornings. (*IP*, 180)

During this period, they 'vaguely' attribute a murder that occurred in a vineyard to Denys. The 'golden age' that accompanied his arrival proves itself to be 'gilded only, after all' as '[p]eople turned against their favorite, whose former charms must now be counted only as the fascinations of witchcraft. It was as if the as if the wine poured out for them had soured in the cup' even though the wine-god himself has not changed (*IP*, 180). However, what has changed is how they view his differences. The otherness he embodies, which once appeared revolutionary and liberating, now appears to have introduced a destructive impurity to their way of life.

This transformation reaches its climax in a 'sequel to that earlier stage-play of the Return from the East in which Denys had been the central figure'. The townspeople go into a 'mad rage', a Dionysian frenzy, inspired by the 'sight of blood' from Denys's scratched lip, which the narrator says, 'brought out in rapid increase men's evil passions' (*IP*, 186–187). Denys' body is 'torn … limb from limb' by the people of Auxerre. Men affix 'little shreds of his flesh, or, failing that, of his torn raiment, in their caps; the women lending their long hair-pins for the purpose' (*IP*, 187). The people of Auxerre reenact the ancient pagan ritual of the *sparagmos*, emulating dismemberment of Dionysus depicted in the preclassical Orphic version of the myth.

Denys's murder at the hands of the Auxerre villagers, whom the narrator now describes as 'savage' and possessing '[a] kind of degeneration, of coarseness', represents the culmination of a sociogenic phenomenon known as the 'colonial mirror of production', as described by anthropologist Michael Taussig (*IP*, 187). This involves an imperial culture projecting notions of ferocity, violence, and barbarity onto a colonised population, and then seeks to counter those forces with its own irrational yet (to them) justified brutality. Taussig explains that

> [t]he terror and tortures [colonists] devised mirrored the horror of the savagery they both feared and fictionalized … it is this very animality projected onto the racial Other that is desired and mimicked as sadistic ritual, degradation, and ultimately in genocide againstthe Other.[38]

Consequently, the irrational violence associated with Oriental, Dionysian excess reveals itself to be more inherent to the European villagers. The collective transformation of their perceptions of Denys, driven by material deprivation, leads them to justify their violent destruction of him by projecting onto him their own tendencies towards violence and destructiveness.

Through his exploration of a Dionysian aesthetic, which he had begun in 'A Study of Dionysus' a decade prior to writing 'Denys', Pater gains an understanding of how our subjective perceptions of the world can justify and normalise racial violence under colonial conditions. This understanding emerges from Pater's nascent understanding of the concept of sociogeny, which emphasises that our perceptions are intimately shaped by our social conditions and the discourses those conditions give rise to. This insight challenges how 'Apollonian' Western aesthetics renders sociogeny invisible by presenting such impressions as mere common sense.

Conclusion

Initially, Pater embraced his culture's dominant Apollonian aesthetics which, in addition to its subversively homoerotic side, rendered whiteness – both the colour and, implicitly, the racial category with which it was inevitably associated by the late nineteenth-century – equivalent to rationality, object-ivity, and neutrality. However, he eventually recognised that this framework imposed unnecessary limitations on one's aesthetic impressions. This led him to begin embracing the formlessness, emotionality, and anti-rationalism associated with Dionysus. Due to the racial politics of Apollonianism, Pater's embrace of Dionysus led him to develop a nascent awareness of the racial violence sustained and justified by Western aesthetic discourse.

He was led to this insight not by a desire for social justice, in my assess-ment, but rather because he was interested in exploring the nature of beauty – the dominant theme of all his writings. Nevertheless, I follow Kristin Mahoney in asserting that one can both assess the racism of aestheticist and decadent writers and what that indicates about their cultural *milieu*, as well as focus on what their work *'can be used for'* when 'engaging in antic-olonial critique' and 'antiracist resistance.[39] By examining Pater's body of work from critical perspectives that foreground the link between aesthetics and politics, we can uncover how the Western aesthetic imagination covertly reinforces racial hierarchies through the normalisation of whiteness and determine how alternative aesthetic sensibilities might allow one to envision a version of human subjectivity that exists beyond Man's overrepresentation.

Notes

1. The critical literature on this topic is extensive. Two of the most influential early studies on the Aesthetic Movement and homoeroticism are Richard Dellamora, *Masculine Desire: The Sexual Politics of Victorian Aestheticism* (Chapel Hill, NC: University of North Carolina Press, 1990) and Linda Dowling, *Hellenism and*

Homosexuality in Victorian Oxford (Ithaca, NY: Cornell University Press, 1994). For a more recent take, see Dustin Friedman, *Before Queer Theory: Victorian Aestheticism and the Self* (Baltimore, MD: Johns Hopkins University Press, 2019).

2. See Robert Stilling, *Beginning at the End: Decadence, Modernism, and Postcolonial Poetry* (Boston, MA: Harvard University Press, 2018) and Kristin Mahoney, *Queer Kinship after Wilde: Transnational Decadence and the Family* (Cambridge: Cambridge University Press, 2022).

3. Walter Pater, *The Renaissance: Studies in Art and Poetry*, ed. Hilary Fraser (Oxford: Oxford University Press, 2025), 199. Hereafter cited parenthetically as *Renaissance*.

4. Ronjaunee Chatterjee, Alicia Mireles Christoff, and Amy Wong, 'Introduction: Undisciplining Victorian Studies', *Victorian Studies*, 62, no. 3 (Spring 2020): 377.

5. David Lloyd, *Under Representation: The Racial Regime of Aesthetics* (New York: Fordham University Press, 2019), 19.

6. Chatterjee, Christoff, and Wong, 'Undisciplining Victorian Studies', 376.

7. Katherine McKittrick, 'Yours in the Intellectual Struggle: Sylvia Wynter and the Realization of the Living', in *Sylvia Wynter: On Being Human as Praxis*, Katherine McKittrick, ed. (Durham, NC: Duke University Press, 2015), 3. See also Sylvia Wynter, 'Unsettling the Coloniality of Being/Power/Truth/Freedom: Towards the Human, after Man, Its Overrepresentation – An Argument', *CR: The New Centennial Review*, 3, no. 3 (Fall 2003): 257–337.

8. See Sylvia Wynter, 'Towards the Sociogenic Principle: Fanon, Identity, the Puzzle of Conscious Experience, and What It Is Like to Be 'Black'', in *National Identities and Socio-political Changes in Latin America*, Mercedes F. Durán-Cogan and Antonio Gómez-Moriana, eds. (New York: Routledge, 2001), 30–66 and Frantz Fanon, *Black Skin, White Masks*, Richard Philcox (trans.) (New York: Grove Press, 2008), xv.

9. Kandice Chuh, *The Difference Aesthetics Makes: On the Humanities 'After Man'* (Durham, NC: Duke University Press, 2019), 19.

10. Sylvia Wynter, 'Rethinking "Aesthetics": Notes towards a Deciphering Practice', in *Ex-Iles: Essays on Caribbean Cinema*, Mbye Cham, ed. (Trenton, NJ: Africa World Press, 1992), 239–240.

11. Chuh, *The Difference Aesthetics Makes*, 6–7.

12. Chatterjee, Christoff, and Wong, 'Undisciplining Victorian Studies', 373.

13. Rei Terada, 'The Racial Grammar of Kantian Time', *European Romantic Review*, 28, no. 3 (2017): 268.

14. Nell Irvin Painter, *The History of White People* (New York: W.W. Norton, 2010), 59.

15. David Bindman, *Ape to Apollo: Aesthetics and the Idea of Race in the 18th Century* (London: Reaktion Books, 2002), 84–85.

16. Painter, *History of White People*, 61.

17. Quoted in Alex Potts, *Flesh and the Ideal: Winckelmann and the Origins of Art History* (New Haven, CT: Yale University Press, 1994), 164.

18. Painter, *History of White People*, 61. Today, archaeologists and art historians know that ancient sculptures were originally painted and lost colour over time. This was already suspected by many in Winckelmann's day. See Bente Kiilerich,

'Towards a "Polychrome History" of Greek and Roman Sculpture', *Journal of Art Historiography*, 15 (December 2016): 1–18.

19. Bindman, *Ape to Apollo*, 221.

20. Immanuel Kant, 'On National Characteristics so Far as They Depend upon the Distinct Feeling of the Beautiful and Sublime', in *Race and the Enlightenment: A Reader*, Emmanuel Chukwudi Eze, ed. (Oxford: Blackwell, 1997), 57.

21. Immanuel Kant, *Critique of the Power of Judgment*, Paul Guyer, ed., Eric Matthews (trans.) (Cambridge: Cambridge University Press, 2000), 120.

22. Kant, *Critique*, 177.

23. Kant, *Critique*, 156.

24. Kant, *Critique*, 163.

25. Emmanuel Chukwudi Eze, 'The Color of Reason: The Idea of "Race" in Kant's Anthropology', in *Postcolonial African Philosophy: A Critical Reader*, Emmanuel Chukwudi Eze, ed. (Oxford: Blackwell, 1997), 117.

26. J. Kameron Carter, *Race: A Theological Account* (Oxford: Oxford University Press, 2008), 89.

27. See Kate Flint's chapter titled 'Pater, Looking' in the current volume'.

28. Walter Pater, *Imaginary Portraits*, Lene Østermark-Johansen, ed. (London: Modern Humanities Research Association, 2014), 272. Hereafter cited parenthetically as *IP*.

29. See Dustin Friedman, 'Sinister Exile: Dionysus and the Aesthetics of Race in Walter Pater and Vernon Lee', *Victorian Studies* 63, no. 4 (Summer 2021): 537–560.

30. Edward Said, *Orientalism* (New York: Vintage, 1979), 57.

31. Said, *Orientalism*, 57.

32. Said, *Orientalism*, 206.

33. Walter Pater, *Greek Studies: A Series of Essays* (London: Macmillan, 1895), 37. Hereafter cited parenthetically as *GS*.

34. Algernon Charles Swinburne, *The Complete Works of Algernon Charles Swinburne*, ed. Edmund Gosse and T. J. Wise, 20 vols (London: Heinemann, 1925–27), 15: 445.

35. Swinburne, *Complete Works*, 450.

36. Stefano Evangelista, 'A Revolting Mistake: Walter Pater's Iconography of Dionysus', *Victorian Review*, 34, no. 2 (Fall 2008): 208.

37. See Kate Flint's 'Pater, Looking' in the current volume.

38. Michael Taussig, *Shamanism, Colonialism, and the Wild Man: A Study in Terror and Healing* (Chicago, IL: University of Chicago Press, 1987), 127, 133.

39. Kristin Mahoney, 'Taking Wilde to Sri Lanka and Beardsley to Harlem: Decadent Practice, Race, and Orientalism', *Victorian Literature and Culture* 49, no. 4 (Winter 2021): 548, 585.

This is a very selective guide to further scholarship on Walter Pater intended to help readers develop their understanding of Pater beyond the present volume. It focuses almost exclusively of work published in the past thirty years. Where possible, hyperlinks are included.

Works

An edition of Pater's *Collected Works* is underway, at the time of writing, published by Oxford University Press, under the general editorship of Lesley Higgins and David Latham. These volumes are comprehensive and therefore invaluable if you are undertaking a major research project on Pater. The list of works published can be found here:

https://global.oup.com/academic/content/series/c/collected-works-of-walter-pater-cwwp/?cc=us&lang=en&

These volumes can prohibitively expensive for personal use, so where possible, modern alternatives are suggested below:

Studies in the History of the Renaissance, ed. Matthew Beaumont (Oxford: Oxford University Press, World's Classics, 2010)

Marius the Epicurean, ed. Gerald Monsman (Kansas City: Valancourt Classics, 2008)

Imaginary Portraits, ed. Lene Østermark-Johansen (London: MHRA, 2014)

Gaston de Latour: The Revised Text, ed Gerald Monsman (Greensboro, NC: ELT, 1995): https://muse.jhu.edu/pub/74/oa_monograph/book/15596

Letters of Walter Pater, ed. Lawrence Evans (Oxford: Clarendon Press, 1970)

Anthologised Works

The following anthologies comprise selected primary texts from the late nineteenth century, including Pater or directly related to his primary concerns.

The Victorian Art of Fiction: Nineteenth-Century Essays on the Novel, ed. Rohan Maitzen (Buffalo, NY: Broadview, 2009)

Strangeness and Beauty: An Anthology of Aesthetic Criticism 1840-1910, ed., Warner, Eric and Graham Hough, 2 vols (Cambridge: Cambridge University Press, 1983)

Decadence: An Annotated Anthology, ed. Jane Desmarais and Chris Baldick (Manchester: Manchester University Press, 2012)

The Fin de Siècle: A Reader in Cultural History, 1880-1900, ed. Sally Ledger and Roger Luckhurst (Oxford: Oxford University Press, 2000)

Biography

Benson, A. C., *Walter Pater* (London: Macmillan, 1906)

Brake, Laurel, *Writers and Their Work: Walter Pater* (Plymouth: Northcote House, 1994)

Donoghue, Denis, *Walter Pater: Lover of Strange Souls* (New York: Knopf, 1995)

Seiler, Robert M., ed., *Walter Pater: A Life Remembered* (Calgary: University of Calgary Press, 1987)

Seiler, Robert M., ed., *The Book Beautiful: Walter Pater and the House of Macmillan* (London: Athlone Press, 1999)

Wright, Thomas, *The Life of Walter Pater* (London: Everett, 1907)

Bibliography

Inman, Billie Andrew, *Walter Pater's Reading: A Bibliography of his Library Borrowings and Literary References, 1858-1873* (New York: Garland, 1981)

Inman, Billie Andrew, *Walter Pater and His Reading, 1874-1877: With a Bibliography of his Library Borrowings, 1878-1894* (New York: Garland, 1990)

Seiler, Robert M., ed., *Walter Pater: The Critical Heritage* (London: Routledge & Kegan Paul, 1980)

Wright, Samuel, *A Bibliography of the Writings of Walter H. Pater* (New York: Garland, 1975)

Journals

English Literature in Transition, 1880-1920 (1957–2020)

The Journal of Pre-Raphaelite Studies (1977 to the present)

Studies in Walter Pater and Aestheticism, formerly *The Pater Newsletter* (1977 to the present): https://walterpater.com/studies-in-walter-pater-and-aestheticism/

Edited Volumes

Bann, Stephen, ed., *The Reception of Walter Pater in Europe* (London: Thoemmes Continuum, 2004)

Brake, Laurel, ed., *Pater in the 1990s* (Greensboro, NC: ELT Press, 1990): https://muse.jhu.edu/book/25279

Brake, Laurel, Lesley Higgins and Carolyn Williams, ed., *Walter Pater: Transparencies of Desire* (Greensboro, NC: ELT Press, 2002): https://muse.jhu.edu/book/11053

Clements, Elicia and Lesley Higgins, eds., *Victorian Aesthetic Conditions: Pater Across the Arts* (London: Palgrave, 2010)

Dodd, Phillip, ed., *Walter Pater: An Imaginative Sense of Fact* (London: Routledge, 1981)

Martindale, Charles, Lene Østermark-Johansen and Elizabeth Prettejohn, eds., *Walter Pater and the Beginnings of English Studies* (Cambridge: Cambridge University Press, 2023)

Martindale, Charles, Stefano Evangelista and Elizabeth Prettejohn, eds., *Pater the Classicist: Classical Scholarship, Reception, and Aestheticism* (Oxford: Oxford University Press, 2017): https://global.oup.com/academic/product/pater-the-classicist-9780198723417?cc=us&lang=en&

Single Author Monographs

Cheeke, Stephen, *Walter Pater and Persons* (Oxford: Oxford University Press, 2024): https://academic.oup.com/book/56361

Hext, Kate, *Walter Pater: Individualism and Aesthetic Philosophy* (Edinburgh: Edinburgh University Press, 2013): www.jstor.org/stable/10.3366/j.ctt5hh2p3

Lee, Adam, *The Platonism of Walter Pater: Embodied Equity* (Oxford: Oxford University Press, 2013): https://global.oup.com/academic/product/the-platonism-of-walter-pater-9780198848530?cc=us&lang=en&

Østermark-Johansen, Lene, *Walter Pater and the Language of Sculpture* (Farnham: Ashgate, 2011)

Østermark-Johansen, Lene, *Walter Pater's European Imagination* (Oxford: Oxford University Press, 2020): https://global.oup.com/academic/product/walter-paters-european-imagination-9780192858757?q=ostermark%20johansen&lang=en&cc=us

Shuter, William F., *Rereading Walter Pater* (Cambridge: Cambridge University Press, 1997): www.cambridge.org/core/books/rereading-walter-pater/532B9EA02275FA040B9AFC48689FF4B7

Whiteley, Giles, *Aestheticism and the Philosophy of Death: Walter Pater and Post-Hegelian Philosophy* (Oxford: Legenda, 2010)

Williams, Carolyn, *Transfigured World: Walter Pater's Aesthetic Historicism* (Ithaca: Cornell University Press, 1990)

Notable Articles and Chapters in Edited Volumes

Brake, Laurel, 'Censorship, Puffing, "Piracy," Reprinting: British Decadence and Transatlantic Re-Mediations of Walter Pater, 1893-1910'. *Modernism/modernity* 19.3 (2012): 419–435. https://dx.doi.org/10.1353/mod.2012.0071

Friedman, Dustin, '"Sinister Exile": Dionysus and the Aesthetics of Race in Walter Pater and Vernon Lee'. *Victorian Studies* 63.4 (2021): 537–560. https://dx.doi.org/10.2979/victorianstudies.63.4.03

Kaiser, Matthew, 'Pater's Mouth.' *Victorian Literature and Culture* 39.1 (2011): 47–64. www.jstor.org/stable/41307850

Kistler, Jordan, 'Walter Pater and Non-Darwinian Science'. *Journal of Victorian Culture* 28.2 (April 2023), 163–177. https://doi.org/10.1093/jvcult/vcaco80

Morgan, Benjamin, 'Aesthetic Freedom: Walter Pater and the Politics of Autonomy'. *ELH* 77.3 (2010): 731–756. https://dx.doi.org/10.1353/elh.2010.0008.

Sutton, Emma, 'Aestheticism, Resistance and the Realist Novel: Marius and Masculinity'. In *The Victorian Novel and Masculinity*, Philip Mallett, ed. (London: Palgrave Macmillan, 2015): https://doi.org/10.1057/9781137491541_8

Roberts, Gabriel, '"Analysis leaves off": The Use and Abuse of Philosophy in Walter Pater's *Renaissance*'. *The Cambridge Quarterly* 37.4 (2008): 407–425. https://muse.jhu.edu/article/254780

Shuter, William F., 'The "Outing" of Walter Pater'. *Nineteenth-Century Literature* 48:4 (March 1994): 480–506.

Viragh, Atti, '"The Keener Touch": Walter Pater and the Hermeneutic Scene of Contact'. *ELH* 89, no. 1 (2022): 185–213. https://dx.doi.org/10.1353/elh.2022.0007

Williams, Carolyn, 'On Pater's Late Style'. *Nineteenth-Century Prose* 24.2 (1997): 143–158.

Pater in Context

Each of the following studies contain at least one chapter on Pater. They effectively read his work in broader literary, cultural, and social contexts.

Adams, James Eli, *Dandies and Desert Saints: Styles of Victorian Masculinity* (Ithaca, NY: Cornell University, 1995): www.jstor.org/stable/10.7591/j.ctv2n7nm7

Brake, Laurel, *Print in Transition: Studies in Media History* (Basingstoke: Palgrave, 2001): https://link.springer.com/book/10.1057/9780230005709

Bridgwater, Patrick, *Anglo-German Interactions in the Literature of the 1890s* (Oxford: Legenda, 1999)

Daley, Kenneth, *The Rescue of Romanticism: Walter Pater and John Ruskin* (Athens, OH: Ohio State University Press, 2001)

Dellamora, Richard, *Masculine Desire: The Sexual Politics of Victorian Aestheticism* (Chapel Hill, NC: University of North Carolina Press, 1990): https://archive.org/details/masculinedesireoorich

Denisoff, Dennis, *Decadent Ecology in British Literature and Art, 1860–1910: Decay, Desire, and the Pagan Revival* (Cambridge: Cambridge University Press, 2021): https://doi.org/10.1017/9781108991599

Dowling, Linda, *Language and Decadence in the Victorian Fin de Siècle* (Princeton: Princeton University Press, 1986): www.jstor.org/stable/j.ctt7zvqqv

Dowling, Linda, *Hellenism and Homosexuality in Victorian Oxford* (Ithaca, NY: Cornell University Press, 1994): www.jstor.org/stable/10.7591/j.ctt1287c6w

Dowling, Linda, *The Vulgarisation of Art: The Victorians and Aesthetic Democracy* (Charlottesville, VA: University of Virginia Press, 1996): https://archive.org/details/vulgarizationofaooooodowl/page/n7/mode/2up

Evangelista, Stefano, *British Aestheticism and Ancient Greece: Hellenism, Reception, Gods in Exile* (Basingstoke: Palgrave Macmillan, 2009)

Evangelista, Stefano, *Literary Cosmopolitanism in the English Fin de Siècle: Citizens of Nowhere* (Oxford: Oxford University Press, 2021): https://global.oup.com/academic/product/literary-cosmopolitanism-in-the-english-fin-de-sicle-9780198864240?q=ostermark%20johansen&lang=en&cc=us

Friedman, Dustin, *Before Queer Theory: Victorian Aestheticism and the Self* (Baltimore, MD: Johns Hopkins University Press, 2019)

Green, Sarah, *Sexual Restraint and Aesthetic Experience in Victorian Literary Decadence* (Cambridge: Cambridge University Press, 2023): https://doi.org/10.1017/9781108917490

Lecourt, Sebastian, *Cultivating Belief: Victorian Anthropology, Liberal Aesthetics, and the Secular Imagination* (Oxford: Oxford University Press, 2018): https://doi.org/10.1093/oso/9780198812494.001.0001

Love, Heather, *Feeling Backward: Loss and the Politics of Queer History* (Cambridge, MA: Harvard University Press, 2007): https://doi.org/10.2307/j.ctvjghxro

Lyons, Sara, *Algernon Swinburne and Walter Pater Victorian Aestheticism, Doubt and Secularisation* (London: Routledge, 2017): https://doi.org/10.4324/9781315097428

Robbins, Ruth, *Pater to Forster, 1873-1924* (Basingstoke: Palgrave, 2003): https://doi.org/10.1007/978-1-4039-3781-0

Russell, David, *Tact: Aesthetic Liberalism and the Essay Form in Nineteenth-Century Britain* (Princeton: Princeton University Press, 2018): https://doi.org/10.2307/j.ctvc778wq

Saunders, Max, *Self-Impression: Life-Writing, Autobiografiction, & the Forms of Modern Literature* (Oxford: Oxford University Press, 2010): https://doi.org/10.1093/acprof:oso/9780199579761.001.0001

Small, Ian, *Conditions for Criticism: Authority, Knowledge, and Literature in the Late Nineteenth Century* (Oxford: Oxford University Press, 1991): https://doi.org/10.1093/acprof:oso/9780198122418.001.0001

Whitely, Giles, *The Aesthetics of Space in Nineteenth-Century British Literature, 1843-1907* (Edinburgh: Edinburgh University Press, 2020): www.cambridge.org/core/books/aesthetics-of-space-in-nineteenthcentury-british-literature-18431907/9029F8AAE22058C191CDA80C90CCE2F5

INDEX

Cambridge Companions to . . .

AUTHORS

TOPICS

For EU product safety concerns, contact us at Calle de José Abascal, 56–1°,
28003 Madrid, Spain or eugpsr@cambridge.org.

www.ingramcontent.com/pod-product-compliance
Ingram Content Group UK Ltd.
Pitfield, Milton Keynes, MK11 3LW, UK
UKHW021920280426
470499UK00017B/317